Sheffield

History & Recollections

The Journal of Muscle Shoals History

Volume XVIII

The Tennessee Valley Historical Society

Officers for 2011
Tom McKnight, President
David Gregg, Vice President
Mary Perry, Secretary
Pat Mahan, Treasurer
William Smith, Counselor

Board of Directors

Term expires in 2011	*Term expires in 2012*	*Term expires in 2013*
Robert Steen	Richard C. Sheridan	Kenneth R. Johnson
Elizabeth "Liz" Anderson	David Curott	Chris Ozbirn
Leo Cobb	Jeffrey Bibbee	C. Cooper King

Publications Committee*:* Richard C. Sheridan (Journal editor). Leigh Ann Wilson, Annie Cooper, Susan Powell, Kenneth R. Johnson, Tom McKnight, and Arthur Weaver.

Scholarship Committee *Chairman:* Jeffrey Bibbee.

Program Committee *Chairman:* David Gregg.

Social Committee *Chairwoman:* Betty Martin.

Manuscripts, documents, or other materials relating to the history of the Muscle Shoals area may be submitted to the Society for publication in this Journal or deposit in the Wesleyan Archives, Collier Library, University of North Alabama. Correspondence regarding the Journal should be sent to Editor, Journal of Muscle Shoals History, P. O. Box 149, Sheffield, AL 35660 or to rcsheridan29@yahoo.com or kennethjohnson10@comcast.net.

© Copyright 2011 by the Tennessee Valley Historical Society

The Journal of Muscle Shoals History ((ISSN 0094-8039) by the Tennessee Valley Historical Society, Post Office Box 149, Sheffield, Alabama 35660

All rights reserved. No part of this publication may be reproduced or transmitted in any form or by any means, electronic or mechanical, including photocopying, recording, or by any information storage and retrieval system, without prior written permission from the Publisher or the Tennessee Valley Historical Society.

ISBN: 978-1-934610-63-3

Published by:
Bluewater Publications, LLC
1812 CR 111
Killen, Alabama 35645
www.BluewaterPublications.

SHEFFIELD
History & Recollections
The Journal of Muscle Shoals History

Volume XVIII   2011

Table of Contents

                                                                                     Page

Contributors 1

Sheffield Historical Context 3
By: Gene A. Ford

'Light Guard' Memorable for Military Focus and Social Activity 32
By: Reynold B. Burt

A Steamboat Named for Sheffield 35
By: Richard C. Sheridan

Early Mayors of Sheffield 38
By: Carole Edwards Driskell

Worthington Was Truly A 'Shoals Man' 61
By: Reynold B. Burt

Sheffield Native's Letters Became a Book 65
By: Richard C. Sheridan

To: James R. Crowe. 67
By: Maud Lindsay

Street Cars Served to Unify Area 68
By: Reynold B. Burt

Lillian Margaret Lee Thomas Schmidt 73
By: Charles L. "Chuck" Beard

Lighting Up Sheffield 80
By: Richard C. Sheridan

H. C. "Chick" Wann's Interview with Chief E. J. Martin, April 18, 1985 83
By: H. C. "Chick" Wann

A History of Nitrate Village One 94
By: John C. Mothershed

Growing Up in Village One 103
By: Stanley Elmore

McWilliams Pure Milk Company 135
By: Robert McWilliams

Streit Milk Company 143
By: Charlie "Bud" Streit

Sheffield Once Had Thriving Coffee Manufacturing Plant 148
By: Richard C. Sheridan

Boyhood Days in Sheffield 1937-1943 151
By: Robert H. Meadows

Dr. George Washington Carver's Lecture Attracted Big Crowd 185
By: Richard C. Sheridan

My Greatest Mission in World War II 188
By: Laverne Mills

Reynolds Ventured into Space 197
By: Richard C. Sheridan

From Northern Lithuania To Northern Alambama 200
By: Sam J. Israel

Index 225

Contributors

Charles L. "Chuck" Beard is a retired Sheffield businessman (Nehi-Royal Crown Bottling Company) and is a former Colbert County Commissioner.

Reynold B. Burt (1910-2004) was a life-long resident of Sheffield and retired from TVA as Director of Chemical Operations. He served as president of the Tennessee Valley Historical Society and edited the book Sheffield: City on the Bluff.

Carole Edwards Driskell lives in Sheffield. She is a former secretary to the Mayor of Sheffield and currently serves as president of SHINE (Sheffield Hometown Interests Needing Energy).

Stanley Elmore, MD grew up in Sheffield and graduated from Vanderbilt Medical School. He is a retired physician and resides in Richmond, VA.

Gene A. Ford is a preservation consultant and architectural historian based in Tuscaloosa, AL. He surveyed the historic buildings and homes of downtown Sheffield in 1997-1998.

Sam J. Israel (1891-1990) immigrated to Sheffield in 1909 from his native Lithuania and became an outstanding citizen, businessman, and philanthropist.

Maud Lindsay (1874-1942) was a famous kindergarten teacher, storyteller, poet, and writer of books for children. Born in Tuscumbia, she resided most of her life in Sheffield.

Robert L. McWilliams grew up in the community of Red Rock on the McWilliams Diary Farm. He distributed milk to homes and stores throughout the Shoals area.

Robert H. Meadows (1926-2005), a salesman, was born on a farm near Athens, AL. The family lived in Sheffield 1937-1954. His autobiography, Papa's Journal, was published in 2006.

Laverne Mills, a long-time resident of Sheffield, retired from Union Carbide as a draftsman and accountant. He moved to Mobile, AL in 2009.

John Mothershed grew up in Village One and majored in history and physical education at the University of North Alabama. He is currently head football coach at Deshler High School.

Richard C. Sheridan, a retired TVA research chemist, is a former president of the Tennessee Valley Historical Society and is the official Sheffield City Historian.

Charlie "Bud" Streit, former owner of the Streit Milk Company, grew up in the family business. A former Sheffield resident, he now resides in Muscle Shoals.

Horace C. "Chick" Wann lives in Sheffield's Village One. He is retired from TVA and holds the rank of Colonel (retired) in the Alabama National Guard.

Sheffield Historical Context [1]

By Gene A. Ford

After the Cherokees and Chickasaws ceded their lands in what is now known as the Tennessee River Valley in 1816, the territory was hastily surveyed, divided into lots and large tracts, and auctioned off at land sales, such as the one held in 1818. Thus began the history of Florence, Tuscumbia, and York Bluff. The great Indian fighters, General Andrew Jackson and General John Coffee, both of whom purchased hundreds of acres surrounding York Bluff, envisioned a magnificent future for their embryonic settlement on the south bank of the Tennessee River. Despite the settlement's ideal location, high profile, and hero status of its founding fathers, their aspirations came not to fruition, leastwise not in their lifetime. Jackson attempted to work the land for a time, but within a few years, he deemed his efforts futile and sold his York Bluff property. Several farmers remained in the area, but nothing more came of the town site until the late nineteenth century.

In 1883, a fateful meeting occurred on the York Bluff town site that overnight literally transformed the bucolic farming community into a major manufacturing center. Captain Alfred Moses, a Montgomery-based banker and real estate developer, had the blind good fortune to meet with Colonel Walter S. Gordon during a business trip in Florence. Gordon convinced Moses to examine a several thousand-acre site on the south side of the Tennessee River and thus was born Sheffield, which took its name from manufacturing giant Sheffield, England (Armes 1910).

Chapter I

Together, Moses and Gordon formed the Sheffield Land, Iron and Coal Company in November 1883. By February 1884, plans were underway to give shape to an actual town site on the river bluff (Friends of the Sheffield Public Library 1985). The executive committee of the Sheffield Land, Iron and Coal

---

[1] Funded by Alabama Trust Fund Survey and Registration Grant Program and the City of Sheffield, March 26, 1998.

Company debated the location of industrial, commercial, and residential sectors as well as the layout of transportation and utility infrastructures and the placement of schools and houses of worship. The task of realizing these plans became the domain of Civil Engineer Charles Boeckh.

Engineer Boeckh translated the specifications of the land company into two-dimensional form, using, for the most part, a grid system. Avenues were oriented in a north/south direction; streets intersected avenues at 90 degree angles. The Sheffield town site grid consisted of sixteen avenues and sixteen streets. Montgomery Avenue, with its superior width of 100 feet, was designated as the main thoroughfare in town (Sanborn Map Company 1889). The other avenues and streets measured 60 feet in width. The blocks north of Sixth Street and east of Columbia Avenue were bisected by a north/south alley and subdivided into twelve parcels; blocks south of Sixth Street and west of Columbia Avenue were cut into four sections consisting of six parcels by the intersection of two alleys, one oriented in a north/south direction, the other perpendicular to it.

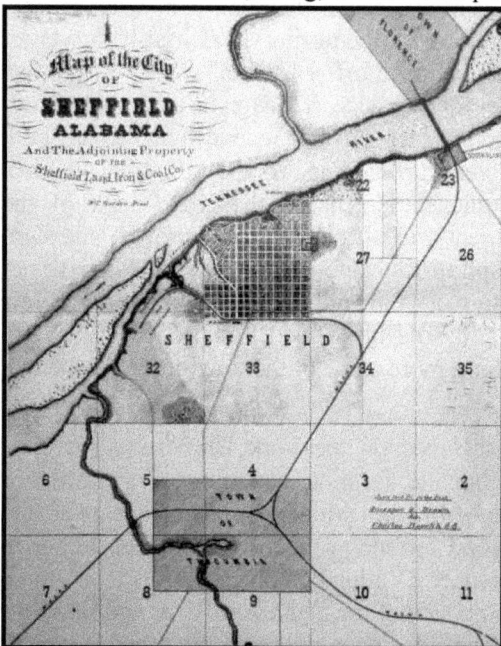

Civil engineer Charles Boeckhl drew this map of the new city in 1885.

In several intriguing instances, Boeckh deviated from strict adherence to the rigid geometry of the straight line and 90 degree angle and standardized parcel divisions. The engineer created a series of serpentine avenues along the river bluff. Hugging the edge of the bluff, the roads conform to the undulating topography of this section of Sheffield, especially the area bounded by Montgomery and Alabama Avenues north of Tenth Street. Alabama Avenue follows a natural ravine that descends from bluff top to river level. The lambent roadways functioned in symphony with River Side Park, providing mystery, frames of pleasing foliage, and dramatic vistas of the Tennessee River for the amusement and recreation of Sheffield's denizens. Boeckh's park aesthetic coincided with the landscape theories and designs of America's leading nineteenth-century park proponents, Alexander Jackson Downing and Frederick Law Olmstead. However, research did not confirm Boeckh's direct link to Olmstead and Downing.

On May 8, 1884, the Sheffield Land, Iron and Coal Company held a land sale, auctioning off 500 lots (Friends of the Sheffield Public Library 1985). While the land company considered the sale a success, many lots were not sold, and many parcels remained undeveloped through the nineteenth century. A circa 1890s photograph of upper Montgomery Avenue, which depicts the Sam Keller – Bishop residence and another Victorian reveals a sparsely built up residential sector. Nonetheless, town building was underway. Sheffield was incorporated in 1885.

After Sheffield was founded, five blast furnaces were established a short distance from the business district in the section of town reserved for industrial plants. Located between Alabama and Georgia Avenues, the industrial area was advantageously situated adjacent to the Tennessee River. A landing with a series of docks was erected along the river, which facilitated the transportation of raw materials and manufactured goods via river to and from major markets. Additionally, the industrial sector was adjacent to major rail lines. In 1886, the Alabama and Tennessee Coal and Iron Company moved its headquarters to Sheffield (Damsgard 1975). The company began operating two furnaces in 1888. A third was completed in 1895, but by then the three furnaces were the property of the Sheffield Coal, Iron and Steel Company. These three furnaces were predated by one built in 1887 by the Sheffield Furnace Company (Adams 1977). Colonel Enoch Ensley, a Memphis magnate, acquired it in 1889, renaming it the Hattie Ensley Furnace. Ensley built another, dubbing it the Lady Ensley Furnace (Nathan 1975). The five furnaces operated infrequently, and all were eventually shut down in the early twentieth century.

Sheffield's industrial zone, which expanded southwest of what was designated as Georgia Avenue in 1884, attracted other industries. An 1889 Sanborn map recorded the presence of a diverse range of plants. Among the factories were the Enterprise Wood Working Company, C. H. Buchanan's Straw Hat plant, A. J. Fould's Shoe Factory, Henderson Flour Mill, Sheffield Ice

Company, Globe Iron Works, Electric Light Works, Sheffield Stove Works, Standard Machine Works, Sheffield Agricultural Works, Sheffield Compress & Storage Company, and the Sheffield Manufacturing Company.

The Old Hattie Ensley Furance, erected in 1887, was replaced by a new furnace and cast house about 1915. It continued to produce pig iron until about 1926 when operations were moved to Birmingham. Courtesy of Richard Sheridan

Concomitant with the rise of Sheffield's iron industry was the development of a transportation infrastructure. Under the aegis of the Sheffield and Tuscumbia Street Railway Company, a rail line was built from the south end of Montgomery Avenue to the Memphis and Charleston depot in Tuscumbia in the late 1880s (Leftwich 1935). The Alabama Improvement Company began construction of a railroad from Sheffield to the ore-rich fields in Franklin County, but the project was halted when financing failed. This line was opened in 1887 as the Sheffield and Birmingham Railroad (Friends of the Sheffield Public Library 1985). The Southern Railway Company represented a major addition to Sheffield's rail system as well as the economy. The company located its shops and a depot just south of Montgomery Avenue and 1st Street in 1898 (Nathan 1975). The Louisville and Nashville line also came to town.

The area bounded by the rail lines, Sixth Street, the industrial sector, and Montgomery Avenue evolved into a transitional zone, mixing small industry with working class residences and commerce. Sanborn maps from 1889 and 1894 depict a number of brick and wood frame dwellings, some of which were occupied by African Americans in the area. Factories included a bottling works, harness and saddlery company, furniture factory, lumber and brick yard, sash and blind warehouse, and livery stables. Bakeries, laundries, grocery stores, and other shops also were established in the vicinity.

Sheffield's upper crust society selected premium lots near the river, especially along Montgomery Avenue north of Sixth Street, on which to build their palaces. Captain Moses built a resplendent Victorian (destroyed by fire) with a commanding view of the Tennessee River at the end of Montgomery. In the late 1880s, Moses was joined on Montgomery by such nabobs as Thos. R. Roulhac, an attorney who later became United States Attorney for the Northern District of Alabama; J. B. Lagomarsino, a real estate tycoon; Major George Keyes, a distinguished lawyer and editor (the oldest brick house in Sheffield); and Dr. Hugh W. Blair, one of Sheffield's leading physicians. W. L. Chambers, general manager of the Sheffield Land, Iron and Coal Company, built perhaps one of the most spectacular of the Victorian residences on nearby Park Boulevard.

In the late 1880s, the middle and upper middle classes built respectable domiciles in the section of Sheffield bounded by the Tennessee River, Austin Avenue, Sixth Street west of Montgomery Avenue, First Street east of Montgomery Avenue, and Dover Avenue. Although the incorporated limits of Sheffield extended beyond Dover Avenue, this area of town was not developed until 1890 when the streets were realigned at a 45 degree angle to Dover. The houses were scattered across the residential section with wide open spaces between many of them. Typical of the upper middle class housing of the era were the two story houses being built on Atlanta Avenue in 1890 (*Sheffield Enterprise* 1890). Erected by a Mobile syndicate (most likely the Mobile Real Estate Company, which had offices in the Mobile Block), the residences represented a stylistically restrained version of the Victorians on upper Montgomery Avenue. According to an article posted in the April 3, 1885 edition of *The Alabamian*, the Mobile Real Estate Company secured enough lumber to build 12 cottages. The article additionally relates that G. P. Humphreys, an architect, and W. A. Rolls, a contractor, were in the process of acquiring machinery to erect a brick works, lime kilns, a planning mill, and general woodworking equipment with which to build houses for Sheffield's daily arriving citizens. Houses of worship erected in this era included: the Methodist Church (1887) on Seventh Street and the Cumberland Presbyterian Church (1891) on Sixth Street.

Housing for employees of the furnaces was erected in the late 1880s in an area of Sheffield situated west of Little Rock Avenue and bounded by Georgia Avenue, Hill Street, 17th Street, and 20th Avenue. Known as Furnace Hill, the community, which consisted mostly of laborers and low level skilled workers and their families, was virtually an entity unto itself (Friends of the Sheffield Public Library 1985). Historic photographs of the quarters depict stock housing types such as saddlebags and prototype front gable bungalows. The saddlebags featured one story, a side gable roof, central chimney with a flanking pen or room, facade bay arrangement composed of two interior doors and a flanking window, shed roof porch, and a rear shed addition. The bungalow prototypes had one story, a front gable roof, interior chimney, a front façade door and window, front shed porch, and a rear shed addition. A number of the dwellings were removed from Furnace Hill during the construction of a nitrate plant in 1917 (Friends of the Sheffield Public Library 1985). The last vestiges of the village were swept away by a public housing project erected in the late 1950s.

For Sheffield, the 1880s represented the palmy days. Spurred by the rise of the iron industry and railroad system, mercantile magnates, development institutions, and independent entrepreneurs flocked to the boom town. The lower portion of Montgomery, Raleigh, and Austin Avenues between First and Sixth Streets evolved into the business district. A number of large, multi-story commercial blocks were erected on Montgomery Avenue in the late 1880s, including the Sheffield Land, Iron and Coal Company (razed in 1979); the Montgomery Block; Ware Building (razed); Cleveland Hotel (razed); and the First National Bank-Blake Building (Friends of the Sheffield Public Library 1985). The Mobile Real Estate Company erected the Mobile Block, an edifice of equal statue and scale to those on Montgomery Avenue, on Raleigh Avenue, and First Street in 1886. These commercial blocks housed numerous merchants and professional offices. Simultaneously small one and two story commercial buildings were erected in the business district.

An 1889 Sanborn map records downtown Sheffield as sparsely developed. According to the map, the northeast corner of A Street (1st Street) and Montgomery Avenue was anchored by two, three-story buildings, one of which is the Ware Building., the other is the Sheffield Land, Iron and Coal Building, construction of which was in progress. The Ware Building was vacant on the first floor while upper floors provided offices for the Alabama Improvement Company (Friends of the Sheffield Public Library 1985), The southeast corner of B Street

(2nd Street) and Montgomery Avenue featured a series of one story, wood frame business houses. They were occupied by several grocery stores, a jewelry shop, a plumber, and other businesses. The map records the presence of the First National Bank-Blake Building. While the Sheffield Hotel was under construction, the Cleveland Hotel was operating at the time of the Sanborn survey. A dry goods business utilized two of the spaces on the bottom floor of the hotel; a third space was vacant. Adjacent to the south side of the Cleveland Hotel was a series of one story establishments that housed a number of saloons, several grocers, an insurance office, a barber, and a tailor. Ensconced in the Montgomery Block were a drug store, hardware business, crockery, an insurance office, and an unspecified office as indicated by the 1889 Sanborn map. A center of mercantile activity, the Mobile Block had under its structural umbrella a saloon, clothing and dry goods operation, wall paper and paints, and several vacant store units on the first floor and the offices of the Mobile Real Estate Company above. The west side of Montgomery Avenue between First and Second Streets was relatively bare save for a two story affair that housed dry goods and notions and a small barber shop. The 1889 Sanborn map documented several offices and a printing shop between Second and Third Streets on the east side of Montgomery. The two story brick, commercial block between 1st and 2nd Streets on the east side of Montgomery Avenue was erected in this era.

Water facilities and education were an integral part of Sheffield's town building in the 1880s. An 80,000 gallon water tank was erected at the head of Montgomery Avenue and a water line constructed along the length of Montgomery Avenue to provide water to the 2,547 who inhabited the emerging manufacturing town in 1888 (Nathan 1975). Considered *au courant* with electric lights and central heating, the Richardsonian Romanesque styled Alabama Avenue School served well the educational needs of Sheffield's students.

The Alabama Avenue School, one of Sheffield's historic landmarks, was completed in 1892. Since classes were discontinued in 1971, the building has been used for storage and offices for administration of Sheffield City Schools. (copied for an old postcard)

Unfortunately, the optimism of the 1880s did not prevail throughout the 1890s. Fate, or more accurately the hard cold facts of reality, dealt the up and coming town a cruel blow. Many of the industries recruited to relocate in Sheffield were unsound, relying on the Sheffield Land, Iron and Coal Company for support (Leftwich 1935). These industries were prime targets for failure in difficult times. Precipitated by a nationwide panic, the Moses Brothers, a major driving force in the Sheffield Land, Iron and Coal Company and ultimately the economy of Sheffield, failed (Adams 1977). A domino effect ensued; the furnaces closed; many industries folded; residences and stores stood empty; and people left town.

An 1894 Sanborn map documents the catastrophic impact of the economic collapse. The following industries closed during the five year interval between 1889 and 1894:

C. H. Buchanan's Straw Hat Factory, Sheffield Stove Works, Standard Machine Works, Globe Iron Works, Sheffield Ice Company's factory, Henderson Flour Mill, Enterprise Wood Working Factory, Sheffield Manufacturing Company, Sheffield Harness and Saddlery Company, and the Eureka Brick Company. The furnaces were idle. According to the 1894 Sanborn map, a woolen mill, a promising enterprise in 1889, never opened.

The business district was equally devastated. The Mobile Real Estate Company found itself as an occupant of an almost entirely empty commercial block. Five out of six of the first floor store spaces stood vacant. Likewise, the Sheffield Land, Iron and Coal Company Building was only partially occupied. Both of the first floor stores were vacant. Vacancy afflicted the adjacent Ware Building. Across Montgomery Avenue and one block north, the Habbeler Block, an amalgamation of the Cleveland Hotel and the stores adjacent to its south side, suffered from a serious lack of mercantile tenants as seven out of eleven stores were empty. Five out of six first floor retail spaces advertises "for rent" signs in the Montgomery Block. Opened in 1893, the wedge-shaped Sheffield Hotel featured several available units. The development firms faced a speculator's worst nightmare: supply far outstripped demand, resulting in dire financial straits. Once bitten, twice shy; the citizens of Sheffield tended toward fiscal conservancy in future decades, often being terribly hesitant to act as the economic morass of the 1890s weighted heavily in their collective conscious.

Chapter II

Sheffield may very well have found itself on the list of Alabama's dead towns were it not for the Southern Railway Company. In 1898, Southern Railway officials decided to locate its headquarters in Sheffield, the culmination of which was the construction of a freight depot and offices at Montgomery and First Street and a freight yard southeast of Dover Avenue and First Street in a section of Sheffield that was opened for development in 1890, but had remained undeveloped until its use by the rail company (Friends of the Sheffield Public Library 1985). Additionally, Southern built shops southwest of Montgomery Avenue and First Street in the industrial section. The rail company became the largest employer in town with a roster of nearly 500 employees (Friends of the Sheffield Public Library 1985). Southern Railway provided a much needed stimulus for the Sheffield economy.

Following the example of the railroad, other businesses and industries chose to settle in Sheffield. Dormant for several years, the furnaces fired up, providing tons of pig iron. A New York-based interest bought out the Sheffield Land, Iron and Coal Company and reorganized it as the Sheffield Company (Leftwich 1961). The Sheffield Company constructed a street railway from Sheffield to Tuscumbia and Florence in 1904 (Adams 1977). The Sheffield Car

Barn was built at this time. A *Sheffield Reaper* article of 1905 (a) boasted of a number of new recruits to the industrial roster, including the Colonial Column Company; S. L. Stansell & Sons, furniture factory; H. W. Berheiser, sawmill and lumber factory; V. Gibb & Son, brass foundry; Edgar Hopeman and W. H. Rodell, hub manufacturer and woodworking plant; and Tuthill and Pettison, hardwood and lumber veneering. By 1906, the newly created Sheffield Cast Iron Pipe and Foundry Company was producing 40 tons of pipe per day (*Sheffield Reaper* 1906). Additionally, a 1903 Sanborn map listed Lowman Stove Works, Sheffield Compress Company, Sheffield Iron Works, Sheffield Rolling Mill Company, Southern Cotton Oil Company, Richmond Cotton Oil Company, and Union Planning Mill among the industrial community. Triggered by the Southern Railway Company's move, a renaissance was underway in the town by the Tennessee River.

The commercial district once again bustled with activity. On May 16, 1905 (b), the *Sheffield Reaper* reported that "More (Business) Buildings Going Up Than At Any Time In The City's History." According to the article, Charles Schall was building a two story business house on Third Street. John Neff was also constructing two stores on Third Street. Several buildings joined those on Montgomery.

Sheffield's resurgence is evident in a 1903 Sanborn map. Merchants occupied all the available spaces in the Mobile Block. All but one of the stores in the Habbeler Block were full. Similar circumstances prevailed in the Ware and Sheffield Land, Iron and Coal Company buildings. Merchants hocking furniture, dry goods, drugs, and groceries filled the Montgomery Block to capacity. Two buildings were built next to Meyer's Opera House (razed). They housed a wholesale grocery, drugstore, and a dry goods store. Two edifices were erected north of the Habbeler Block. Raleigh, Nashville, and Frankfort Avenues were home to a small scatter of business houses. Across the street from the Habbeler Block, a two story, brick commercial block was built to house a hardware store. A cluster of two story structures went up on the northeast corner of Montgomery Avenue and Third Street. The buildings ensconced several general stores, two dry goods places, a druggist, and a furniture store. A series of one and two story, commercial blocks fleshed out the business district on the west side of Montgomery Avenue.

According to a 1908 Sanborn map, much happened in the intervening years between 1903 and 1908. Between Nashville and Columbia Avenues on A

Street, the Union Railroad built a passenger depot. The west side of Montgomery Avenue was packed with buildings offering a wide range of goods. Grocery stores, restaurants, and dry goods abounded. Jewelers, furniture stores, and pool halls were in no short supply. On the east side of Montgomery Avenue, a hotel was erected adjacent to B Street. Off Montgomery Avenue began to attract business as well. Two of the buildings serviced a bicycle repair shop and sewing machine shop while there were several vacancies in the other buildings. Second Street between Montgomery and Nashville Avenues became the permanent home of a string of one-stories that housed a confectionery, restaurant, tailor, warehouse, and a grocer. Development occurred on Raleigh, Frankfort, and Pittsburgh Avenues as well.

Sheffield's industry enjoyed continued growth in the interval between 1903 and 1908. The *Sheffield Reaper* announced the construction of a brewery and ice plant on November 23, 1905 (e). Completion was slated for spring of 1906. In 1907, the Sheffield Coal and Iron Company, formerly of Pennsylvania, declared its intention of locating its headquarters in Sheffield (*Sheffield Reaper* 1907 b). Southern Cotton Oil Company stated that it would construct a fertilizer plant in 1907 (*Sheffield Reaper* 1907 c). A 1908 Sanborn map listed a number of newcomers to Sheffield's manufacturing scene. They include the Cudahy Packing Co., H. Marks Lumber Yard, Pratt Bottling Works, W. G. Richardson Coal Yard, Sheffield Boiler Works, Standard Hardwood Lumber Company, and Thomson and Smith Coal Yard.

While commercial and industrial construction moved at a brisk pace during the first decade of the twentieth century, new home starts lagged behind demand. Sheffield was a city on the move with a population that doubled from 2,500 in the early 1890s to 5,000 in 1905 (*Sheffield Reaper* 1907 a). Five hundred joined the census by 1907. Despite this influx, the *Sheffield Reaper* (1905 c) reported that "No appreciable effort is being made to provide homes for the many people who are to come…Every available house is occupied." Later in the same article, the *Reaper* urged those refusing to sell or develop lots to do so for "patriotic" reasons. For whatever reasons, patriotic or capitalistic, contractors began to meet the demand.

Contractor A. D. Thomson, an enterprising man, purchased between 40 and 50 small dwellings at Smiths mines in Lawrence, Tennessee with the intention of dismantling and rebuilding them in Sheffield (*Sheffield Reaper* 1905 d). In an article entitled "Building Activity," the *Sheffield Reaper* (1906 b) proclaimed the erection of many new houses throughout Sheffield. George Henderson was in the process of building two cottages near the car barn. W. S. Hatch had two cottages on Fifth Street on the rise. Max R. Block was building a two story house on Eighth Street and Nashville Avenue. In October of 1906 (c), the *Reaper* announced construction of four more homes near the car barn. A number of cottages on Dover Avenue and Twelfth Street were nearing completion. The Sheffield Concrete and Tile Company was constructing two houses on Montgomery Avenue in October of 1906 (*Sheffield Reaper* 1906 c). These houses featured rusticated concrete block construction. Other residences were in the works, especially in the vicinity of the car barn. Houses of worship built between 1903 and 1908 included the Grace Episcopal Church (1903) on Montgomery Avenue and Seventh Street and B'Nai Israel Temple (1908) in the 800 block of Atlanta Avenue.

The area roughly bounded by First and Sixth Streets and Frankfort and Little Rock Avenues witnessed some residential development between 1903 and 1908. A number of individual T- shaped and rectangular dwellings were scattered about the area as documented by the 1908 Sanborn map. Flats, a series of connected, one story apartments, were developed. The Pittsburgh Flats occupied the southwest corner of Pittsburgh Avenue and Third Street. The southeast corner of the two streets featured the Frankfort Flats. On the northwest corner of Third Street and Frankfort Avenue stood the Iron Flats; so designated for their iron cladding. These dwellings may very well have been home to Sheffield's growing African American population as a black lodge and M.E. Church were located between Third and Fourth Streets on Pittsburgh Avenue.

The economic momentum generated by Southern Railroad carried on into the second decade of the twentieth century. From 1907 to 1920, the population of Sheffield climbed to 6,682 (Friends of the Sheffield Public Library 1985). In order to meet the needs of the citizens, contractors continued to erect buildings. Between 1909 and 1915, two churches were built: the First Presbyterian Church (1911) on Fifth Street and the First United Methodist Church at 710 Montgomery Avenue. Eleven mercantile edifices rose during this period. Homes went up on vacant lots throughout Sheffield, including the areas bounded by 30th and 1st Streets and Dover Avenue in the eastern section and 16th and Montgomery Avenues in the southwestern corner, both of which were opened for development in 1890.

Chapter III

Despite the infrequent operation of the furnaces in the early twentieth century, Sheffield continued to bustle with activity. That activity greatly increased when it was learned that the Muscle Shoals area was selected as the site for a hydroelectric dam and two nitrate plants in 1916. Critical to the development of munitions, the nation's nitrate supply, which was supplied by South America, was threatened by Germany. Thus, it was deemed necessary to establish a domestic supply at the outbreak of World War I. A readily available source of hydroelectric power, i.e. the Tennessee River, a well developed river and rail infrastructure, and many industrial resources made the Muscle Shoals area an idea choice for the dam and nitrate plants (Friends of the Sheffield Public Library 1985). In 1917, construction began on two nitrate plants; Nitrate Plant No. 1 was established on the west side of Sheffield; Nitrate Plant No. 2 on the east side of town. The two plants, dam, construction of which began in 1918, and support facilities attracted an additional 30,000 people to the area (Friends of the Sheffield Public Library 1985).

Construction of the two nitrate plants began in late 1917. The undertaking necessitated the acquisition of thousands of acres of land. An article in the *Sheffield Standard* (1917 a) urged land owners to be reasonable in their negotiations with the federal government lest the project sour. For Plant No. 1, a total of 1900 acres was acquired; Plant No. 2 surpassed that with a total of 2306 acres (Friends of the Sheffield Public Library 1985) (Figure 4). Plant No. 1 opened on September 16. 1918 while Plant No. 2 opened at 20% capacity on October 26, 1918 (Friends of the Sheffield Public Library 1985).

The two manufacturing centers required a large working force. Plant No. 1 employed nearly 800 men; Plant No. 2 had a larger force of 19,263 (Friends of the Sheffield Public Library 1985). Sheffield was unprepared for the housing logistics of such a large force. To alleviate the housing crisis, the federal government committed to the construction of 1800 houses (*Sheffield Standard* 1918 a). Adjacent to Plant No. 1, 26 bunkhouses, a large mess hall, and 110 cottages, all of which were temporary, were erected (Friends of the Sheffield Public Library 1985). A more permanent village of 85 houses of stucco construction and tile roof was constructed. Known as the Liberty Village for its Liberty Bell configuration, the village is presently extant and is listed on the National Register. Temporary quarters went up at Nitrate Plant No. 2. A collection of more permanent dwellings was also fabricated. These homes were moved to the Highlands section of Sheffield after World War II (Friends of the Sheffield Public Library 1985). Several tent cities were pitched in the vicinity of the two plants (*Sheffield Standard* 1918 b).

New construction starts escalated. *The Sheffield Standard* (1917 b) declared "The boom is on!" The article stated that it was near impossible to keep track of all the property transactions as certain choice parcels changed hands two to three times in one day. In January of 1918 plans were underway to build a number of apartment houses (*Sheffield Standard* 1918 c). Four apartment houses dating to this period were identified in the residential survey. Residential construction associated with the nitrate plant boom is synonymous with the bungalow. Hundred of these residences with their distinctive low pitched roofs, emphasis on craftsmanship, and ample porches were built in this era. The bungalow genre represents the largest classification of buildings identified in the residential survey with a total of 207 houses. Victorians, which are associated with the initial phase of development and Sheffield's turn-of-the-century renaissance, constitute the second largest classification with 146 houses. A June 7, 1918 (*Sheffield Standard* c) article announced the construction of many bungalows along the car line. According to the article, Mr. John W. Johnson was building a bungalow on Montgomery Avenue and Eighth Street. Mr. John F. Funke was also building a bungalow next door to Mr. Johnson.

The business district welcomed many newcomers during the nitrate plant boom. The Sheffield Hotel planned an ambitious addition of 71 rooms (*Sheffield Standard* 1917 b). Judge Nathan indicated that he planned a two story business house for the corner of Montgomery Avenue and Fourth Street (*Sheffield Standard* 1918 d). The building was completed circa 1920. Mr. J. J. Kienker declared his intent to build on Montgomery Avenue. The two story edifice, proclaimed the "Handsomest Store in North Alabama," was open for business in April of 1919 (*Sheffield Standard* 1919 a). The Henderson Land and Development Company entertained the construction of three buildings (*Sheffield Standard* 1918 c).

The nitrate plant boon was short lived, lasting for only a two year period. The five furnaces, most of which had been rebuilt, continued to operate infrequently, and all would be closed permanently by the 1930s (Friends of the Sheffield Public Library 1985). In 1919 both nitrate plants were put on standby status; construction of Wilson Dam, which picked up some of the slack from the nitrate plant closures, ceased in 1921. A March 18, 1919 (*Sheffield Standard* b) article declared that "The boom has passed." A short lived recession or what the *Standard* termed a lower business volume, prevailed in the early 1920s.

A 1921 Sanborn map reflects both Sheffield's rapid growth during the nitrate plant boom and subsequent recession. The Chamber of Commerce was a new face on Montgomery Avenue. A two story, commercial block at 509 Montgomery Avenue, which was erected between 1908 and 1921, ensconced a garage and a furniture store, but its one story neighbor stood vacant. Built in 1918, the Red Cross Building (razed) occupied the corner of Montgomery and Alabama Avenues. The Sheffield Hotel had several vacancies and parts of the additions were unfurnished. Work on the new city hall was suspended indefinitely. The present city hall replaced it in 1926. While a skating rink at 508 Montgomery Avenue was vacant and in dilapidated condition, the E. C. Carter Garage (razed) at 501 Nashville Avenue was open for all of Sheffield's automobile needs. All of the available retail spaces in the Montgomery Block were full. The block immediately east served as a ball field. Completed in 1918, the offices of the Southern Bell Telephone Company resided in a building at 411 Nashville Avenue. All but one of the commercial blocks on the east side of the 300 Block of Montgomery Avenue had businesses; however, five out of six of the units at 105 – 115 East Third Street stood empty. The even numbered edifices on the 200 Block of Montgomery Avenue enjoyed favorable mercantile occupation. The 100 and 200 Blocks of East Second Street were a mixed bag of vacancies and no vacancies. Three of Sheffield's nitrate plant boom hotels were located on the east side of Montgomery Avenue in the 100 Block. Southeastern Express Company and American Railway Express had joined the Union Passenger Depot on East First Street.

On the 100 Block of the west side of Montgomery Avenue, four out of eleven commercial blocks were vacant. A shoe shop, barber, pool room, lunch room, seed and feed wholesale, clothing, and dry goods occupied the other units. Half of the spaces in the Mobile Block ensconced merchants. The Henderson Hotel, another boom hotel, utilized the second floor of 113 Montgomery Avenue. Six spaces of the erstwhile Habbeler Block, which had been acquired from Mr. Henry Habbeler in 1918, wanted for merchants. A two story, commercial block built circa 1917 housed a drug store at 215 Montgomery Avenue. The 200 Block of Raleigh Avenue featured a steam laundry. Erected circa 1920, the edifice housed the Quality Cleaners, then Pride's Cleaners. Few buildings claimed a west side 300 Block address on Montgomery Avenue. The 100 Block of West Third

Street offered a number of services and goods. An automobile garage, the Miller Building, which was constructed in 1919, was stationed at the southwestern corner of West Fourth Street and Raleigh Avenue. The area bounded by First and Sixth Streets and Austin and Little Rock Avenues featured a number of dwellings and warehouses, such as the Swift Company warehouse and the Philip Olim and Company warehouse. The Gulf Refining Company of Louisiana built a warehouse on First Street and Frankfort Avenue. A wholesale grocery business stood north of the refining company. The building was constructed circa 1915-1920.

The 1921 Sanborn map documents several subdivisions in Sheffield. Developed around the time of the boom, the Oak Hills Subdivision featured stunning views of the Tennessee River. A number of bungalows and Colonial Revival houses were crafted on wooded lots on Park Boulevard. The River Bluff Subdivision was evidently in the planning stage in 1921 as no roads had been mapped out in the area contained within the borders of the Tennessee River and Alabama and Georgia Avenues.

The 1921 Sanborn map clearly establishes the presence of an African American community in the southeast section of Sheffield. Bounded by Atlanta Avenue South and 21st Street S. E., the "Colored Neighborhood," as it was designated by the Sanborn Map Company, contained numerous L and rectangular shaped dwellings. A recent, cursory drive through of the area revealed that many of the dwellings are of the bungalow typology. A small number of Victorian cottages are extant. The M. E. Baptist and First Baptist Churches provide African Americans opportunities for organized worship services. A grade school and several stores were counted among the built environment of Sheffield's African American community.

Chapter IV

News of the automobile manufacturing magnate Henry Ford's interest in utilizing the nitrate plants and dam in a scheme to build a 75-mile long city along the Tennessee River, the focus of which would be the production of cars, ignited speculation frenzy in the Muscle Shoals. Real estate investors from Detroit, Chicago, New York, and other areas flocked to the area to buy and develop real estate (Friends of Sheffield Public Library 1985). A boom ensued.

One of the biggest Sheffield real estate transactions during the 1920s involved Mr. John J. Nyhoff of Troy, New York. An entrepreneurial mogul, Nyhoff, it seems, made a career of capitalizing on Ford's and others' industrial plants. He created nine large developments in Troy, New York where Ford was in the process of building a $15,000,000 tractor factory (*Sheffield Standard* 1922 a). Nyhoff also engineered large developments in Gary, Indiana, the Steel City, and Detroit, Michigan. Nyhoff, a March 3 1922 (a) *Sheffield Standard* article asserted, was quite assured that Ford would get the Muscle Shoals properties and Sheffield would become the largest city in the South. Toward that goal, Nyhoff purchased a fifteen acre site sandwiched between Nitrate Plant No. 2 and the Tennessee River at the eastern edge of Sheffield. With its proximity to Wilson Dam and Nitrate Plant No. 2 and the passage of the Jackson Highway and electric car line through it, the property was ideally situated.

Nyhoff developed a subdivision with a series of streets on the north and south sides of Jackson Highway. In 1924 (a), the *Sheffield Standard* carried the headline, "Nyhoff Properties Steadily Improving." The article stated that water line taps to 23 lots had been completed. Three residences stood ready for occupation. Twenty to thirty residences would follow in the next month. Nyhoff built two commercial buildings in his subdivision (Friends of the Sheffield Public Library 1985). Upper floors of a three story, brick building housed apartments and offices for the Nyhoff Real Estate Company while the bottom floor housed retail space. A furniture store occupied this space for much of the building's history. Nyhoff built another building on the opposite side of Jackson Highway. This two story, brick edifice originally served a Buick-Cadillac dealer. In the 1930s, it was a popular restaurant and night club (Friends of the Sheffield Public Library 1985). Adjacent to Nyhoff's buildings, the Elks built a three story, brick lodge.

A 1928 Sanborn map records the status of the Nyhoff subdivision in the late 1920s. In all, 39 dwellings, many of which are of the bungalow typology, were scattered about Nyhoff's development. Six commercial buildings, five of which faced the Jackson Highway, were among the built environment. One religious building, the M. E. Church, existed at the time of the Sanborn survey.

A spirit of economic optimism launched a serious residential construction campaign that spread throughout Sheffield. In May of 1923 (a), 25 houses were under construction according to a *Sheffield Standard* (1923 a) article. The newspaper projected that 200 new homes would be required to accommodate the population increase. In 1924, Sheffield boasted of a population of approximately 10,000 (*Sheffield Standard* 1924 b). By 1925, it was estimated that 400 residences were built in the Muscle Shoals district (*Sheffield Standard* 1925 a). The River Bluff Subdivision was open for development in the late 1920s (Sanborn Map Company 1928). The two and a half story, brick and stone Tudor Revival mansion on Riverbluff Drive was built circa 1925. Bungalows were standard residential fare at this time.

Commercial ventures abounded in this period. In 1926, A. L. Howell purchased three lots on Montgomery Avenue adjoining the Sheffield Hotel (*Sheffield Standard* 1926 a). Construction of the Airdome Theater, which would feature movies and vaudeville shows, was in progress at the corner of Montgomery Avenue and Fifth Street in 1924 (*Sheffield Standard* 1924 c). The Ritz Theater opened July 9, 1928 (*Tri-Cities Daily* 1928). Dr. H. A. Griffith built an office building on Nashville Avenue in 1928. Even the City of Sheffield found itself caught up in the boom. City officials had City Hall built in 1926.

A 1928 Sanborn map documents a number of additions to the business district. Attesting to the rising popularity of the automobile in American culture, three filling stations were built on East 2nd Street. Two still stand at opposite corners of East 2nd Street and Nashville Avenue. The third station at the corner of Columbia Avenue and East 2nd Street was replaced by a modern gas station in recent years. A two story, brick building (the Griffin Building) served an automobile sales and service outfit. The Sheffield Shirt Company, Inc. had a new building on the northeast corner of Columbia Avenue and East 2nd Street. Piggly Wiggly occupied one of the stores in the east side 400 Block of Montgomery Avenue. Across the street, the Airdome Theatre was open for Sheffield's entertainment.

Commercial development occurred on the west side of town as well. Between 1921 and 1928, a filling station came to occupy a triangular lot at the corner of Raleigh and Alabama Avenues. A large, two story brick edifice, which was divided into three retail spaces and storage, was built on the south side of the Ritz Theatre. It faced Raleigh Avenue, but was later razed. The Grand Theatre, an entertainment hall that catered to African Americans in the early 1920s, sat vacant in 1928. Montgomery Avenue buildings did not lack for tenants. Frankfort Avenue claimed Sheffield's wholesale business. Wholesale produce, groceries, and feed and seed occupied a series of buildings between West 2nd and

West 3rd Streets. Numerous dwellings occupied lots between Austin and Little Rock Avenues

Industry enjoyed gains during the 1920s. Dr. W. J. Galloway, a druggist, purchased property on Austin Avenue and First Street with the intention of constructing a factory in 1923 (*Sheffield Standard* 1923 b). Galloway planned to produce "Galloway's Embrocation" at his plant. A lead battery plate plant was slated for opening on March 1, 1923 (*Sheffield Standard* 1923 c). The King Company announced it would build a plant in Sheffield in 1926 (*Sheffield Standard* 1926 a). The King Company, manufacturers of White Way standards, anticipated a pay roll of a half million dollars. In 1928, the Nehi Company was in the process of equipping a plant in Sheffield (*Sheffield Standard* 1928 a). Nehi, however, postponed the opening for a number of years.

Were it not for the Sanborn Map Company, little would be known about the African American section of Sheffield. Historic texts mention next to nothing about the town's black history. Newspaper accounts tended to ignore blacks unless their misfortunes or transgressions were deemed newsworthy. Fortunately, the Sanborn Map Company documented the southeast section of Sheffield in 1928. According to the map, the number of residences dramatically increased from approximately 90 in 1921 to nearly 200 in 1928. Counted among the houses of worship were the Brown Temple C.M.E. Church, Calvary Baptist Church, Presbyterian Church, Baptist Church, Bethel M.E. Church, and the First Baptist Church. A one story structure on 20th Street S.E. and 13th Avenue S.E. served as a grade school in 1921 and was afterward converted to an undertaker's office. A much larger, two story building was built on 11th Avenue S.E. and 19th Street S.E. for the education of African American youths. C.D. Whitfield Lumber Company took over the former site of the Nitrate Coal and Grain Company on 21st Street S.E. and 13th Avenue S.E. Powell Coal and Grain Company maintained its location across the tracks. The Alabama Oil Company moved in one block southeast of C.D. Whitfield. The King Company occupied an entire block between 8th and 9th Avenues S.E. and 20th and 21st Streets S.E. In 1928, Sheffield's African American neighborhood was quite a vital community.

Ford's plans for the Muscle Shoals area were never realized. Senator George Norris of Nebraska opposed Ford's privatization of the Muscle Shoals properties, believing that the government facilities should remain in the public domain (Friends of the Sheffield Public Library 1985). Norris attempted to thwart Ford's efforts to acquire Wilson Dam and the nitrate plants by authorizing the Norris Bill, which called for government operation of the facilities. Ford tired of Norris' opposition and withdrew his proposal in 1924. Nonetheless, Sheffield capitalized on the automaker's vision for the Muscle Shoals area.

Chapter V

Sheffield was not immune to the deleterious effects of the Great Depression. The banks closed; people lost their jobs; businesses closed; and college students were forced to withdraw from school and return home to find whatever jobs were available (Sepmeier 1977). Succor came to Sheffield in the way of the Tennessee Valley Authority (TVA). Established in 1933, the TVA addressed a six-fold mission: improve manageability of the Tennessee River and provide flood control by the construction of dams; generate electrical power for the Tennessee River Valley; reforest denuded lands; provide for agricultural and industrial development; operate Muscle Shoals properties for national defense; and manufacture fertilizer (Headrick and Schafer 1993). The nitrate plants and Wilson Dam went into full production. Construction of Wheeler Dam several miles east of Wilson Dam began in earnest in 1933. TVA provided a boost to the Sheffield economy in the 1930s.

A 1936 TVA map provides compelling evidence as to the presence of the TVA in the Muscle Shoals district. Flanking the west and east sides of Sheffield were U.S. Nitrate Plants No. 1 and No. 2. Wilson Dam Village No. 2, a community of several hundred workers cottages, was situated just southeast of Nyhoff's Subdivision. Operated by the TVA and Civilian Conservation Corps (CCC), the Muscle Shoals Nursery lay southeast of U.S. Nitrate Plant No. 2. Although there had been several units of CCC companies supervised by TVA during the early 1930s, by 1936 CCC Company 4499 – "Camp Ala. TVA Project No. 2 of the U.S. Forest Service" - became the official permanent camp to occupy and work on the TVA reservation in Muscle Shoals. It was stationed northeast of Nyhoff's Subdivision. TVA central offices were ensconced in a building north of the CCC-TVA camp, which was re-designated in 1937 as Camp TVA-13.

Many in the Shoals district credited the New Deal with resuscitating the local economy. "Yesterday, depression, Today, a New Deal, and more business, more employment, and more money circulating," claimed a *Sheffield Standard* (1934 a) story after the newspaper conducted a survey of bankers, merchants, professional men, farmers, and laborers. The TVA employed 3,100 men on projects from Decatur to Tupelo, Mississippi. The CCC enlisted 1,000 young men in local conservation projects (*Sheffield Standard* 1934 a). In one pay period, the TVA accounted for a ¾ million dollar payroll in the Shoals (*Sheffield Standard* 1935 a). Approximately 4,200 men were employed in the construction of Wheeler Dam with a monthly payroll of $450,000. Another 2,600 men worked on clearing the Wheeler Dam reservoir with an aggregate payroll of $300,000 per month. The Public Works Administration (PWA) underwrote $230,000 for Sheffield's municipal power plant (*Sheffield Standard* 1935 b). Sheffield's power company building was a result of the PWA project. Among other activities, the TVA's nursery produced 40,000,000 seedlings that were ultimately planted in the Tennessee Valley as part of the TVA-CCC efforts to prevent soil erosion (*Sheffield Standard* 1935 c). Sheffield was the first of the Shoals' cities to provide its citizens with TVA produced power. Its White Way system was flooded with light generated by TVA power for the first time on March 19, 1936 (*Sheffield Standard* 1936 a). Sheffield won first place in the Alabama League of Municipalities contest having accomplished the most good with WPA money for cities with populations 5,000 to 25,000. In 1936, the PWA sponsored a $50,000 harbor project in Sheffield (*Sheffield Standard* 1936 b).

Through the 1930s, Sheffield attracted manufacturing enterprises. In 1932, the Robbins Tire and Rubber Company announced that it would acquire the erstwhile Rubber Products Corporation in Muscle Shoals City (*Sheffield Standard* 1932 a). The Robbins Tire and Rubber Company employed 100 men. The Union Carbide Company entertained plans to develop a plant in the Shoals district (*Sheffield Standard* 1938 a). Woburn Industries Farm Bureau planned a facility to process castor beans in Sheffield (*Sheffield Standard* 1939 a). Not missing a beat in the 1930s, the King Company rolled out White Way standard after standard. In 1930, the manufacturer filled a government order for 1200 post lamps (*Sheffield Standard* 1930 a). The company operated a six day, nine hour shift, employing many local men. In 1931, the King Company was awarded a contract to supply 219 White Way standards for the George Washington Bridge in New York (*Sheffield Standard* 1931 a). The King Company's White Ways were also featured on the Arthur Kill Bridge, Galveston Bridge, Texas Causeway Bridge, and Lake Ponchartrain Bridge in Louisiana.

Evidently, little new development occurred in the business district as there was a dearth of such news in the *Sheffield Standard*. According to a 1934 story, Swoopes Tailors, which was located on Second Street, was gaining a reputation "famed for its alterations and pressing and dry cleaning services" (*Sheffield Standard* 1934 b). P.B. Swoopes was a leading African American business man. J. Spielberger and Sons, Inc., located at 217 Montgomery Avenue, invited the public to visit the largest department store in Sheffield (*Sheffield Standard* 1935 d). Spielberger and Sons had been a Sheffield institution since it moved from Florence in 1898.

Sheffield faced yet another housing shortage in the 1930s. "Quite a shortage of desirable houses and apartments" in the Muscle Shoals area was reported by the *Sheffield Standard* (1934 c). That reopening of the Nitrate Plant No. 1 and No. 2 villages would relieve the problem was hoped by many. The Sheffield City Commission established a Housing Authority in order to find solutions to the housing crisis in 1935 (*Sheffield Standard* 1935 e.) A residential construction campaign was initiated in April of 1935 (*Sheffield Standard* 1935 f). In 1936, the Martin Home was built on a Park Boulevard lot overlooking the Tennessee River (*Sheffield Standard* 1936 b).

In the absence of new construction, Colbert County's Better Housing Program initiated a campaign to repair and remodel the existing building stock. "Clean Up, Paint Up Week" was quite a success in Sheffield in April of 1935 (*Sheffield Standard* 1935 g). Unfortunately, Colbert County's Better Housing Program encouraged residents to give their homes a youthful makeover (*Sheffield Standard* 1935 h). A more up-to-date and streamlined appearance could be obtained by the removal of gingerbread ornaments or fancy trim and the application of modern cladding, according to the housing authority. Thus it was that many Victorians were stripped of their quintessential stylistic details, a point that is not unnoticed by today's viewer. Many porches were streamlined during this period as well. For this reason, many Victorians have featured bungalow like porches for the last sixty years. Nonetheless, housing continued to be a problem throughout the remainder of the decade. In 1938, Judge Carmichael urged the construction of more homes (*Sheffield Standard* 1938).

A 1936 TVA map provides a sketch of Sheffield's development in the 1930s. The Nyhoff Subdivision appeared much as it did in 1928. Very little development occurred south of Jackson Highway between 1928 and 1936. The area bounded by Dover Avenue, 2nd Street, and 27th Street featured many residences which were erected between 1890 and 1936. That bounded by 27th, 31st, and 2nd Streets was sparsely populated by houses and a few commercial buildings. These buildings were built between 1924 and 1936. On the south side of 1st Street, the African American district was replete with residences, churches, stores, and industries. Several stores stood on Ashe Street south of the Southern Railway tracks. Commercial buildings abounded in the business district between Atlanta and Pittsburgh Avenues and Ashe and Sixth Streets. Hundreds of dwellings occupied lots from Dover Avenue to Park Boulevard and 1st Street to the river. Sandwiched between U.S. Nitrate Plant No. 1 and Park Boulevard were dwellings and industry.

Chapter VI

The direct link between TVA facilities and national defense kept life bustling in Sheffield during World War II. Reynolds Metal Company built a plant near Sheffield in 1941 (Friends of the Sheffield Public Library 1985). Additional chemical plants were constructed on TVA property. These plants and others in Muscle Shoals operated around the clock producing munitions and other wartime goods for the allied cause. With plentiful employment, the Sheffield population swelled from 7,933 in 1940 to 10,767 in 1950 (Friends of the Sheffield Public Library 1985). Housing was in great demand. People added on to their homes and converted garages in order to accommodate those requiring shelter. TVA built 250 prefabricated units throughout the area (Rosenbaum 1993). Sheffield contributed many resources to the war effort.

A calamity in 1938 led to development in the vicinity of 18th and 19th Avenues and 30th Street in the 1940s. On April 21, 1938, conflagration consumed the Sheffield High School on Atlanta and Annapolis Avenues and 9th and 10th Streets, which was built in 1923 (*Sheffield Standard* 1938 c). The City School Board issued a $104,000 bond to match a PWA grant of $123,000 with which to build a new high school (*Sheffield Standard* 1938 d). Hailed as modern in every detail, including its PWA modern design, the new high school opened for classes in March 1940. The school was situated between 28th and 30th Streets and 18th and 19th Avenues. The junior high was built on the previous high school site. Residential construction soon embraced the new high school.

In 1941, efforts were made to ameliorate the housing crunch. Sheffield Homes, Inc. built 65 homes in the High Point Subdivision (*Sheffield Standard* 1941 a). Constructed for defense workers, the houses were located in the vicinity of 30th Street and 17th Avenue near the high school. The Defense Homes Corporation bought 40 acres between 12th and 16th Avenues and 31st and 33rd

Avenues in 1941. The corporation contracted the Rust Brothers of Birmingham to erect 160 dwellings in what came to be known as York Terrace (*Sheffield Standard* 1941 b). Featured in the subdivision were 120 Type A two bedroom models; 24 Type B two bedroom models; and 15 Type D three bedroom models. The houses came with an electric range, electric refrigerator, electric water heater, base cabinets in the kitchen, oil burning floor heater, and tub and shower (*Sheffield Standard* 1941 c). Opened as rental units for defense workers in 1943, the houses were sold to the public in 1944.

For many areas nation-wide, the end of World War II meant the end of the war industries that fueled the economy. Such was not the case for the Muscle Shoals. In 1944, the U.S. Department of Labor predicted a roseate future for the Tri-Cities (*Sheffield Standard* 1944). Nitrates, phosphates, and aluminum, the Shoals contributions to the war cause, promised to be as vital in rebuilding the world as they had been in defeating the Axis powers. "An expected age of light metal would bring with it brisk demand for the area's aluminum" (*Sheffield Standard* 1944). TVA's fertilizer development facilities would be instrumental in helping feed the world's hungry.

Sheffield's bright future grew brighter when the industrial scene expanded. In 1946, the Union Aluminum Company (UALCO) opened for business. Located in a large plant that extended from Raleigh Avenue to Pittsburgh Avenue, the company manufactured aluminum casement widows (*Tri-Cities Daily* 1948). UALCO, which secured its raw materials from Muscle Shoals based Reynolds Aluminum, shipped its products nation-wide as well as to Cuba, Canada, the Philippines, Brazil, Argentina, and Puerto Rico. UALCO locally distributed its products through its affiliate Southern Sash. Southern Sash operated out of a facility on the south side of First Street. Together, UALCO, the world's largest manufacturer of aluminum casement windows, and Southern Sash employed 150. The J.A. Jones Construction Company of Sheffield was awarded a contract to manufacture artillery shells in 1945 (*Tri-Cities Daily* 1945). The shell maker would have employed approximately 1,500 people, but never went into operation as the war was nearly over. In 1945, TVA announced that is was moving the headquarters of its chemical operations to the Muscle Shoals (*Sheffield Standard* 1945 a). A Lime Cola plant was built at 703 South Montgomery Avenue in 1946 (*Sheffield Standard* 1946). Sheffield bustled with industrial activity in the late 1940s.

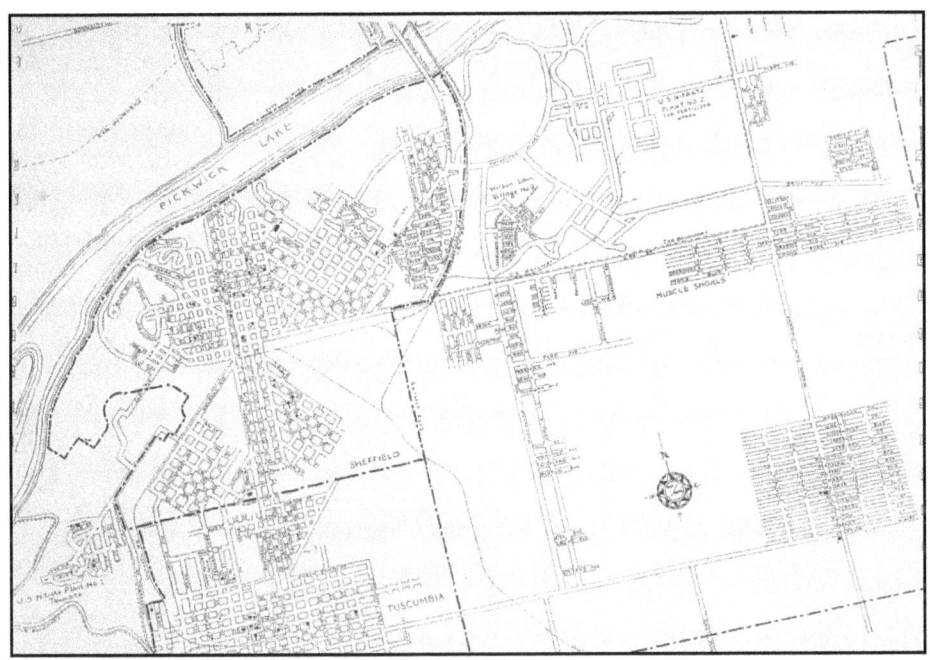
This 1948 street map shows Sheffield's boundaries before Village One was annexed.

In response to the prevailing economic optimism, many applied for building permits in 1945. New homes popped up all over the High Point and York Terrace Subdivisions (*Sheffield Standard* 1945 b). A number of homes were built of concrete blocks. At this time, Alabama Court was opened for development. Located near Park Boulevard and the Tennessee River, Alabama Court became the address of six, wood frame houses of the Colonial Revival genre in the late 1940s. Half of the Colonial Revival dwellings documented during the residential survey were added to Sheffield's housing stock in this time frame. In 1949, Southern Sash marketed the Lustron House for distribution in the Shoals. Constructed of prefabricated metal parts, the Lustron House was hailed as a breakthrough in house design. Only two were erected in Sheffield, one across from Village One and the second on the east side of town.

Unfortunately, conflagration destroyed a major fixture in the business district. The Sheffield Hotel burned to the ground on June 14, 1948 (Friends of the Sheffield Public Library 1985). The historic hotel was replaced by another in 1950 on the opposite side of Montgomery Avenue. Designed by local architect Howard A. Griffith, architect of the Sheffield High School, the Muscle Shoals Hotel features a sleek, stylistically simple modern design. The Water Department Building, another Griffith creation, was erected on Nashville Avenue in 1949. Four commercial buildings were constructed on Raleigh Avenue in the 1940s.

With a strong industrial foundation, Sheffield enjoyed relatively sound growth over the next five decades. Better late than never; the Ford Motor Company built a plant in the Shoals in the 1950s. The Rivermont Subdivision was developed west of Nitrate Plant Village No. 1 during this decade. While the African American section of town expanded southward, the open land between the Jackson Highway and the Tennessee River began to give way to development with each successive decade. Unfortunately, the construction of a number of shopping malls along South Montgomery Avenue in the 1960s and 1970s displaced a number of long time Montgomery Avenue businesses which sought more modern environs; but in the late 1980s, that trend began reversing itself as the City of Sheffield began preserving its historic resources.

References Cited:

Adams, Mrs. Harvey. "Sheffield, Its Early Beginnings." *The Journal of Muscle Shoals History:* Vol. V, p. 99-105. 1977.

The Alabamian, "Sheffield Construction." April 3, 1885.

Ames, Ethel. *The Story of Coal and Iron in Alabama,* Chamber of Commerce. Birmingham. 1910.

Damsgard, H. T., "The Iron Industry in Sheffield, Alabama." *The Journal of Muscle Shoals History:* Vol. III, 40-45. 1975.

Friends of the Sheffield Public Library. *Sheffield: City on the Bluff, 1885-1985.* Sheffield. 1985.

Headrick, Leslie Mowitt and Daniel Schafer. *A Peace Time Army: The Tennessee Valley Authority – Civilian Conservation Corps,* 1933 – 1942. Knoxville. 1993.

Leftwich, Nina. *Two Hundred years at Muscle Shoals.* Privately Published. Tuscumbia. 1961.

Nathan, Joseph H. "Town Building: The Case of Sheffield, Alabama." *The Journal of Muscle Shoals History:* Vol. III, p. 65-75. 1975.

Rosenbaum, Alvin. Usonia: Frank Lloyd Wright's Design for America." The Preservation Press. Washington, D.C. 1993.

Sanborn Map Company. Sanborn Fire Insurance Map of Sheffield, Alabama. 1889, 1894, 1903, 1908, 1921, and 1928. New York.

Sepmeier, Mrs. Emma Jane McKee. "Reminiscences of Life in Sheffield, Alabama, 1931 – 1934." *The Journal of Muscle Shoals History:* Vol. V, 112-120. 1977.

Sheffield Enterprise, "Cottages Being Built on Atlanta Avenue." September 14, 1890.

Sheffield Reaper, "Sheffield Attains Its Majority," June 15, 1905 a.
- "Sheffield's Growth." May 16, 1905 b.
- "Sheffield's Problem." August 3, 1905 c.
- "To Build Residences." July 20, 1905 d.
- "Brewery and Ice Plant." November 23, 1905 e.
- "Perfect Pipe Being Cast." August 2, 1906 a.
- "Building Activity." September 27, 1906 b.
- "Building Notes." October 25, 1906.
- "Census is Practically Complete." April 18, 1907 a.
- "Sheffield To be Headquarters." June 20, 1907 b.
- "Manufacturer of Fertilizer." August 29, 1907 c.

Sheffield Standard. "All Land Owners Must Co-operate." October 5, 1917 a.
- "Big Boom On." December 14, 1917 b.
- "Will Build Cantonment." June 7, 1918 a.
- "Living In Tents." February 15, 1918 b.
- "Buildings Going Up." June 7, 1918 c.
- "Business Houses." April 26, 1918 d.
- "Handsomest Store In North Alabama Opens." April 4, 1919 a.
- "High rents and business." March 28, 1919 b.
- "Big Realty Deal." March 3, 1922 a.

"Building Drive on In Sheffield." May 25, 1923 a.

"Another Factory To Be Erected." February 16, 1923 b.

"Another Industry For Sheffield." February 23, 1923 c.

"Nyhoff Properties Steadily Improving." April 11, 1924 a.

"Sheffield, City of Ten Thousand." August 22, 1924 b.

"Sheffield Gets Open Air Theater." June 27, 1924 c.

"Tri-Cities Enjoy Prosperous Year." January 9, 1925.

"Round About The District." April 16, 1926 a.

"Work On New Industry To Start In a Few Days." January 8, 1926 b.

"Nehi Company Opens Plant Here." July 27, 1928 a.

"Another Government Order Goes to King." August 8, 1930 a.

"Sheffield Industry Is Awarded Eastern Job." July 10, 1931 a.

"New Rubber Industry Soon to Operate Here." February 19 1932 a.

"TVA Seen as Base for All Improved Conditions Locally." 1934 a.

"Swoopes Tailoring Firm is Pioneer of Kind in City." December 21, 1934 b.

"House Shortage Here." May 25, 1934 c.

"TVA Spending Almost Million Dollars in District." June 21, 1935 a.

"Contracts Have Been completed in Every Detail." April 19, 1935 b.

"TVA Activities Developing Valley Interestingly Told." June 28, 1935 c.

"J. Speilberger and Sons, Inc." December 6, 1035 d.

"City Commission Approves Set Up of Housing Body." March 15, 1935 e.

"Many New Homes Are Under Construction: Remodeling Reported." April 5, 1935 f.

"Clean-Up, Paint-up Week Meeting with Success in Cities." April 19, 1935 g.

"New Exterior Makes Old Home Look Young." June 21, h.

"Sheffield White Way flooded With TVA Current Tuesday." March 20, 1936 a.

"Sheffield Harbor Being Constructed by PWA and board." July 31, 1936 b.

"Much Building Under Way in Muscle Shoals district in '36." November 27, 1936.

"Location of New Plant at Shoals First Step to It." November 11, 1938 a.

"Judge Carmichael Urges the Building of More Homes Here." April 8, 1938 b.

"Fire Departments of Entire District Fight to Ave Plant." April 22, 1938 c.

"City Commission Endorses Bond Issue for School Building." Spetember 16, 1938 d.

"Plant to Progress Castor Bean May Be Located Here." May 19, 1939 a.

"Sheffield Homes, Inc., to Build 36 More Modern Residences in City." August 15, 1941 a.

"160 Attractive New Rental Homes To Be built in Sheffield by U.S. Government Agency." November 28, 1941 b.

"Defense Housing Project Is About Ready For Workers." June 22, 1943 c.

"Alabama's Northwest Corner Said Rosy by U.S. Dept. of Labor." May 19, 1944.

"TVA's Main Office Coming to Muscle Shoals: Other Cities in Valley Will Retain Offices Too." June 29, 1945 a.

"Sheffield Has Construction Spurt." October 12, 1945 b.

"New Lime Cola Plant Located in Sheffield." August 23, 1946.

Tri-Cities Daily. "Theatre Opening." July 10, 1928.

"1,500 Employees Will Be Required to Fill Jobs in New Factory." January 26, 1945.

"The Story of Our Industry." August 24, 1948.

'Light Guard' Memorable for Military Focus and Social Activity[1]

by Reynold B. Burt

The Sheffield Light Guard, officially designated Company J., 2nd Regiment, Alabama State Troops, was organized July 10, 1888.

The membership included 55 energetic and entrepreneurial young men who had come to Sheffield to start new businesses. The Alabama State Troops had been established by the state legislature in 1877 to fill the need for a voluntary militia during the period following reconstruction. Like the Sheffield Light Guard, most of the state militia units were social as well as military in character.

The Sheffield Light Guard elected J. V. Allen, captain; H.J. Jones, secretary; and L.W. Dimic, treasurer. The Light Guard held regular meetings at which they practiced drilling and other military procedures. Target practice and proper care of firearms were important training requirements.

Joseph V. Allen served as Sheffield Light Guard and as Mayor of Sheffield in 1891-1893. Courtesy of Harold Damsgard

Uniforms – light blue with gold trimming and black hats – were purchased and the Light Guard began to make public appearances both to stimulate interest in the Guard and to render public service. On June 18, 1889, the Sheffield Daily Enterprise, reporting on a recent excursion to Huntsville, wrote "the Sheffield Light Guard wore their uniforms and put on a magnificent appearance. They show the proficiency of veterans."

When a group of prospective investors from New England came to Sheffield, the Light Guard acted as official hosts. They escorted the visitors to the

---

[1] Reprinted from Times Daily (Florence, AL, March 3, 1994.)

important industrial developments. After dinner at the Cleveland Hotel, they were entertained at a dance held in the Ware Building. The Light Guard was in charge of celebrations on public holidays such as the Fourth of July and Labor Day. An early appearance in their new uniforms was attendance as a group at Grace Episcopal Church, where Dr. B. Weddell, guard chaplain, was pastor.

Soon after they were organized, the Light Guard set an objective of building an armory. As fund-raising activities, frequent dances were held to which friends and acquaintances were invited. These dances, called "germans," honored various members of their group such as officers and public officials. A "german" was a reel-type dance with a caller. Music was provided by a string band.

On May 20, 1890, the Light Guard was in the parade at Richmond, Virginia at the unveiling of the statue of General Robert E. Lee.

On August 7, 1891, the Light Guard held a dance in the ballroom of the newly completed Sheffield Hotel in honor of one of their members, Dr. W. E. Proctor, who had been married recently to Lena Waddell of Florence. This occasion was a highlight of the social season.

Support groups came to the assistance of the Light Guard. Mrs. Sam Lata of Tuscumbia arranged an entertainment at the Opera House for the benefit of the Light Guard.

On July 20, 1889, the Light Guard left Sheffield en route to Montgomery to attend the annual encampment of the 2nd Regiment of the Alabama State Troops. In Birmingham, they were entertained at dinner by Major Campbell at the Opera House Hotel. The company arrived at Montgomery the next morning and went to Camp Hall at Highland Park. The following companies and their commanders attended:

Company A, Montgomery Greys, Lt. Watson; Company B, Oats Rifles, Troy, Capt. Shackford; Company C, Tuskegee Light Infantry, Capt. Cloud; Company D, Montgomery Blues, Lt. Davis; Company E, Woodstock Guards, Anniston, Capt. Agee; Company F, Warrior Guards, Tuscaloosa, Capt. Foster; Company G, Jefferson Volunteers, Birmingham, Capt. Clark; Company H, Lee Light Infantry, Opelika, Capt. Dean; Company J, Light Guard, Sheffield, Capt. Allen; Company K, Birmingham Rifles, Capt. Weakly.

Regimental officers included Col. Thomas D. Jones, commandant; Lt. Col. B.L. Corner, Capt. and Adj. J.O. Saffold, Capt. and Qtr. Mas. B. Holt, Sgt. L.L. Hill, and Asst. Sgt. R.L. Watkins. Staff was Sgt. Maj. R.D. Willow, Qtr. Mas. Sgt. Mike Graham, Com. Sgt. W.W. Heron, Color Sgt. C.C. Doud and Courier Jim Holtzclaw.

Each company was assigned an area with tents for the personnel and a mess tent for the company. The tents for the regimental officers and staff were at the camp's front.

On the evening of arrival at the camp, Adj. J. R. Saffold addressed the assembled regiment and announced that Commandant T. Jones had ordered a drill for 5:30 a.m. the next day. Daily schedules were posted announcing sessions for drilling, target practice, and firearm maintenance as well as recreation and free time.

The regimental band gave concerts each evening and these as well as the regimental drills were attended by many visitors from Montgomery.

On the evening of the fourth day in camp, the Sheffield Light Guard was entertained at its evening mess by the Montgomery brothers of Capt. Alfred Moses of Sheffield.

They brought oysters, fruit, and cigars to supplement the evening meal. This occasion, referred to as the "Moses Mess" was greatly enjoyed by the Guard and its visitors.

A battalion drill was ordered by Jones for the evening of the last day of the encampment. This drill was reviewed by the commandant and the governor of Alabama, as well as many visitors and friends.

The Sheffield Light Guard returned to Sheffield and was greeted at the railroad station by Joseph Nathan and many friends. The Light Guard then led a parade up Montgomery Avenue.

The Light Guard continued to represent Sheffield as Company J, 2nd Regiment of Alabama State Troops until the system was changed to the Alabama National Guard in 1899.

A Steamboat Named for Sheffield[1]

By Richard C. Sheridan

The first steamboat to arrive in the local area reached Florence in March 1821. The steamboat *Osage* delivered large quantities of lead, coffee, nails, sugar, tea, molasses, mackerel, and bar iron from New Orleans. Regular steamboat service on the lower Tennessee River began in 1822.

During the golden age of steamboats on the Tennessee River, the St. Louis and Tennessee River Packet Company operated several boats between 1887 and about 1930. Their steamboats carried passengers and immense amounts of freight with regularly scheduled trips to Sheffield and Florence.

Business was good in 1890, and the company contracted to have a new steamer built at Jeffersonville in May 1890. With a length of 185 feet and a width of 35 feet, she was considerably bigger and a little faster than most riverboats. The Louisville Courier-Journal reported Nov. 25, 1890, that "The beautiful new *City of Sheffield* was tested yesterday, found to perform perfectly, and will depart in a few days for her new home in St. Louis." According to the St. Louis Globe, the *City of Sheffield* arrived there on Dec. 3 with a cargo of Tennessee River lumber from Paducah. The St. Louis paper also described her as "beautiful" with 22 "lovely" stateroom cabins for passengers. The owners gave a luncheon the next day for merchants, boatmen, and others while the vessel was being loaded. She departed that afternoon on her maiden voyage to the Tennessee River.

She was unable to get to Sheffield, her namesake, and turned around at Riverton because of low water on the Colbert and Bee Tree Shoals. Rising water enabled her to continue on to Sheffield in late December where she was greeted by a large crowd. After a short trip to Florence, the *City of Sheffield* returned to spend the night.

The next day an elegant banquet for 75 ladies and gentlemen was held in the steamer's dining room. Champagne, ice, fruit, and conserves were served along with more substantial food. Speeches were made by Sheffield's city fathers as toasts were made to the new vessel and the ladies. And the city presented a very pretty set of "colors" to Captain Todd and his crew. The crew included a

---

[1] Reprinted from the Times Daily, Florence, AL. May 15, 2005,

master, two clerks, two pilots, two engineers, two mates, carpenter, watchman, and steward.

The steamboat "City of Sheffield" carried freight and passengers between St. Louis and Sheffield in the 1890s. The vessel was 185 feet long and 35 feet wide. It was destroyed by fire about 1896. Courtesy of Area Research Center, University of Wisconsin – La Crosse.

By the summer of 1891, a trip on the Tennessee River aboard the new steamboat had become a favorite excursion for St. Louis people. One group had such a good time on the *City of Sheffield* that they gave a picnic for the crew. The fare was only $12 for the 8-day round trip.

When Shiloh National Military Park opened in 1894, the *City of Sheffield* and other steamers were engaged to take old soldiers to the battlefield from St. Louis, Florence and other ports along the way. Many veterans traveled to Florence on the L & N Railroad and were taken to the battlefield site by the *City of Sheffield.*

The river steamers sometimes sank due to fires, explosions, or running into snags or sandbars. And the ***City of Sheffield*** suffered the same fate. In the late summer of 1895, she hit an obstruction in the Mississippi River and sank near Mound City. But she was quickly raised and put back into service. A year or so later, the ***City of Sheffield*** was destroyed by fire at Grand Tower, IL. Other steamboats continued to ply the Tennessee River well into the 1920s. But river traffic virtually came to an end during the Great Depression.

Early Mayors of Sheffield
The First 50 Years
1885 to 1935

by Carole Edwards Driskell

Thirty-three men have served as Mayor of Sheffield during its 126-year history. This list of dedicated civic leaders includes four lawyers, two doctors, a pharmacist, a teacher, a dentist, and many successful businessmen. Many were veterans of the military, including the Confederate Army through World War II. One mayor, Lewis Timberlake, was a highly decorated Naval aviator, receiving the Navy Cross for extraordinary heroism in World War II. Three mayors died in office and one resigned. Five were appointed to fill vacancies. From 1885 to 1912, the city's form of government was the Mayor and Aldermen. The citizens of Sheffield voted on August 19, 1912 in favor of the following proposition:

> Shall the Proposition to Organize the City of Sheffield under the Commission Government Act of the Legislature of Alabama of 1911, Applicable to Class D Cities be adopted.

The city's form of government then became the Commission form of Government and a board of three commissioners were elected with the board naming its "President of the Board of Commissioners" who was known as the Mayor. In December,1928, a petition was presented to the Probate Judge of Colbert County, asking that:

> The proposition of abandoning the Commission form of Government of the City of Sheffield and returning to the Aldermanic form of government as it existed in the said city at the time said Commission form of government was adopted, be submitted to the voters of said City.

This proposition was defeated, and the Commission form of Government remained in effect until 1988, when the Mayor and Council form of Government was approved by the voters of Sheffield. None of the early mayors were natives of Sheffield because they came from other parts of Alabama and nearby states to seek their fortune in the new and growing "Steel City of the South." One mayor,

Phil Campbell, was born in Liverpool, England. All of them tackled with energy and determination the problems that they faced in running the city during economic depressions as well as boom times. This article presents biographical information on those mayors who served from the founding of Sheffield to the beginning of World War II.

Captain Alfred Huger Moses (1885-1887): After Sheffield was incorporated on February 17, 1885, Governor Edward A. O'Neal appointed Alfred Moses as the town's first mayor. Colbert County Probate Judge John A. Steele, administered the oath of office to Captain Moses and he, in turn, administered the oath to the aldermen on February 25, 1885. Alfred Huger Moses was born in Charleston, South Carolina in 1840 to Levy and Adaline Moses. In 1860, after graduating from the College of Charleston, he moved to Montgomery, Alabama where he apprenticed in a local law office. When the Civil War erupted, Moses became the clerk of the Confederate District Court in Montgomery and a member of the Alabama Rebels, a civil defense volunteer militia company. Toward the close of hostilities he was made captain of a company, and saw service in and around Pensacola and Mobile. After the war his two brothers, Mordecai and Henry, joined him in Montgomery; and the three entered the city's real estate market. By the 1870's they developed the successful Moses Brothers Banking & Investment Firm. He was married November, 1871, to Janett Nathan, sister of Joseph Nathan; and five children were born to them: Sarah A. , Alfred II, Adaline L. , Lee J. and Joseph W.

Captain Alfred Huger Moses, founder of Sheffield, was appointed mayor when the town was incorporated in 1885.
Courtesy of Sheffield Public Library

In 1883 Moses visited Florence with the thought of investing in land near Florence because of a projected new railroad to run from

Kentucky to the Southeast via Florence and the iron ore, coal, and limestone deposits in the area. On the second day of his visit he was invited by Colonel Walter S. Gordon to stay an additional day and tour the area on the south side of the Tennessee River. Upon the completion of the tour of Colbert and Franklin Counties, Moses envisioned building an iron-producing city greater than Birmingham; and he would call it Sheffield, after the great steel producing city of Sheffield, England. By the end of that day, Moses and Gordon had agreed to joint ownership of 30,000 acres of iron ore land in Franklin County and the area between the river bluff and Tuscumbia (known as York Bluff). The newly organized Sheffield Land, Iron and Coal Company was authorized to do business on December 5, 1883, and Captain Moses was named Vice President and General Manager. Beginning on May 8, 1884, the "Great Land Sale" was held. The three-day sale was well attended. Five hundred lots were sold and the sale realized $350,000. By 1889 five blast furnaces were in operation or on the drawing board.

Mayor Moses was known to be a gentleman of polished address and superior education, who made a pleasant and agreeable impression on everyone. He had a beautiful home built at the head of Montgomery Avenue at the river bluff. Sadly, in 1891, due to a recession and bank failure combined with Moses' miscalculating the willingness of railroads to expediently link Sheffield with major cities and his over-estimating of the region's iron ore supply, the enterprise failed along with the Moses family bank in Montgomery. When the market price for iron dropped below $12.00 per ton, less than the cost for Sheffield's foundries to produce and deliver it, the town's furnaces were banked and most of its residents departed. Moses and his family removed to St. Louis where they lived for about 30 years in greatly reduced circumstances, his dreams destroyed by the boom-and-bust cycle of the Gilded Age. He died in St. Louis in 1918. He and his wife were buried in Montgomery where he had enjoyed his greatest success, rather than Sheffield, a city he envisioned, built, and then lost. The Moses History Room at the Sheffield Public Library is named for Mayor Moses.

Sources: Northern Alabama-Historical Biographical, Sheffield City on the Bluff, Jewish World Review & The American Jewish Historical Society

Charles Thomas Morris (1887-1889) was a medical doctor—a graduate of the University of Kentucky. He was the second mayor of Sheffield and was the first elected mayor (as the founder of the City of Sheffield, Alfred H. Moses, was appointed mayor by the Governor of Alabama.) Dr. Morris was born May 18, 1857, and was married to Mary Ida Payne of Auburn, Alabama, June 9, 1880. They apparently came to Sheffield in 1885 or 1886. They were the parents of the first white child born in Sheffield, Cornelius VanCleef Morris, on August 22, 1886. Other children born to the couple were: Mary Elizabeth—Dec. 15, 1881; Alma Bertrand—July 6, 1884; Ida Caroline—March 8, 1891; Charlotte Naomi—Sept. 29, 1894, and Jane Warren—August 31, 1898.

Dr. Charles T. Morris, a Sheffield physician and drug store owner, was Sheffield's first elected mayor.
Courtesy of Charles Morris Mead

The family home was located at 708 North Nashville Avenue, and stands there today in excellent condition (in 2008 the house was restored to near its original appearance). He operated a drug store in Sheffield for a time. From his hand-written annual report for the first completed year of his term, Mayor Morris reports:

> I am exceedingly glad to be able to state that the City has grown very rapidly for the last twelve months and has increased from three or four hundred to over three thousand inhabitants.

In his report he recommended, "that a suitable lot be secured and a house be built on it to be used for a colored public school." In November, 1905, Dr. Morris's daughter, Mary Elizabeth Morris Mead (Mrs. W. J. Mead), was killed when the buggy in which she and her two-year old son and her younger sisters, Charlotte and Jane Morris, were riding was struck by a street car on Atlanta Avenue between Seventh and Eighth Streets in Sheffield. The horse was frightened and stepped on the tracks as the express car approached. Charlotte

Morris was seriously injured while the younger children escaped serious injury. Dr. C. T. Morris died July 22, 1919. Both Dr. & Mrs. Morris are buried in Sheffield Oakwood Cemetery.

Sources: The Morris family Bible provided by Mr. Charles Morris Mead, great grandson of Dr. Morris, a hand-written report for the year May, 1887 to May, 1888 and the Sheffield Enterprise

George T. McGregor (1889-1891): The following comments were taken from an 1890 article in the *Sheffield Enterprise*:

> The Honorable George T. McGregor is a native of Mississippi where he was a successful businessman, but determined that Sheffield was the place for a progressive man to rise, and so was among the very first to buy property at the original sale in 1884. He embarked in the grocery business with two houses and surprised even himself by the sales. He then branched out and opened the largest dry goods store in the city; and seeing a bargain bought out a feed business, owning and operating all simultaneously. He is one of the largest property owners in the city in 1890. Many of his friends, seeing his business qualifications, induced him to make the race for Mayor. He did so and was elected. He served without salary; and, as a public officer, is as successful a mayor as he is a businessman. As a citizen, he is for Sheffield and her interests at all times. Any public move met his endorsement, his encouragement and his aid. One could carry to him any scheme for the advancement of Sheffield and it would gain the aid of this Mayor. His administration is one that is marked with disagreements and dissensions; but there is not a man in the city who could beat him today for Mayor. As a citizen he is for Sheffield and her interests at all times. Any public move meets his endorsement, his encouragement and his aid. Carry to him any scheme for the advancement of Sheffield and it will gain the aid of her mayor. As a private gentleman, he is generous, charitable, honorable and manly. Sheffield, in his hands, is safe.

He removed to Memphis in 1918 and returned to Sheffield in 1928. Mr. McGregor died in April, 1929 at the age of 79 at the home of his daughter, Mrs. R. Y. Sibley, at 1111 Dover Avenue in Sheffield following a "lingering illness of six months." He was buried in Sheffield Oakwood Cemetery. He was the grandfather of Mr. Ray Azbell, Manager of the Sheffield Utilities Department from 1971-1986.

Sources: Sheffield Enterprise-1890 and Raymond Azbell, grandson

Joseph Virginius Allen (1891-1893): Joseph V. Allen was born to ex-Confederate General William W. Allen and Susan Pendleton Ball Allen in Montgomery on June 9, 1866. Joseph was one of nine children. He went to a private school in Montgomery while growing up and did not attend college. He went to work in the office of the Mobile and Montgomery Railroad and later worked for the Louisville and Nashville Railroad. Also, he worked as a cashier for 3 ½ years for the First National Bank of Montgomery. In 1887 he came to Sheffield as a private secretary to Captain Alfred H. Moses, (founder and first Mayor of Sheffield and Vice President of the Sheffield Land, Iron, and Coal Company). Allen was elected Treasurer of the Sheffield Land, Iron, and Coal Company in 1888 and became an officer in many of the companies organized in the new city.

In November of 1891, at the age of 25, he was married to Annie Lou Weakly; and he was elected Mayor of Sheffield the same year. He was "a remarkable young democratic candidate for Mayor of Sheffield that even the Republicans supported." Captain and Mrs. Allen lived in the Sheffield Hotel in a suite of rooms. Two children were born to the Allen family in Sheffield—Porter and Annie Louise, who died as an infant. Their first child, a son, Porter Weakly Allen, was born in the Sheffield Hotel. The proud father promptly went down to the desk of the hotel and registered his son and said of the baby, "he was sent from Heaven." Another child, a daughter, Annie Louise, was born in Sheffield, but died while still an infant. Two other children-Joseph, Jr. and Harriet Elanore-were born after the family moved to Birmingham. Allen was Captain of the Sheffield Light Guard, a militia company. On January 31, 1893, a special session of the City Council was called for the purpose of tendering Mayor Allen's resignation. The Clerk read the resignation to take effect after the election and qualification of his successor. After remarks, the resignation was accepted according to the terms offered. The following day, February 1, 1893, at the regular meeting of the Council, Mayor Allen announced a vacancy in the Mayor's office. Alderman James C. Harris received the majority of votes cast and was declared the duly elected successor in office. Mayor-elect Harris was sworn in by retiring Mayor Allen. Harris took the chair and read a resolution regarding J. V. Allen:

> Whereas, J.V. Allen has decided to remove from Sheffield and therefore resign his office as Mayor of Sheffield; and Whereas, the City Council of Sheffield appreciated his vigorous administration in this, a young and therefore difficult City to govern, and his marked financial ability in guiding the City through the financial crises of the first year, which has been the most difficult in the City's history and his generosity in declining the salary due him under the ordinances, is desirous of officially expressing such appreciation; Therefore, be it resolved by the City Council of Sheffield that it expresses its gratitude to Mayor Allen for his courteous, dignified, and highly creditable conduct in serving the City as its Chief Executive and accepts his resignation with keenest regret and extends to him sincere wishes for prosperity and every success in his chosen home.

Mayor Allen was the youngest Mayor of Sheffield, the only mayor to be married while in office, and apparently the only mayor to resign that position. The family moved to Birmingham where Captain Allen worked for the Ivy Coal and Iron Company. He later became the secretary of the Coal Operator's Association in Birmingham; and Governor O'Neal appointed him as Tax Collector of Jefferson County. He died May 26, 1917, at the age of 50, in Birmingham and was buried there in Elmwood Cemetery.

Sources: Sheffield City Minute book & Sheffield Library researcher Betty Dyar

James Craig Harris (1893 and 1903-1905): Born in Tippah County, Mississippi, October 19, 1860, Mr. Harris came to Sheffield in 1890, to practice law. His law office was located in the 300 block of North Montgomery Avenue, downtown. He was active in the City's civic and church activities. In 1895 he was elected President of the Land Company and further engaged in buying and selling real estate. He was elected by the City Council to complete the unfinished term of Mayor J. V. Allen upon his resignation in February, 1893. He was elected to a full term in 1903 and served until May of 1905. The following Street Tax Ordinance of 1904 was unanimously adopted April 6, 1904:

> Be it ordained by the City Council of Sheffield, Alabama, that all male inhabitants of the City of Sheffield over the age of eighteen years and under the age of forty-five years, shall be required to work on the streets of the city for six days during the year 1904, at such time and place as may be ordered, under the direction of the City Marshal or some person appointed by the Street Committee. Provided, that any person paying to the City Collector the sum of three dollars shall be relieved from such work. Be it further ordained, that any person liable to work on the streets, who shall be notified by the Marshal, or officer appointed by the Street Committee to appear at a certain time and place to work on the street, who fails to appear and do the work, or to pay the sum of three dollars to the City Collector, shall be guilty of a misdemeanor, and on conviction must be fined not less than five nor more than twenty-five dollars, and may be sentenced to hard labor on the streets not more than ten days, either or both.

In 1945, Mr. Harris contributed $5,000 toward the completion of the basement room to house the Men's Bible Class at the First Methodist Church of Sheffield. The class was named the Harris Class in his honor for his contribution, as well as for his many other philanthropic endeavors. A picture of Mr. Harris still hangs in the Men's Bible Class in the basement of the church. He died January 17, 1956, at the age of 95, and is buried in Sheffield Oakwood Cemetery.

Source: Old church history records compiled in 1983 by Harold Damsgard and Sheffield City Minute Book

Philip Campbell (1893-1895): Born December 8, 1848, in Liverpool, England, it is not known when Phil Campbell immigrated to the United States of America. In 1880 he was employed as a railroad construction superintendent in Evansville, Indiana. A few years later, he moved to Sheffield to supervise the construction of the Birmingham, Sheffield & Tennessee River Railroad. Campbell was appointed to the first board of aldermen for the new city of Sheffield in 1885. In a prepared written statement, upon taking the oath of office as mayor Campbell stated:

I favor all public improvements, Schools, Public Buildings, Streets, Sewers, etc., but first the finishing of the School Building, so that it may be opened as rapidly as possible to meet the pressing wants of the children of the city. I favor a wise and conservative administration of the different branches of the city government, and the enactment of all ordinances necessary for the just and proper government of the city.

Mayor Campbell also stated that he would ask the cooperation of the citizens in doing what was best for the city and also harmony in the council. In the 1880's when Phil Campbell was overseeing the construction of the railroad near a developing town in Franklin County, he was approached by a prominent merchant, Mel Allen, with a deal: If Campbell would bring the railroad by the town (which had no name) and establish a depot and a side track there, the town would be named for Campbell. This statement led to Phil Campbell being the first town in Alabama to have the first and last name of a person. Shortly before 1900, Campbell left Sheffield and located in New Orleans where he met and married a young woman, Catherine Flynn, and three children were born to them. Though Catherine was 20 years younger than her husband, she died when the children were toddlers and Campbell was in his late 50's. He did not remarry; and he reared the children alone. In later life, he worked as a real estate agent. He died in 1932, at the age 84, in New Orleans and was buried there.

Sources: Research by Richard Sheridan, Sheffield Historian, Phil Campbell Reflector, The Sheffield Reaper, and information collected by Kathrine Cottrell and Walter T. Gamard, grandchildren of Phil Campbell

Thomas B. Woodard (1895-1898): Thomas B. Woodard was born in Tishomingo County, Mississippi, August 3, 1854, and was reared on a farm. He was 24 years old when he took up a commercial life. After spending a few years in business in his native state, he came to Sheffield in February, 1887, and entered the business world. He was elected Mayor in 1895. When the classes opened that year the City funded the School Board $175.00 per month. The City School Fund was exhausted January 2, 1896. Mayor Woodard was responsible for the board sidewalks being taken up and replaced with "gravel sidewalks, leveled and smoothed down, not less than 4 feet wide and 4 inches deep." It was during Mayor Woodard's term in office that the controversy concerning the question of the City owning its water and power systems or allowing an independent contractor to build and own the systems. This controversy continued for several more years. He was a popular Mayor of Sheffield who was re-elected 1897 but did not complete his second term. His health had begun to fail and after a trip to Hot Springs, Arkansas, he returned looking splendid, but after a while the disease took a fresh hold and he again went to the Springs, but this time its curative powers could not stay the malady. He returned to his home where loving hands could administer to his needs. His obituary read:

> Soon he had to take to his bed, then the battle of medical skill and vitality against the destroyer was waged. Yet, withal, the call must be obeyed, and the spirit of Mr. Woodard went before its God. He died at 5:45 p.m., Wednesday, June 8, 1898. The first Mayor of Sheffield to die in office. He lacked one month and 26 days of being 44 years old. He had a genial nature, a kind heart, and many friends.
>
> He was buried near Corinth, Mississippi, in the old family cemetery.

Sources: The Sheffield Reaper, June 11, 1898 and Sheffield City Minute Book

Richard J. Thurmond, Jr. (1898-1903): Mr. Thurmond was born April 26, 1867, in Mississippi and came to Sheffield in 1891. He had a nice home built at 1100 North Montgomery Avenue in 1893. He began a contracting business in Sheffield and became very much involved in civic and social life of the city. He was elected to two terms as Mayor of Sheffield, after completing the un-expired term of Mayor Woodard, who died in office. His performance as mayor during his incumbency gave universal satisfaction. During his administration the sexton's house was built on the Cemetery grounds. The following ordinances passed by the council during 1898 and 1899 reveals problems experienced by the City during Mayor Thurmond's administration:

> After 15 October 1898, any unmarried woman, not being a member of a supporting family and having a reputation for lewdness, or having no visible means of support, shall be deemed guilty of vagrancy or lewdness and arrested, and upon conviction shall be fined not less than $5.00 for the first offense, $10.00 for the second offense, and $20.00 for the third and each subsequent offense.

An ordinance forbidding Sunday sales of liquor was passed with a $25.00 fine charged for each violation of the ordinance as well as a new ordinance concerning livestock:

> It shall be the duty of the City Marshal or other Police Officers of the City finding any horses, mules, goats, or hogs roaming at large within the City limits to take up such animals and impound the same.

After leaving the mayoralty, he remained in city government having been elected in 1903 as a member of the Aldermanic board. He was a member of the Order of Knights of Pythias, of the Independent Order of Odd Fellows, of the Brotherhood of Elks, and others. On August 8, 1889, Mr. Thurmond married Miss Dora Harris of Ripley, Mississippi. Three children were born to them. He died September 24, 1908, and was buried in Sheffield Oakwood Cemetery.

Sources: Sheffield of Today 1903, Sheffield City Minute Book, and Sheffield Library Researcher Betty Dyar

Dr. Hugh W. Blair (1905-1909): A native of Georgia, Dr. Hugh W. Blair, was born in Savannah on October 2, 1862. He was a graduate of the University of Tennessee and Cumberland University. He graduated first in his class at Vanderbilt Medical School in 1885. Upon graduation, he began practicing medicine in Carthage, Tennessee, and in a short time was made President of the County Board of Health. He and his father, Dr. Hugh A. Blair, came to the young and growing town of Sheffield in March of 1887 and began a remarkably successful medical practice in the Montgomery Block building. Young Dr. Blair served for many years as surgeon for all the railroads and large corporations of the district. In 1901 Dr. Blair invited Dr. Wyatt H. Blake, his former Vanderbilt Medical School classmate, to join his medical practice in Sheffield. Dr. Blair was also a successful businessman, owning many valuable properties in the City and an elegant home on Montgomery Avenue. The City was in poor financial condition in 1905 when he was elected Mayor of Sheffield, but when he left office the City owed no debt and a sizable reserve had accumulated. Upon his retirement as Mayor of Sheffield in 1909, the following resolution was introduced by Aldermen Cosper and Schaut:

> Be it resolved by the City Council of Sheffield that: Whereas, our Mayor, who has given the City of Sheffield four years of able and faithful services, is about to retire from office; and Whereas, during all these years of his Mayoralty, he has been courteous and thoughtful, while at the same time, firm and positive in discharge of his important duties; and Whereas, in the discharge of his duty to the public, he has by building up, and strengthening the financial condition of the City, promoting its sanitation, conserving its morality, enforcing its laws, enlarging its system of sewerage, enhancing the effectiveness of its system of fire protection, improving its streets, and establishing a system of sidewalks second to none in Alabama; and Whereas, by all of his official acts and conduct, he has earned the love and gratitude of this body and of the great body of our citizenship; Now Therefore, be it resolved, that this preamble and resolution be unanimously adopted by this body and that they become a continuing testimony, not only of the appreciation of his fellow workers, but of the appreciation and esteem of all of his fellow citizens for his splendid, wise, and efficient administration of the duties of his responsible office.

An excerpt from retiring Mayor Blair's reply follows:

> All of these things and much more, my dear friends…for your comfort and welfare has only been made possible by your encouragement and assistance; and on retiring I want to briefly say

that it has been said that somewhere in the human heart there blooms a flower, which cannot be seen by the human eye, and which no human hand has ever touched—the flower of gratitude. This flower I lay at the feet of you, my friends, tonight, as an everlasting token of my love and esteem for you, and with the same spirit of loyalty that has prompted you to assist me with your wise council in sunshine as well as in storm.

His death by suicide on June 12, 1917, was described in the *The Sheffield Standard* as a "Deplorable Tragedy" and "A shock beyond expression" to the community. His funeral was conducted at Columbia Avenue Presbyterian Church in Sheffield; and he was buried in Sheffield Oakwood Cemetery.

Sources: Sheffield City on the Bluff, Sheffield Standard—June 16, 1917, and Sheffield City Minute Book

Captain Washington Rose Weston (1909-1910): W. R. Weston, a prominent businessman of Sheffield, was born at Weston, Georgia, March 24, 1847. In December, 1861, at the age of 14, he left school to enlist in the Confederate Army. He was seriously injured in the Civil War's Seven Days' Battle in front of Richmond and was discharged. Following his recovery, he rejoined the army in the Sixty-fourth Georgia Regiment, in which command he remained until 1864, when he was captured by some of General Grant's men; and because of his very young age, he was sent to Washington, where he subsequently took the oath of allegiance and remained until the close of the war. After the war ended in 1865, and until he came to Sheffield in 1886, he was variously employed in railroading, attending school, farming, manufacturing, orange-growing, milling, and merchandising. In Sheffield he was engaged in the lumber business, and was one of the incorporators of the Sheffield Manufacturing Company, of which, he became secretary-treasurer and business manager and held those same offices at the Sheffield Ice Company. He served as Sheffield City Treasurer in 1889. He was Mayor of Sheffield for slightly over one year from May 2, 1909, to May 8, 1910. His obituary read:

> He became ill on Saturday, April 30, after emerging from an exciting and strenuous campaign for nomination for Judge of Probate, in which he worked unremittingly for several weeks, exposing himself to various forms of weather. The attack was

malignant from the beginning and little hope was given his family and friends by the physicians. He was the second Mayor of Sheffield to die in office; and Robert H. Wilhoyte was appointed to serve out his term. Weston was 63 years of age. Under an escort of Confederate veterans of Camp W. A. Johnson, of which Capt. Weston was a member, his remains were borne from the family residence to the First Methodist Church in Sheffield where the funeral took place Sunday afternoon at 3:00 o'clock. The concourse was one of the largest ever before seen in Sheffield, the building being crowded and many being forced to remain on the outside during the services, which were conducted by Rev. L. F. Stansell of the Methodist Church and Rev. Joseph Hardy of the Episcopal Church. The officials of the city were present in a body, the five members of the City Council and the City Clerk acting as pall bearers. At the conclusion of the religious services the Masonic fraternity took charge and conducted the obsequies at the grave.

The minutes of the May 14, 1910, Sheffield City Council meeting carried the following resolution:

Whereas, under Divine dispensation, Hon. W. R. Weston, Mayor of the City of Sheffield and our honored Co-Laborer has been called from the activities of office after just one year of service; therefore, be it resolved by the City Council of Sheffield, Alabama, in adjourned session assembled, that we hereby deplore the sad providence which has taken him from his unfinished work in which he had taken such active and intelligent interest. Resolved further, that the City has lost a faithful and painstaking official; the City Council, a congenial and courteous presiding officer; and the executive branch, a diligent and just coadjutor. To his bereaved and stricken family, we tender our heartfelt condolence and sympathy, assuring them of our warmest interest and deep sorrow, because of their loss. We hereby order that the City Hall be draped for thirty days as a badge of mourning for his death, and that a copy of these resolutions be spread upon the Minute Book of this Council, a copy published in the Sheffield Standard and the Tri-

Cities Daily; and that a copy be forwarded to his family under the Seal of the City.

He is buried in Sheffield Oakwood Cemetery.

Sources: Sheffield Standard—May 13, 1910, Northern Alabama Biographical and Historical, and Sheffield Library Researcher Betty Dyar

Robert H. Wilhoyte (1910-1912): R. H. Wilhoyte was born December 31, 1848, at Owensboro, Daviess County, Kentucky and educated in the common schools of Owensboro. He was the son of Benjamin Allen and Nancy Snyder Wilhoyte of Oldham County, Kentucky. He was married December 18, 1879, at Brownsville, Tennessee, to Etta Curd Cowan of Wilson County, Tennessee. They had three children. He read law while a clerk of the court at Brownsville, and practiced as attorney-at-law in Memphis from 1883-1887, and in Sheffield from 1887 to the time of his death. Wilhoyte was on the board of directors of the Sheffield Brewery, which was built in 1892. The company collapsed and never made a drop of beer. The facilities were purchased by J.B. Lagomarsino and converted into an ice plant. It was during Mayor Wilhoyte's administration that the citizens of Sheffield voted to end the Mayor and Alderman form of government and adopt the Commission form of government. The question was:

> Will the City of Sheffield adopt the Proposition to Organize the City of Sheffield under the Commission Government Act of the Legislature of Alabama of 1911, Applicable to Class D Cities.

The election was held August 19, 1912, at the Council Chambers of the City Hall on Raleigh Avenue, which was upstairs and over the City's Fire Department. The vote was 173 in favor and 152 against the proposition. Mayor Wilhoyte served on the Sheffield School Board, was a member of the Christian Church, and a Freemason. He died in Sheffield on September 17, 1945, and was buried in Owensboro, Kentucky.

Sources: Sheffield Library Researcher Betty Dyar and Sheffield City Minute Book

Andrew D. Thomson (1912-1915): A. D. Thomson was one of the early citizens of Sheffield. When he was born, he had no middle name. This seemed to trouble his wife, the former Bettie Blair; and she decided that he needed a middle name.

She gave him the middle initial of "D." The story goes that she and Mr. Thomson could not settle on what name the "D" should stand for; so he was simply called A.D. They had a lovely house built on Park Boulevard. A.D. and Bettie had four children: Margaret, Elizabeth (Beth), Hugh Blair, and Louise. He was a prominent merchant who dealt in coal, iron, flour, and grain. Mr. Thomson served as an Alderman for several terms. In 1909, as an Alderman, Thomson proposed an ordinance prohibiting cows from running at large. This passed on the first reading and was to become law at the next meeting. He had "fought down the opposition to his cow law and had at last triumphed in what seemed to be a hopeless undertaking." On November 19, 1912, the Mayor and Commissioners received a request from the chairman of the Triangle Improvement Committee (which had donated so much time and attention to the civic interests of our City, especially to the improvement of the Triangle) that "a mounted cannon of suitable size be secured from our government and be placed in the Triangle, or Hotel Park" (in the vicinity of today's Love Plaza). The City Commission approved the request and pledged to "cooperate with the ladies of the Civic Improvement Association in their efforts to secure this relic of the Earlier Conflict" (Civil War). A June 2, 1913, letter from the "Civic Improvement Club" informed the Mayor that they had gotten the Triangle in good condition and were turning the project over to the City, "…thereby relieving themselves of all responsibility to attendant thereto." The commission issued a letter of thanks to the committee: "for your care, time, interest and pride you have exercised in beautifying the Triangle, and regret that you feel that you should in any measure relinquish future active interest in its upkeep."

June 3, 1913, the following resolution was passed:

> Be it resolved that in compliance with the communication and petitions which have come to us in regard to placing a cannon, donated to the City by the federal government, in the Triangle, and the generous offer of certain citizens to defray all shipping and mounting expenses of said cannon, we hereby authorize said cannon to be placed in said Triangle as a monument and souvenir and we hereby instruct the City Clerk to get into communication with the proper authority and have the cannon shipped at once.

A. D. Thomson was born on May 19, 1857, and died January 24, 1924. He, his wife, and their four children are buried in Sheffield Oakwood Cemetery.

Source: Sheffield City Minute Book and Sallie Muhlendorf, granddaughter

William H. Habbeler (1915-1916): Mayor William (Will) H. Habbeler was the son of W. Henry Habbeler, the owner of most of the land previously known as "York Bluff." It was this property that was a large part of the acreage that Col. Walter Gordon and Capt. Alfred H. Moses purchased for development of the new city of Sheffield. The Habbeler family home was the first to be built (1885) on North Montgomery Avenue and stands in beautiful condition today. During Mayor Habbeler's term in office the Furnace Hill Kindergarten School was started and the City of Sheffield donated $10.00 to this project. Also, the City paid expenses for dogs for trailing burglars who burglarized Belue and Nelson's Store. His wife Julia was active in organizations and community activities. An article in the *Sheffield Standard* reveals that:

> Mrs. W. H. Habbeler of Sheffield has been appointed President of the Alabama Division of the Women's National Rivers and Harbors Congress, an auxiliary of the National organization for the promotion of waterway improvement. Mrs. Habbeler attended the convention of the congress in Washington last December and has taken a lively interest in the work for Tennessee River improvement. The honor was worthily bestowed."

After his father's death William Habbeler and his wife enjoyed traveling at home and abroad. They had no children. They eventually settled in California, where Julia died in 1949. In 1957, William died at the age of 93 in Los Angeles, California.

Sources: Sheffield City on the Bluff, Sheffield Standard—February 5,1915, and Sheffield Library researcher, Betty Dyar

Samuel Claiborne Cooke (1916-1917, 1920-1921, 1922-1923 and 1927-1928): Sam Cooke was born (possibly in Tennessee) in 1869. He married Caroline R. Robinson in 1890 in Tennessee and moved to Sheffield in 1898. They had no children. They lived with Caroline's parents in the "Big House" at 910 North Montgomery Avenue, until they built a new house in 1923 at 1000 North

Montgomery Avenue. Sam and Caroline sold their house in 1940 to the Charles L. Beard family (Beard later became a mayor of Sheffield) and moved back into the "Big House" to live out their lives. Sam had his own business downtown at 306 North Montgomery Avenue. First he ran a men's clothing store and then an insurance and brokerage business. He was an outstanding citizen, a member of the Rotary Club, the Chamber of Commerce, and served as Mayor of Sheffield four times. In October, 1916, as a result of many citizens of the city expressing the desire for the Riverfront and Park grounds to be beautified and improved, the Commission gave permission to a group of citizens to erect buildings as needed to make the park an appropriate place for holding picnics and public entertainment. This is the present-day park lying north of Gordon Drive and between Montgomery and Atlanta Avenues.

March 29, 1921, marked an historic event; the City and County Hospital (a public hospital) was formed in Sheffield:

> Whereas, all deeds and contracts relating to the purchase of hospital and equipment, having been prepared and presented to the City Commission for approval, the same were examined and were found to be in accordance, heretofore, made in regard to same property on motion the sum of one thousand dollars is hereby appropriated by the commission to meet the City's part on the first payment on said property, and all other contracts relating to equipment are to be placed on the minutes of the commission and filed with the clerk.

At the same meeting a resolution was adopted providing for the appointment of three Trustees on the part of the City, who, with the same number of Trustees appointed by the county, were to have control and supervision of the hospital and its operation. The County of Colbert having agreed that it will appropriate an amount equal to that paid by the City and the Citizens of Sheffield on the purchase of the property, and the purchase price of twelve thousand dollars would be payable at two thousand dollars cash and two thousand dollars per year. Also, Dr. W. H. Greer signed an agreement:

> Being personally and financially interested in the establishment of a public hospital in Sheffield, Alabama, and in consideration of my financial interest and of the agreement on the part of Colbert

County, Alabama, and the City of Sheffield, Alabama, to purchase a hospital building, paying therefore the sum of twelve thousand dollars, payable two thousand cash and two thousand dollars in one, two, three, four and five years, I do hereby agree that during the time the said County of Colbert Alabama and City of Sheffield Alabama are paying for the said property, I will donate to the said hospital to be controlled and maintained by the County and City, all of the equipment of the hospital owned by me, an inventory of which is herein attached.

This hospital was later named Colbert County Hospital and is known today as Helen Keller Hospital.

Sam Cooke died at his home on September 7, 1946, of a malignancy. He is buried in Sheffield Oakwood Cemetery.

Source: Script from oral interview with Caroline Morris, Sam Cooke's niece and Sheffield City Minute Book

Allen Jones Roulhac (1917-1920, 1921-1922, and 1923-1927): Allen Jones Roulhac was born July 6, 1876, in Greensboro, Alabama, the son of Judge Thomas Ruffin Roulhac and Julia Erwin Jones Roulhac. He was a lawyer in Sheffield and Colbert County for more than 40 years having located to Sheffield as a youth. He was active in political and community life. At one time he was Colbert County Probate Judge. He served 15 years on the Sheffield Board of Commissioners, being President of the Board (Mayor) for eight years. He was very active in civic activities and traveled to Washington D.C. with a delegation of Shoals dignitaries to try to acquire funds for the area. During his last term as Mayor, the Sheffield Municipal Building, located at 600 North Montgomery Avenue, was completed. March 12, 1918, the Sheffield and Tuscumbia Telephone Exchange signed a contract with Southern Bell Telephone and Telegraph Company to provide:

A modern, common-battery control energy telephone exchange in Sheffield and furnished its subscribers with first class and efficient telephone service replacing the present 'magneto' telephone system.

The rates ranged from $2.00 per month for a residential two-party line to $4.00 per month for a business special line service. Judge Allen Jones Roulhac died at 10:30 a.m., November 7, 1947, at Colbert County Hospital. Funeral services were conducted at his home at 809 North Montgomery Avenue. Officiating were Rev. Richard Fell, Rector of Grace Episcopal Church and Rev. W. Glenn Bartee, Pastor of First Methodist Church of Sheffield. His wife, Mrs. Annie Bee Cohen Roulhac, survived him. He is buried in Sheffield Oakwood Cemetery.

Source: Standard and Times-November 14, 1947, Dr. Wyatt Blake, Sheffield City Minute Book and UNA Library/Archives

Herbert Marshall Kinnard (1928-1930): H. M. Kinnard was a native of Murray County, Tennessee. He came to Sheffield in 1902 and lived here for 65 years. His home was located at 706 North Raleigh Avenue in Sheffield. He was a member of First Methodist Church. He served one term as Mayor of Sheffield during the commission form of government. He was a partner with Harvey Adams in the Adams-Kinnard Hardware at 210 North Montgomery Avenue from 1918 until the business closed in 1965. The building is still standing and in good condition. During his administration a petition was presented to the Colbert County Probate Judge asking that:

> The proposition of abandoning the Commission form of government of the City of Sheffield and returning to the Aldermanic form of government as it existed in the City at the time the commission form of government was adopted, to be submitted to the voters of Sheffield for a vote on December 17, 1928.

The proposition was defeated by a vote of 636 to 177. April 10, 1929, a contract with the Alabama Power Company to provide the electricity to be used for the White Way system (lighting for main thoroughfares) in the City of Sheffield was continued for two years. It appears that problems with animals continued as an ordinance was passed to:

> Give the police power to control and regulate premises upon which certain domestic animals are confined; and to provide for the control and disposal of manure from said animals.

Herbert Marshall Kinnard died in Colbert County Hospital (now Helen Keller Hospital) in Sheffield in December of 1967 at the age of 81 years. He was buried in Rose Hill Cemetery, Columbia, Tennessee.

Sources: Florence Times-1965, Tri-Cities Daily-December 18, 1967, Sheffield City Minute Book, and Sheffield Library researcher, Betty Dyar

William Hal Richeson (1930-1931, 1932-1935, and 1936-1937): W. H. Richeson was born in Russellville, Alabama, on August 5, 1886. He was an officer of the People's Bank in Sheffield, at the northwest corner of Third Street and North Montgomery Avenue. At the March 3, 1931, city business meeting, Dr. Burkett, Colbert County Health Officer, was granted the privilege of the floor to speak on behalf of bettering sanitary condition in general and especially in behalf of the cleaning and removal of shacks along the river front between the powerhouse and the ice plant. The commission immediately moved that:

> The City Attorney be and is hereby instructed to draw-up legal notices and same to be served on person having and owning shacks along the riverfront, to remove their places of abode within the legal time allowed by law.

An ordinance passed May 5, 1931, concerning personal conduct is as follows:

> Any person or persons when shall, within the corporate limits of the City of Sheffield, Alabama, quarrel in a loud tone or use profane language in a public or private place, loud enough to be heard by neighbors, or who shall act in an indecent, riotous, or disorderly manner in the streets, or in any place within the corporate limits of said city shall be fined not less than one dollar, nor more than one hundred dollars.

Some years after serving as Mayor of Sheffield, Richeson worked for the Department of Industrial Relations in Montgomery, Alabama, until his retirement in 1958. He died August 11, 1959, in Montgomery where his funeral was held at 9:30 a.m.; and he was buried in Russellville at 4:00 p.m., the same day, in the Knights of Pythias Cemetery.

Sources: U.S.A. Census records, World War I Draft Registration Card, Sheffield City Minute Books, and The Franklin Citizen-August 18, 1958

Richard Randolph Hill (1931-1932): R. R. Hill lived at 800 Austin Avenue in Sheffield. He was in the hardware business for 27 years and served on the Sheffield City Board of Commissioners 21 years—one year as the President of the Board (Mayor). The November 3, 1931, business meeting revealed that the effects of the "Great Depression" were very much evident in the lives of the citizens of Sheffield as well as throughout the nation. A resolution was approved as follows:

> Whereas, the City of Sheffield, Alabama was desirous of payment of the school teachers for the month of September, 1931, and whereas, the City's funds were insufficient to take care of said payroll without securing money from the Sheffield National Bank, and due to the fact that the President of the Commission and City Clerk were verbally authorized and instructed to secure the amount as needed to meet said payroll. Therefore, be it resolved that said President of the Commission and the City Clerk were empowered to issue a note to the amount of $4,250 to secure sufficient funds for the payroll of teachers for the month of September, 1931.

At the same meeting the Salvation Army Officer addressed the Commission concerning co-operation from the city in helping take care of the transients, as well as the needy people of the city. It was agreed that this question should be studied closely by a committee and arrive at an understanding in the near future.

Mayor R. R. Hill, was born on January 1, 1871, and died at 11:30 a.m., January 10, 1944. He was a member of Grace Episcopal Church, Sheffield. Funeral services were conducted by C. J. Alleyn, Rector of the church. He is buried in Sheffield Oakwood Cemetery.

Sources: Sheffield Library Researcher Betty Dyar, Sheffield City Minute Book, and The Florence Times—January 10, 1944

Hoyt Greer (1935-1936, 1937-1938 and 1940-1941): Hoyt Greer came to Sheffield in 1923, at the age of 28, and opened a drug store. During the 20-year period of operating Greer Drug Co., he made many friends, many of whom received free medicine from him during the "Great Depression." He was elected to the Sheffield City Commission in 1931 and served 12 years, three times being

President of the Commission (Mayor). It was during this period of time that TVA was established in the Muscle Shoals District, and he immediately foresaw and instigated the municipal ownership of the power and water systems; with the city owning the systems, he realized there was an excellent probability of new industries and lower taxes. He was among those taking the first steps that led to the erection of the O'Neal Bridge.

At the outbreak of World War II, Greer resigned as a city official and turned his talents toward national interests. As many newcomers moved into Muscle Shoals District communities to work in the defense plants, he was among those instrumental in obtaining a defense homes development to house the new residents, and served as property manager of the subdivision known as York Terrace in Sheffield from 1943 until 1947, when the corporation was liquidated and the homes sold to veterans and former tenants. Throughout his lifetime he pursued civic obligations; he helped found and served as the first president of the Muscle Shoals Chamber of Commerce. Being interested in bringing new industry here, he served as president of the North Alabama Industrial Development Association, Inc. Other organizations with which he was affiliated included Kiwanis and Rotary clubs, American Legion, Veterans of World War I, 40 and 8, Colbert County Chapter of the American Red Cross, County Board of Equalization, County Jury Commission, and Lodge No. 503 F. and A.M. He and his wife, the former Reba Garrett, had two children: James Julian Greer, who was a doctor in Birmingham, and Betty Jean Greer Mefford. Born January 18, 1895, Hoyt Greer died April 21, 1968, and is buried in Sheffield Oakwood Cemetery.

Source: Tri-Cities Daily Editorial, May 1968, Joe Baber, and Sheffield Library Researcher Betty Dyar

Worthington Was Truly A 'Shoals Man'[1]

by Reynold B. Burt

John Warren Worthington was known best as a successful lobbyist in Alabama and Washington, D.C. He was an able promoter in the development of Sheffield but is best remembered for his activity in the development of the hydroelectric potential of that part of the Tennessee River known as Muscle Shoals. He was indeed "a Shoals man."

Worthington was born near Trussville on January 14, 1856 and grew up during the Civil War. He graduated from the University of Alabama with a degree in civil engineering in 1882. He participated in the development of Birmingham, where he and his partner, Henry Debardeleben, operated a company building railroads and transporting iron ore from the mines to the furnaces in Birmingham.

When Sheffield was founded in 1885, iron blast furnaces were built to operate on iron ore mined in Franklin County, about 25 miles south of Sheffield. Worthington became interested in the Sheffield development in 1889 and was involved in several projects in early Sheffield. He was a principal investor in an electric power plant, a water distribution plant, a pipe foundry, a bank and trust company, and the Sheffield Hotel. In 1898, Worthington was employed by the Sloss-Sheffield Steel and Iron Company as manager of their Sheffield operations. Through his association with

This picture of John Warren Worthington was probably taken during his student days at the University of Alabama.
Courtesy of G. Clopper Almon

---

[1]Reprinted from <u>Times Daily</u> (Florence, AL), November 11, 1993.

the investors in this company, Worthington was able to influence northern capitalists to make investments in Sheffield.

Among these was the Parsons family of New York and Maine. George Parsons and his sons, Henry and Charles, had substantial investments in Birmingham and had railway and electric power utility interests in South Carolina. At Worthington's suggestion, the Parsons organized the Sheffield Company and built an electric generating plant in Sheffield that supplied electric power to Sheffield, Florence, and Tuscumbia. An electric streetcar line was built, connecting the three towns and a new water plant was built in Sheffield. The Sheffield Company also had extensive real estate holdings in Sheffield and purchased the National Bank. Worthington was employed as general manager of the Sheffield Company.

Living in close proximity to the great Muscle Shoals soon led to Worthington's interest in developing the power potential the Shoals presented. In 1906, he organized the Muscle Shoals Hydroelectric Power Company to develop the Muscle Shoals. The bill proposed that three dams would be built providing for power generation and navigation. It was also proposed that the project would be undertaken by a partnership between the U.S. Government and the Muscle Shoals Hydroelectric Power Company. The Army Engineering Corps proposed several technical changes in the plan submitted. The proposed partnership between the government and the company was not agreeable to Congress, so the bill was tabled.

In the summer of 1911, the Muscle Shoals Hydroelectric Power Company merged with the Alabama Power Company. Worthington assumed leadership of Muscle Shoals lobbying activity for the combined companies.

To increase the effectiveness of local lobbying activity on Congress, Worthington organized the Tennessee River Improvement Association. Members were businessmen, state and local government officials, and private citizens from the Tennessee Valley and adjoining territory. John H. Patten of Chattanooga was president, C. W. Ashcraft of Florence was the first vice-president, John D. Rather of Tuscumbia was a district vice-president, and J.H. Nathan of Sheffield was on the executive committee.

In May of 1915, the association conducted a visit by 60 congressmen and government officials from Alabama and Tennessee. The group visited points of interest at Muscle Shoals and were entertained at a barbeque lunch at Lock Six on the Muscle Shoals Canal. The group then visited Chattanooga and Knoxville before returning to Washington.

The participants in this visit were presented with an elaborate brochure that gave the case for development of Muscle Shoals. Worthington's lobbying activity on the Muscle Shoals question produced no action by the Congress at this time.

When Worthington heard of Henry Ford's interest in Muscle Shoals, he visited Ford in Detroit in June 1921. The two men, with Ford's engineers, soon visited Muscle Shoals to inspect the facilities. With Worthington's assistance, Ford prepared an offer for purchase of the Muscle Shoals facilities and the offer was submitted to the government on July 8, 1921.

While Ford's offer was under consideration by Congress, Ford made another visit to Muscle Shoals accompanied by Thomas Edison, a close friend. On this visit, Ford made several appearances before groups of citizens and related his impressive plans for development of the Muscle Shoals facilities. When Ford's proposal was not approved by Congress within a reasonable time, Ford withdrew his offer on October 18, 1924.

Construction of Wilson Dam was completed in 1925. The Alabama Power Company had constructed a power transmission line from its Gorgas generation plant on the Warrior River west of Birmingham to supply power to Wilson Dam during its construction.

When it was completed, the dam generators needed a receptor into which the electric power could be transmitted during the generator-testing period. The connection with the Alabama Power Company served this purpose and the testing was completed in 1926.

In January 1926, the government renewed its efforts to lease the Muscle Shoals facilities. A proposal was submitted by the Associated Power Companies of the South, a group of 13 power companies led by the Alabama Power Company. This proposal was supported by Senator Underwood and Senator Heflin of Alabama. Worthington continued his lobbying activity for this proposal.

In the late 1920s and early '30s, Muscle Shoals development became a major political football.

The conservationist group led by Senator George Norris of Nebraska, who favored government control of hydroelectric developments, became the dominant influence in this activity. This was culminated by the Tennessee Valley Authority Act adopted by Congress and signed by President Franklin Roosevelt on May 18, 1933.

Worthington, more than any other individual, was associated with efforts for the development of Muscle Shoals during the first third of the 20th century. He can be credited with keeping this subject before the Congress and the public during this period.

Worthington's unique contribution included the technical concepts of the use of high dams and the development on a whole river basis.

The concepts, originated by Worthington, were developed in collaboration with the U.S. Army Engineers and became the basis for evaluating proposals for the Muscle Shoals development and are reflected as basic considerations in the TVA Act.

Worthington believed that the cost of the Muscle Shoals development in accordance with these concepts would be too great for any private company to absorb. He felt that a partnership arrangement would be logical in which the government would bear the cost of the basic structures and the provisions for navigation and the company would bear the cost of facilities for power generation and transmission.

In the early 30s, with the realization that the development of Muscle Shoals was finally being carried out in accordance with the concepts he had originated, Worthington, then an old man, retired to his home in Tate Springs, Tennessee. He died April 4, 1942 and, in accordance with his instructions, his body was cremated and the ashes were spread onto the waters of Lake Wilson.

Sheffield Native's Letters Became a Book[1]

by Richard C. Sheridan

In 1919, a book entitled "Pat Crowe, Aviator" came off the press. It was composed of letters written from France by Lieutenant James Richard Crowe, Jr., a Sheffield native. One critic pronounced it the best of all American war books, based on its literary and human values.

Crowe was born March 4, 1889, less than two years after his parents Isabella and James R. Crowe, Sr. moved here from their former home in Pulaski, Tenn. His father was a Confederate veteran and a Sheffield businessman. The Crowe home still stands in good condition at 101 Park Blvd.

After receiving his elementary education in Sheffield, Crowe attended Castle Heights School to prepare for college. Then he enrolled in Vanderbilt University in 1907. In college, he made many friends with his old-time Southern manners and participated in several clubs, such as the Glee Club, the Dramatic Club, and Kappa Sigma Fraternity. He was a member of the track team for two years.

Jim Crowe (as he was known at Vanderbilt) loved the open road and went on many hikes. On one occasion, he hiked from Nashville to Sheffield in four days. After his junior year, Crowe went to Europe and visited several countries. Upon graduating from Vanderbilt in 1911, he taught one year at Henderson-Brown College and coached the football team to the state championship.

Crowe was attracted to journalism, and in 1912 he became a reporter on the Memphis **Commercial Appeal.** Later, he worked for the Hattiesburg *News*, and from there he moved to the New York **Sun** where he was able to satisfy his love of music, the drama, and fine writing.

When the United States entered World War I in 1917, Crowe. expressed a desire to join the army. His mother sent him a telegram from Sheffield, saying "Enlist, my boy, and God bless you." He enlisted August 31, 1917, and volunteered for the aviation service. After preliminary training in this country, Crowe went to France to be commissioned and to complete his training as a pursuit pilot.

---

[1] Reprinted from the TimesDaily (Florence, AL), December 14, 2003.

Lieutenant Crowe's many friends in New York knew him affectionately as "Pat." He wrote numerous letters and stories from France to them and also to his mother in Sheffield. One story entitled "Birdman's St. Francis" was highly praised for its beauty and fine writing. His story about Jacqueline, a lovely French girl who resided in a chateau where he made a forced landing and then many other landings was a classic. The editor of *Times Magazine* described it as the "prettiest thing I've seen out of this war—a delight and a joy in every line."

The young pilot's tragic death occurred at Issoudun, September 30, 1918, on the eve of his departure for the front. He had never had an accident, but his airplane fell to the ground from a height of 7,000 feet. The army ruled that Crowe "was killed in the faithful performance of his duty" but no one could say exactly what went wrong.

Shortly after Crowe's death, his writings were collected and edited by W. B. Chase, an editor with the New York *Times*. In the foreword, Chases expressed thanks to Mrs. James R. Crowe, Sr. for permission to use her son's letters and to the Sheffield *Tri-Cities Daily*. The book was published by the New York firm of Nicholas L. Brown.

When Sheffield's American Legion Post No. 27 was organized in 1919, it was named in memory of James R. Crowe. A few years later, Miss Maud Lindsay, who had watched Crowe grow up near her home in Sheffield, wrote a beautiful poem about this gallant young soldier as a Memorial Day tribute. Mrs. Joseph H. Nathan (a sister of Miss Maud) pasted a clipping of the poem from an unidentified newspaper in her personal copy of <u>Pat Crowe Aviator</u>. The poem is reprinted below in honor of both the soldier and the poet.

To: James R. Crowe.

I love to think his spirit sometimes goes,
Through the wild woods he loved so well,
When sap begins to flow and buds to swell,
When, like the elusive colors of a dream,
Scarlet, and bronze, and emerald faintly gleam,
From oak, and elm and towering chestnut tree,
Perhaps he comes to see.
When mocking birds with magic throats a tune,
Fill all the green moon-lighted aisles of June
With melody he loved so well to hear,
Perhaps he lingers near.
Perhaps, when autumn flaunts,
Barbaric splendor in his old-time haunts,
And nature is half joy and half pain,
He drinks deep draughts of beauty once again.
Or when leaves in rustling cadence fly,
And, challenging all dauntless hearts and high,
The winter wind its summons loudly blows
Perhaps—oh, who can tell?
His spirit on the wings of heaven goes,
Through the wild woods he loved so well.

Maud Lindsay (Sheffield, Alabama, May 30, 1923)

Street Cars Served to Unify Area[1]

by Reynold B. Burt

The street car system built by the Sheffield Company in 1904 that ran between Florence, Sheffield, and Tuscumbia was recognized immediately as more than just a mass transit system.

Prior to this time, travel between the three towns was mostly by horse and buggy and was quite limited. From the beginning, the new street car system was widely accepted by residents of all three towns. On July 4, 1904, the first holiday after completion of the system, the street car company reported that the street cars handled 10,000 passengers. The growth of the feeling of community that prevailed among the people in the three towns could be attributed to the increased contact afforded by the programs carried on at the Tri-Cities Park in the woods east of Sheffield. The park was provided to stimulate the use of the street cars and, therefore, had a profit motive. The people were very appreciative of the beautiful recreational area.

The car barn at Little Rock Avenue and Sixth Street in Sheffield was the base of operation for the street car system. It consisted of two brick buildings and a large shed. One brick building housed offices and a shop area. It had large arched doors and a track by which cars could be brought in. The other brick building housed a warehouse for equipment and supplies for the power house and water works at the river front as well as the street car system. The shed had a steel frame with steel sides and roof. Track was provided for storage of cars.

Two types of street cars manufactured by the American Car and Foundry Company of St. Louis, Missouri were used – a closed car used most of the year and an open car used during the hot summer months. The cars were 60 feet long and carried 90 passengers when fully loaded. They were painted yellow and beige. A motorman and conductor, dressed in blue serge suits and caps with patent- leather visors, operated the cars. The motorman drove the car by means of a large rheostat that controlled the power to the motors driving the cars. He also operated the brakes, the air horn, and the bell used to indicate the approach of the car to a loading station and also to warn animals that might have wandered onto

---

[1] Reprinted from the Times Daily, Florence, AL (January 21, 1993.)

the tracks. The conductor collected the fares and handled chores such as throwing track switches and raising and lowering the trolley pole.

People identified in this 1908 pictures, snapped on Main Street, Tuscumbia, are W.E. Matthew and Calvin Highfield with bicycle and Lewis Matthew who is leaning on a post behind the street car. Courtesy of Margaret Matthew Anderson

    The closed car had windows and seats that ran along each side of the car. The seats were upholstered with split cane. The open car had no sides and wooden slat seats that ran across the car from side to side. Passengers boarded the open cars directly onto the seats by stepping up onto a running board that ran along each side of the car. The conductor collected fares in the cars by walking along the running board while holding onto the metal frame that supported the roof of the car. Riding in the open summer cars was delightful. They offered an unobstructed view of the country side and passengers received full benefit of the breeze resulting from the movement of the car.

    The street car system also had work cars which, under their own power, could proceed at any point in the system for maintenance work on the track or the trolley wire that ran above the track.

    The street car track ran from the car barn to downtown Sheffield via Sixth Street and Montgomery Avenue. At First Street it tuned east to Atlanta Avenue and then turned north and ran up Atlanta Avenue to Twelfth Street and ran into the open country where Sheffield High School now stands. The open country east of Sheffield with its rolling meadows fringed by large pine, oak, and chestnut trees was the most beautiful area through which the street car track passed. After a run of about a mile through the open country, the track passed through a switch and entered the railroad track that ran north onto the bridge across the Tennessee River. After crossing the bridge, the track ran through another switch, turned west and ascended the steep hill by a circuitous route to downtown Florence. It traveled north up to Court Street to the college and then east on Nellie Avenue. It then turned south on Poplar Street and, via Tennessee Street and Royal Avenue, went to East Florence. At the end of Royal Avenue, it made a loop around by the railroad station and returned.

Street cars crossed the Tennessee River on the railroad bridge. (Taken from an old postcard.)

The street car track to Tuscumbia left the car barn on Little Rock Avenue and ran south into the Furnace Hill area. Here it crossed a large trestle over the furnace area and turned east around the Plant One area and entered Wilson Dam Avenue. It turned off Wilson Dam Avenue onto Blackwell Road and continued south about a mile, passed under the railroad trestle over Spring Creek, and entered Tuscumbia on South Jefferson Street. It turned east of Jefferson Street to

Fifth Street and continued on to downtown Tuscumbia. It made a loop around Main Street and Sixth Street via Water Street, back to Fifth Street and returned.

As the street car system was completed in each of the three towns, ceremonies were held. A car carrying company officials and their wives proceeded to the main street where they were greeted by the mayor. After appropriate speeches by city officials, they and other prominent citizens and their wives were taken on an introductory ride. Then regular service was initiated. Fares were very reasonable and an hourly schedule was followed.

For employees at the blast furnaces and the Southern Railway shops, the street car service was very convenient and economical. For Florence, a similar situation prevailed. East Florence was the largest suburb of Florence and was an industrial area. Street car service was important to the people of East Florence.

Riding the street cars, particularly for the first time, was very pleasant and somewhat thrilling. The smoothness of the ride depended upon the roadbed and the speed of the car. As the speed picked up as it inevitably did on long stretches, minor undulations in the track caused a gently swaying of the car that increased to a pitching movement described by some as "galloping." These conditions were not particularly unpleasant and were readily controlled by the motorman.

The ultimate thrill came from one's first ride across the river bridge in an open summer car. While enjoying the beauty of the river, as the speed of the car increased, one's gaze dropped toward the track and saw only open water rushing by 50 feet below. The instantaneous reaction was to grasp the edge of the seat and move closer to the center. This sensation soon passed as the car completed the crossing and speed was reduced to normal.

The street car company built a trolley park east of Sheffield (first called Forest Park and later changed to Tri-Cities Park) at the present site of the River Oaks Subdivision. They erected a pavilion with a stage at one end. Surrounding the pavilion was a playground-picnic area with the numerous tables and benches. Refreshments and ices were available and on most weekends some form of entertainment was provided. People in the area responded by riding the street cars to the park in large numbers. Other sites such as Spring Park in Tuscumbia, always an attractive spot, were a regular destination for street car riders.

A newspaper advertisement on July 16, 1904 announced an "open air concert will be held." The program included vocal and instrumental music, recitations, and dialogues by the "best local amateurs." Admission was free and refreshments were 25 cents. Ladies had literary club meetings at the park and young people held regular dances there. A "German at the Park" was reported for July 10. It was led by Mr. and Mrs. Warren of Florence. A "german" was a reel type dance very popular with the young adults.

During the spring of 1905 a theater was constructed at the park and improvements were made to the lighting and other facilities. On July 15, 1905, the Jefferson Stock Company opened a two-week engagement offering both matinee and evening performances. Special performances were planned for children at which refreshments were to be served. Free entertainment was continued for the weekends.

The success of the street car system continued. As the growth of the Tri-Cities increased, it became an important service for the communities. In 1917, when World War I began and construction of the nitrate plants and Wilson Dam commenced, the street car system provided an invaluable service. The population of the area increased to triple its normal size with the influx of workmen to build the wartime facilities.

Housing this mass of people was a major problem and moving them about would have been impossible without the street car system. A spur track was built from the park to Nitrate Plant No. 2 and regular service was extended to that area. To handle the great number of passengers, trailer cars were installed behind the regular cars and schedules were changed as necessary to handle the loads.

In 1925 the facilities of the Sheffield Company, including the electricity generating and distributing system for the Tri-Cities and the street car system, were sold to the Alabama Power Company and were included in their statewide system. Alabama Power Company continued to operate the street car system until 1933, when the effect of the Great Depression and the increased use of personal automobiles reduced the use of the street car system to an unprofitable operation and it was discontinued.

The car barn complex in Sheffield is the only part of the system remaining today. These old solid masonry buildings, still in good condition, remain as a reminder of an important part of life of the Tri-Cities only a few years ago.

Lillian Margaret Lee Thomas Schmidt
Artist and Pioneer for Woman's Rights[1]

By Charles L. "Chuck" Beard

Lillian Margaret Lee was born in Columbus, Ohio, on August 5, 1875 to James and Sarah Miller Lee. Prior to her birth the Lees moved to Columbus from Virginia, where he was a builder. He established a business in Columbus, Ohio, where a sizable amount of development was taking place. Being born with several talents, Lillian played the piano and violin, becoming a member of a Columbus orchestra as a teenager. As for education, given her choice, she chose to take art lessons. She graduated from the Art School of Columbus and continued her study at the Art Institute of St. Louis, Mo. After completing the course, she took a job teaching in a St Louis high school.

During this phase of her life she met a very personable vaudeville entertainer and eloped with him over the objections of her family. Her parents were "high church" Episcopalians and they expected all Lees to marry auspiciously so as to be a credit to the family name. Her husband, a Mr. Thomas, though talented and charming, turned out to be a compulsive gambler. This led to insurmountable problems. As she kept on painting and trying to deal with his problems as best she could, he wound up deep in debt. Threatened with death over his gambling debts, he took up with a gang of robbers and attempted unsuccessfully to rob a railway mail car. He was caught and convicted. This being his only criminal action, Lillian went to high public officials seeking lenience for him. Finally, she went to President McKinley, who was from Ohio, seeking a pardon. Though this effort failed, she did wind up painting a portrait of the President, which was displayed in the meeting room of the Ohio Society in Washington, DC.

After painting President McKinley's portrait and securing a divorce, Lillian Thomas opened a small studio in New York City. Hiring an agent in New York and Paris, her professional art career was well underway. Spending her summers in London and Paris, she became well known as a portrait artist in the cities of New York, Washington, London, and Paris. It was on one of these trips to

---

[1] This paper was prepared for Sheffield Founders Day, June 8, 2008. It is based on personal knowledge and family records in possession of the author (a grandson of Mrs. Schmidt).

Europe that Lillian, upon her return, boarded an English ship. The first evening she was seated for dinner across from a young German man, Curt Schmidt, who was coming to America to, as he put it, seek his fortune. The language spoken on the ship was English and since he couldn't speak the language, he was having trouble communicating with the waiter. Lillian perceived his problem and spoke to him in French, helping him order his meal. Curt, my grandfather, often would relate this story to me, telling how she saved his life by keeping him from starving.

These portraits of Curt and Lillian Schmidt, Sheffield artists, were shown along with other examples of their work in a 2009 exhibit at the Tennessee Valley Art Museum.
Courtesy of Lori Curtis

They were married in New York City on October 8, 1901. Four years and several ocean crossings later a daughter, Therese Augusta Schmidt was born on October 9, 1905, being named for two of her German aunts.

Settling in New York, Curt got a job representing a German automobile factory and Lillian pursued her passion for art. During this time she became a member of the exclusive Professional Woman's League. In the years leading up to World War One she pitched into civic work, ever pursuing her love of art. Using her connections with the professional women and work with the schools she showed inexhaustible energy in promoting art for the betterment of society.

In the early 1900's she taught Curt to paint. They opened a small art gallery where they sold their paintings along with the works of their friends. Later they carried lines of imported chinaware, sculpture, and later some pottery imported from Spruce Pine, Alabama. In addition to the gallery, Lillian had a very large picture frame built which she covered with gold material to make it look carved. She painted backdrops of famous paintings, sewed and made costumes, found well-to-do society members to pose and presented a program she called Tableaux Vivants[2] in various New York hotel ballrooms. Many fashionable groups and organizations hired her to put on her Tableaux Vivants to raise money for their favorite charities.

At one of the fundraising events Lillian wrote to Samuel Clemens, aka Mark Twain, who at this time had moved from New York to Redding, Connecticut, asking him for some autographs to be auctioned off. Upon receiving a positive response, she invited him to speak at one of the Galas. He respectfully declined through his secretary, a Miss Lyons.

In 1913 Curt Schmidt received his citizenship papers becoming a naturalized citizen. Curt was extremely proud of his new homeland; in fact I often heard him say in response to being queried about his age, that he was born in 1901, the year he came to America and married Lillian. The year 1913 also saw Lillian continuing with her Tableaux Vivants for many worthwhile fund-raising efforts.

The years 1914 through 1920 turned out to be most eventful for Curt and Lillian, as well as for the Muscle Shoals and the United States. World War 1 in Europe broke out in 1914 with the U.S. becoming directly involved in 1917. This saw the construction of the Nitrate Plants and Wilson Dam in the Muscle Shoals in 1918. Feelings of patriotism broke out all over the land. In New York City,

---

[2] This term is French for "living picture." It describes a group of suitably costumed actors or artist's models, carefully posed and often theatrically lit. During the display, the people do not move or speak. The technique combines the art form of the stage with those of painting/photography. The *tableau vivants* were popular forms of entertainment before radio, film, and television.

Lillian was right in the middle of things. She was instrumental in forming the National School Children's Garden League to encourage children to learn to grow vegetables to help out with the war effort.

In 1919 there was a very strong movement for giving women the right to vote, an issue that had been smoldering for many years since the Civil War. Lillian was right in the middle of the campaign in New York City. Congress passed the 19th Amendment and it was ratified in 1920.

With the ending of the hostilities, work ceased on Wilson Dam and the Nitrate Plants. The economy in the Muscle Shoals area turned sour. The issue of the unfinished Wilson Dam and the Nitrate Plants bounced around the halls of Congress until in 1921 Henry Ford and Thomas Edison visited the Muscle Shoals and Ford made an offer to Congress to purchase the facilities. This started a battle over whether the resources should be developed privately or publicly. It also started a tremendous speculative land boom in the Muscle Shoals area. Several northern financiers and real estate developers jumped on the bandwagon. Among them were names such as J.J. Nyhoff and the Fowler Brothers. Fowler Brothers had offices in Detroit and New York. With a slowdown in the economy in the east the art business came almost to a standstill. Lillian looked at other ways to earn a living. After working in one of the corporations in New York for a short time, she went to work for Fowler Brothers, a real estate company.

In those days real estate was primarily a man's world. However, it didn't take Lillian long to break into the business. After traveling to Muscle Shoals by Pullman several times escorting prospects, she conceived the idea that she and some of her unemployed actress friends from the Professional Woman's League could form a real estate company and compete with the other firms. She left Fowler Brothers and started the L. T. Schmidt Real Estate Organization, acquiring several tracts of land in the Shoals and forming four real estate development corporations.

While this was taking place she continued her art work with a prominent display in The Exposition of Women's Arts and Industries held at the Hotel Astor in October of 1927. Let me read a quotation from the program: "Lillian T. Schmidt, artist, clubwoman, globe trotter, was the originator of unique ballroom entertainments. Her "Tableaux Vivants" being in a class by themselves. At the close of the war, Mrs. Schmidt turned to a business career. She organized the woman's sales force for the Brooklyn Edison Company. She was then at the head of several corporations composed almost exclusively of women who were successful Real Estate operators. In her judgment, the real estate field was exceptionally adapted for development by women of high intellect. She also encouraged women to enter the manufacturing field."

On one of Lillian's trips to Muscle Shoals, she saw some examples of very unusual pottery that was being made in Spruce Pine, Alabama. In 1927 she entered into a contract to sell the entire output of the company in New York through a company she and her husband, Curt, started. [3]

At the same time these events were transpiring, Lillian was embroiled in lobbying the U.S. Senate to take action on the Ford proposal. I have copies of many letters that she wrote to senators, urging them to take positive action on the proposal. However the politics of the times turned against privatization. Under the leadership of Senator Norris of Nebraska and the political campaign of Franklin Roosevelt the tide turned toward public development. I find it extremely interesting that she was strongly in favor of the private development of Wilson Dam and the Nitrate Plants. In 1953, her son-in-law, my father, C. Leonard Beard, two years before her death, was on the other side of the fence. As Mayor of Sheffield, Alabama and President of Citizens for TVA, he lobbied strongly and successfully for the defeat of the proposed Dixon-Yeats deal that would have been, as many believed, the beginning of the end of TVA and public power in our area.

Speaking of Leonard Beard, in 1928 he graduated from the University of North Carolina. The year before, as a member of the glee club, he took part in a concert in New York City where he met Lillian's daughter, Therese Schmidt. After graduation, Leonard and Therese were married in New York on June 21, 1928. Facing a scarcity of jobs in the New York area, they decided to move to Sheffield to manage Lillian's interests. They moved into a small bungalow at 109 31st Street which was next door to Sterchi Brothers Furniture Co. On June 13, 1929, I was born at Colbert County Hospital.

Lillian had rented out the land on the various properties she controlled along with a couple of houses she had acquired. Leonard and Therese were to collect the rents, pay the taxes, and oversee the sale and cutting of timber. For a short time Leonard worked as a salesman for Sterchi Brothers. Later, he worked surveying timber to be cut in connection with the construction of Wheeler Dam.

---

[3] For information on this pottery, see Ann Z. Wrenn, "Bits and Shards About Spruce Pine Pottery and its Potters," <u>Journal of Muscle Shoals History</u>, Volume XIII, 102 (1993).

The month of September, 1929, changed the course of history for Muscle Shoals in a way nobody ever expected. Almost everything went overnight from boom to bust. Thus the New Deal was ushered in. In the presidential election of 1932, a young man from New York named Franklin Delano Roosevelt was swept into office vowing to bring an end to the great depression that had engulfed the nation. At the same time a U.S. Senator from Nebraska had picked up the fight for the public development of the Tennessee River and other natural resources. The U.S. Senate refused to approve the sale of Wilson Dam and the Nitrate Plants to Ford. A bill was introduced in Congress to establish the Tennessee Valley Authority as a dual purpose project of generating electricity and providing flood control and inexpensive river transportation to the area for the benefit the nation and specifically the Tennessee Valley. This has recently been commemorated with the dedication of the beautiful monument at the corner of 1st Street and Montgomery Avenue, honoring Roosevelt's visit to Sheffield and Wilson Dam. Roosevelt went back to Washington determined to see the Tennessee Valley Authority become a reality. On May 18, 1933, Congress passed the TVA Act and Roosevelt signed it into law.

Back in New York, Lillian and Curt felt the full impact of the depression. They closed their art studio because of a lack of business. In 1934 an opportunity arose to purchase a bankrupt business in Sheffield and Lillian and Curt along with Therese and Leonard Beard entered into a partnership to revive the Nehi Bottling Company and rented a building on 2nd Street from Mr. Blackwell, who operated a laundry across the street.

Because of the economic impact of work started in Muscle Shoals and the new business, in 1935, Lillian and Curt decided to pack up and move to Sheffield. They had acquired a small house fronting on 32nd Street behind the cottage of the Beards. Upon arriving they immediately built an addition to house their studio and art gallery. Lillian started teaching art classes and had a number of students, including Nora Thompson, Catherine Maddox Owen, a Mrs. Jordan, Reba Greer, the wife of future mayor Hoyt Greer, Ethel Davis, Katherine Boyd Rice, and many others. Lillian became involved with the community, belonging to The Mother's Club and forming the Muscle Shoals Art league. She and Curt became affiliated with the Alabama Art League and conducted showings of their work both in Montgomery and Birmingham.

An article in <u>The Montgomery Advertiser</u>, Sunday, May 25, 1941 concerning The Alabama Art League and their annual exhibition reads: "Notable among exhibitions were portraits by Mrs. Lillian Schmidt of Sheffield, who painted the picture of Gen. 'Fighting Joe" Wheeler in the Museum's Confederate Room. Like her husband, Curt Schmidt, who is known for his portrayals of the Alabama negro, Mrs. Schmidt has studied for many years in Europe." In 1946 Curt gave the Montgomery Museum of Fine Arts one of his paintings entitled "Sermon on the Mount".

In 1948, shortly after Dr. E. B. Norton was named President of Florence State Teachers College, Lillian gave him another painting of "Fighting Joe" Wheeler to hang in his office. This painting at my last notice was hanging in Pope's Tavern in Florence.

At this point Lillian was suffering from severe cataracts on her eyes and a series of operations in Montgomery proved unsuccessful, bringing to an end her years of painting. Curt continued his painting of southern scenes for several more years until his eyesight also failed.

In 1953 the only remaining real estate from Lillian's original holdings, Norris Park Subdivision, lying south of 6th Street in the City of Muscle Shoals, north of Highway 20, was condemned and taken by the State of Alabama for the extension of Woodward Avenue to become U.S. Highway 43.

On January 21, 1955, after several months of illness, Lillian Schmidt died at the age of 80 in Colbert County Hospital, bringing to a close the life of a most remarkable lady, one who had been a pioneer for women and their rights all of her life.

Lighting Up Sheffield[1]

by Richard C. Sheridan

Shortly after World War I, the Tri-Cities began to install a modern system of street lighting known as the "White Way." It featured electric lamps enclosed in white globes mounted on large, fluted metal posts called standards.

Sheffield's first White Way was installed along Montgomery Avenue from First Street to Fifth Street in early 1920. The lights were immediately proclaimed a progressive step toward a bigger and better city.

In late 1925, the Sheffield-Tuscumbia Chamber of Commerce announced that the King Company of St. Joseph, Missouri, and Chicago, Illinois, would build a plant in Sheffield to manufacture White Way posts, brackets, and bases. The company had recently contracted to install their standards around the White House and the Lincoln Memorial in Washington, D.C.

White Way standards being prepared for shipping at the King Company plant in Sheffield (late 1920s) Courtesy of Matt Dixon

---

[1] Reprinted from the TimesDaily (Florence, AL), May 16, 2002.

Tuscumbia Mayor E. H. Clifford handled negotiations with the company, assisted by officials of the Sloss-Sheffield Steel and Iron Company, Alabama Power Company, L & N Railroad, and others. Bonds were sold to local individuals to raise the $100,000 needed to purchase the land and begin construction of the plant.

Operations began August 17, 1926, with J. L. Andrews, president of the Chamber of Commerce, pouring the iron for the first casting. The plant was located in blocks 174, 190, and 208, with a railroad frontage of one-fourth mile.

It was housed in a building measuring 140-by-400 feet, used Sheffield pig iron, and employed more than 300 workers in three shifts. Some of the workers were transferred from the company's Missouri plant after it closed. The most modern machinery and laborsaving devices were used.

Orders from all parts of the country poured in, and production was increased to 250 posts per day. Sales agencies were maintained in several cities, and the Western Electric Company was a general agent for the King Company. By 1929, its lighting system was in use in major cities such as Detroit, Kansas City, Cincinnati, and Los Angeles.

This old street light, made in Sheffield, is preserved in the backyard of Kenneth and Carolyn King in Sheffield's Rivermont subdivision.

The King Company reorganized in 1929 and moved its general offices from Sheffield to Canton, Ohio, but continued to operated the local plant. In May 1929, the plant was running 10 hours daily, five days per week, with a work force of 187 men in the shop and 12 men and women in the office.

Sheffield installed 78 new King lamps of 318 watts each in the spring of 1929 along Montgomery Avenue, on First Street from Columbia to Montgomery, and on Third Street, between Columbia and Raleigh Avenues. All of those lights burned with the same intensity, whereas the earlier system grew dimmer with increasing distance from the power source.

When O'Neal Bridge opened in 1939, the local standards were used to provide a White Way from Nyhoff Corner[2] to the south end of the bridge. The next year, shipments were made to the Pensacola Naval Air Station and to the U. S. Submarine Base in Connecticut.

The fortunes of the King Company declined after World War II, and the company dissolved January 8, 1951. The King standards on Sheffield's streets have been replaced by newer street lights, but the lamp posts that King made for the entrances to the municipal building are still in use. A few of the old standards and lamps are owned by members of the King family.

---

[2] The intersection of Jackson Highway and Plant Street was known as Nyhoff Corner. It was named for John J. Nyhoff who developed residential and commercial property along Jackson Highway in the 1920s and 1930s

H. C. "Chick" Wann's Interview with Chief E. J. Martin, April 18, 1985

Transcribed and edited by Richard Sheridan

Wann: This is Chick Wann. I am in the home of E. J. Martin, the former Chief of the Public Safety Service out at TVA. Chief Martin came here as a young man and witnessed the construction of Nitrate Plant No. 1 and Village One. The purpose of this interview is to preserve the history and historical data of Village One. And Chief Martin is one of the experts on it and I guess is "the expert" living today. And he has graciously consisted to come down for this interview. We are thankful to him for taking time to grant this interview.[1]

This TVA Police & Fire Station was located at Nitrate Plant No. 1. From left to right: Chief E. J. Martin, L.L. Stanford, W.L. Butler, S.L. Rogers, John Duncan, John R. Stewart, -- McMurry, -- Smith, ---Jones, G.O. Stewart, W.G. Stanford, Joe Horton, M. Sanderson, Y.J. Clark. Louie Clemons and Nick Fago. Courtesy of Nancy Stewart King

---

[1] Elmer Jackson Martin lived at 400 Watts Bar Street in Village One. He was born Oct. 15, 1898 and died Sept. 16, 1993 and was buried in Sheffield Oakwood Cemetery.

Wann: Chief, I understand that you came here at a very early age.

Martin: I came here the second day of February 1918 during the midst of the worst flu epidemic I think that we have ever had. I arrived at the depot in Sheffield, which was down on First Street, and you could hardly walk for the coffins that were waiting to be shipped out. And there was snow almost up to your knees. It was a miserable place. The streets were all chert. I came out to Plant #1 and got a job in the personnel office. Well, I didn't like that very long, and I decided that I would get a job on the guard force, which I did. I saw the whole thing go from out here in the Village and the Plant almost from the ground up. J. G. White Engineering Corporation was the principal contractor and J. G. Munsom[2] was the general superintendent. Plant #1 was built for the production of ammonium nitrate. My understanding was that the formula was obtained by an American army officer from a German army officer who failed to give the whole formula. They went ahead and built the plant and it operated for a very short period due to the fact that the armistice was signed and the production ammonium nitrate then was stored in bags. It was supposed to be used for ammunition but it turned out to be a fertilizer—ammonium nitrate fertilizer—and the plant shut down. In the meantime, the Liberty Bell Village was under construction and I saw it go from sewers and cisterns and cornfields up to where it is today.

W: Chief, you mentioned the Liberty Bell shape of this village. Can you expand on that just a little bit?

M: Well, it was known as the Liberty Bell Village--in the shape of a bell--with commons, parks, and everything including the clapper of the bell which is in the end of the circle.[3]

W: Okay, we have heard--now of course I am one of the youngsters around here compared to you people--we have always heard that these Village One houses were constructed here as army officer quarters. Is that correct?

M: Built solely for the army officers.

---

[2]The spelling of this surname is unconfirmed.
[3]Although the bell is commonly believed to have a Liberty Bell design, recent research suggests that the designer, Harold A. Caparn, of New York City, used an English handbell as his model. Oliver Chamberlain, Jr., "An Historic Village at Sheffield, Alabama—Its Town Planner, Architects, and Symbolic Design," unpublished manuscript in possession of editor.

W: And I feel like what is commonly known as the apartment house now—I believe that you told me one time that was bachelor officer quarters.

M: Bachelor officer quarters, built for the single army officers.

W: Right oh. And to catch the overflow, they added a second bath to what is now the G. O. Summers house. Is that correct? To take care of the overflow of the bachelor officers quarters?

M: Well, the Summers house was just used as a guest house. It was known then as House 40. And we had three houses....

W: In what we call the big circle.

M: Yeah. In the bell part of the village, there were three houses there--one for the commanding officer and two for the lieutenant colonels.

W: Was the commanding officer a general officer?

M: The commanding officer was a Captain Hempfield at the time. And of course we had Col. Ware, and Col. R. B. Chambliss was the last full colonel army officer. He was a lieutenant colonel and he lived in what was known as the colonel's house.

W: I see. Is that the one the Winkles live in now?

M: No, that was a major's house. Arthur Kirkby (who used to operate the Shoals Hotel) bought the colonel's house. That is one of the biggest houses in the Village.

W: And when you first came in, you told me about—I believe that you said you came here from Tennessee, is that right?

M: No, I came from Hopkinsville, Ky. My hometown is Hopkinsville. And when I first came down here, I was just out of school and nobody could tell me anything. I knew everything but I soon found out that I was just about as ignorant as they come. (laughter).

W: Well, I understand during one of our conversations prior to this, there was quite a bit of meanness and mischief going on and your parents tried to get you to come back home. Is that correct?

M: Oh, yes. I had a sister who lived at the Sheffield Hotel. Her husband was general distributor for Miller & Hartz meats at that time and this was his headquarters. Of course, that was the reason why I came to Sheffield, and she used every wile she had to make me go back home but I refused to go back. Ha! Ha!

W: Well, I guess you are glad now that you stayed.

M: Oh, yes, I am glad that I stayed because I saw the thing go up and shut down. Only 11 families lived out here in the 100 houses.

W: Is that the total number of houses?

M: Yes, there were supposed to be a hundred houses.

W: We younger people have also heard that a house or two might have burned. Is that correct?

M: One house burned up on Norris Circle. Of course that was back when the Ordnance Department. was renting a few of them. And this holy roly preacher—it was in the dead of winter—so he forgot to shut the draft off. And he went somewhere to preach and when we got out there with the fire truck, the house was falling in. Another house out here on Norris Circle, fourth house from the corner of Pickwick, termites ate it up and the Army tore it down and filled up the foundation.

W: Was that back before the days of all these fancy termite exterminators? Did they have termite control?

M: Under the Army Ordnance control, none of these houses were ever treated for termites, but when TVA sold them, everybody that bought them had to have them treated because they had never had any termite treatment of any type from anybody.

W: I understand that all this property in here where these houses were constructed was farmland in the beginning.

M: Yes, it was farmland and it was also part of Sheffield. The streetcar line used to run through here and it was known as the old Cherokee Pike, which is still the Cherokee Pike. Now it is known as Blackwell Road. The streetcar line there belonged to the Alabama Power Company.

W: And went down to Tuscumbia.

M: Went to Tuscumbia, turned around and went all the way to Florence, turned around in East Florence, and came back.

W: I remember that we used to (ride it) from old Village 2

M: Yeah, used to go straight up through Greenbriar (a street in Village 2).

W: And the Junction was over there about where the putt-putt golf course is now (on Nathan Blvd.).

M: That's right.

W: (People would) ride out there and transfer.

M: The old Cherokee Pike used to run right through Plant 1. So they bypassed it and made the present road. And that is still known as the old Cherokee Pike on county maps. It was a mail route. It came on down to what is known as Pickwick Street now, and right on across Spring Creek. At that time this reservation consisted of 2300 acres but there was 1550 acres across Spring Creek, It was all farmland and it was bought for future farming and this, that, and other. Anyway, these houses were laid out in rows of four to six at a time. And you could just see them jump! I have never seen as many carpenters in my life! And there were quite a few subcontractors here but not as many as there were over at Plant 2. There were about 15 or 20 over there but here there were about 8 or 9. They would complete about three houses a day. And seemed like it just jumped from block to block. In the meantime, all the construction on the streets, water lines, and sewer lines was being put down at the same time. And there were so many sinkholes out here, and cisterns too, that they used the debris left over to fill them up. Consequently, in a lot of places you can't dig down too far without digging up part of the old system.

M: We used to train out here on horses. All the guards did this. We had a very tough Lieutenant Egbert of the Army Ordnance Department. and we used to run into barbwire fences (laughter). The Village was never occupied completely because of the war ending. Now up on Pickwick Street, we had what was called the "Snuff Row." It was temporary housing and it was for non-commissioned officers. And there are still quite a few of the old red houses that belonged to various people and they remained there for quite some time. The big construction camp, right on the corner of the old Cherokee Pike streetcar stop, ran back quite a distance and the mess hall and fire hall. They had a bunch of soldiers here and they had barracks. They had barracks for the workers. We had a large military commissary where one could buy almost anything he wanted. When it closed down, everything began to fold up.

W: Chief, do you remember Mr. Stewart who used to live where Summers lived and rode horses? Wasn't he one of the first people in here?

M: That was John Righty Stewart—there never was a finer man[4]

W: Was he Ocie's daddy?

M: Yeah, Ocie and Mose—remember Mose? They had two daughters—one was named Sarah. Mose is dead—he was a guard up at Wheeler Dam.

W: He used to drive a bus, didn't he?

M: Yeah, he sure did. But John Righty was quite a man. Under Major Anthony Poyet, who was a warrant officer that come in here, sent in by the Ordnance Department. Col. John W. Clement was the commanding officer at both plants; he kept receiving orders to lay off and close things down but he never did. His wife was the social leader of the Tri-Cities (laughter). And they lived on what was known as Proctor Farm then—a big house overlooking everything.

W: Where was that?

M: That was at Plant No. 2.

W: You know, when I was just a young fellow, we come when I was just five years old.

The old fire station was out there on the Wilson reservation—a stucco building with a big siren on top and the largest flag that I had ever seen in my life.

M: I remember it very well. We used to put the flag up at sunrise and take it down at sunset.

W: Now that is the first time that I can remember I ever saw you. Do you remember that? It had a little three-stall garage of a thing. And an old gasoline pump.

M: We operated that for the poor people. We didn't sell gas to anybody but employees, or wasn't supposed to, but we sold a lot to personal friends. I was Major Poyet's personal representative and he kept me on the day shift out there. And I had charge of the gas station.

W: That is the first time that I saw you—pumping that gas!

M: I had an old pump. Ed Engels of the Alabama Oil Company. I bought oil from Fred W. Robertson, who was the chief administrative officer. At Christmas,

---

[4]John Righty Stewart, a Spanish-American War veteran, is buried in Sheffield Oakwood Cemetery. He was born Sept. 29, 1877 and died May 13, 1969.

we would take the gas money and buy groceries and deliver them around in the Tri-Cities to the poor people whose names we got from the Associated Charities. And Mrs. Joe Jacks was the head of that then. Just take what profit we made--and it was quite a lot—and buy groceries. That went on for quite a number of years until it got to where we could not handle it due to the fact that so many people to whom we delivered big baskets on the day before Christmas would be back the day after Christmas demanding more. Finally, the little committee out at the plant decided to turn the profits over to various charities--the Salvation Army and the Associated Charities--and let them do it. It seemed like the more we gave, the more they demanded.

W. Getting back to Major Poyet, I remember him, He had two daughters didn't he?

M: Three daughters.

W: Well, I remember two of them. And I believe that you told me during WWI, Poyet was a major in the army.

M: Yeah. He was a colonel on General John J. Pershing's staff. Major Poyet was a full-blooded Frenchman. And when he got excited, you could not understand him, and he used to holler out at me and he called me "Mar-tin." And I taught him how to drive his first car. That was an old 1918 Dodge, and he was the only man I ever saw that could make one squat in the middle when he would start or stop.

W: Laughter.

M: We had a mechanic then--Johnny Williams. We had about 117 cars there and it kept Johnny busy replacing his car. We finally got him where he would just mash down on the accelerator and take his foot off the clutch. And boy, it would jump! But he managed to hold on to it. He was one fine fellow.

W: I remember your fire trucks out there had solid tires.

M: Oh, yeah. They were American LaFrance trucks. We had three.

W: Later on, I remember Chief Watts had a—I guess you would call it a truck.

M: It was a GMC truck You had to crank it. He would always leave it on a hill. He lived on the corner of Florence and Tombigbee (in Village 2). He would park it there and when it would not start, why he would let it roll down the hill. I inherited that thing when I was make chief in 1933. I lived on Possum Trot and

Elmwood out there 22 and a half years. TVA sold the house and that was the only way to get me out of it. But I didn't keep that truck too long. I inherited it from Capt. Riley (who was an engineering officer at the dam). When they consolidated the guard force—we used to have two guard forces here, one was ordnance and one was engineering. When TVA came in, they consolidated the two forces and I was given Capt. Riley's car. It had these puncture-proof tires on it, and I used to drive it to Waco where the old limestone quarry was. You could get up to 40 mph and I mean it would swing and you could not tell if you were going or coming (laughter).

W: Well, lets see now, Mr. Fred Robertson, you said that he was an administrator and worked out of old First Quarters.

M: Oh, yeah. That is where Major Poyet's headquarters was. There were four people in there

W: Before I retired from TVA, I found an old drawing, a blueprint. It listed the old First Quarters as a hotel.

M: It was used for the workers. It was a hotel. It had individual rooms and baths but only for employees, mostly army people. Back during the CCC days, we were gifted with quite a bunch of CCs. They brought the first kudzu in here. They were using it to repair erosion, and, boy, we have never been able to get rid of it since. We had never heard of kudzu until the CCC planted it.

W: You know that big drainage ditch over behind the State Trooper office, on Hatch Blvd? I remember where we were kids, we used to play in there and there was no kudzu there then.

M: Of course, you did Yeah, the CCC came in there and we didn't know what kudzu was.

W: Wonder where they got that stuff?

M: I don't know. It was part of the Civilian Conservation Corps and somebody came up with the idea. It was good for soil erosion but it choked everything else out. It you got a little of it on the ground, you could not get rid of it, even if you dug it up.

W: Well, that is quite interesting. That is the first time that I have heard that.

W: You were talking about John Williams. He was a machinist down in the plant until he retired.

M: That is right. There were three brothers—John, Dennis, and Warren. And Warren and Dennis were on the Fire Department with us. And, of course, we had a guard force and part of them were guards and part of them firemen. We were known as fire fighter/policemen. Dennis was the younger brother—boy, he was a rounder (laughter). There was nothing sacred to him. Warren was the oldest; he was more sensible But he developed something—I don't know just what it was-- and never got over it.

W: Chief, when they started construction of Village One, were the old furnaces at Furnace Hill in operation?

M: Three of them. The Hattie and the two Cole furnaces.. Bruce LeMay was the general superintendent--Ralph LeMay's father. Those furnaces operated for quite some time All of the pig iron that they made was shipped to Birmingham. And that is where all the slag came from, for the roads around here. You have never seen such slag pits on the banks of the Tennessee River and when they emptied one of those pots, they illuminated Sheffield and you could see the red fire from Tuscumbia and Florence. They operated for a long, long time at Furnace Hill.

W: Well, we finally got rid of the furnaces and the shacks or houses for the workers. They got in bad shape and they tore them down and put in public housing.

M: Yes, Furnace Hill used to be a disgrace to the Tri-Cities.

W: Chief, have you seen a copy of the new book that the Friends of the Sheffield Library are putting out for the centennial this year? You know this is the 100th birthday of Sheffield.

M: No, I haven't.

W: They have a lot of old pictures in there that you would really enjoy seeing. I have a copy of the book and will bring it sometime for you to see.

M: Good! I have been reading about it. I am not able to read too much because I can't read much without a magnifying glass. The glass is getting weaker—not my eyes (laughter). And of course, my arm has gotten too short (laughter).

M: Back when they shut down everything, Alabama Power Company was represented in the Tri-Cities by a fellow named Jackson, a very fine fellow. And he lived out here in the Village and he was the general manager. The dam was operating then, not very much, and they were paying 3 cents per kw for power, and from the large steam plant down on the river, and turning around and selling it to people in the Quad-Cities for ten cents. And of course, TVA came in and bought all the lines and everything. They operated the steam plant for a while but they finally tore it down because it was unprofitable. Eleven families lived out here in the Village until TVA took it over. They were spaced where you were responsible for looking after so many houses.

W: I see. For fire and vandalism?

M: Right. Major Poyet lived in No. 114, the big house up there in the bell. And he had three daughters: Garnette, Evangeline, and Isabell. Evangeline was a full colonel in the Nurses Corps. Isabell married Bill Mead, Morris Mead's brother. Bill died and Isabell married a Coast Guard man and left. And Garnette married a newspaper man in Nashville. When Major Poyet retired, he and his wife went to San Francisco and he died out there.

W: Well, I didn't know what ever happened to the man.

M: He was one fine man.

W: He always seemed like he was. We had a lot of fun.

M: Of course, he had a terrible job. When a warrant officer relieves a full colonel! And he sold everything. You remember how many old houses, barracks, and everything there were out at Plant No. 2?

Wann: As we finished side A on the tape, Chief Martin was becoming fatigued. He was real old and I regret very much that we did not get to finish the interview. Chief Martin had his niece down at his house taking care of him until her death and then Chief went into a nursing home where he finally passed away Chief Martin was some character himself. He got some of his army officers mixed up. He jumped Poyet from Warrant Officer to Lt. Colonel to Colonel and back to Major.[5] But I thought, he being as old as he was at the time, his memory was remarkable. I have talked to some of the senior citizens of Sheffield and they pretty well were of the same opinion as Chief Martin was about the construction of this Village.

When TVA came in, they opened a school for children living out here in Village One. And Burns Bus Lines in Sheffield ran buses from Wilson Dam to

---

[5]Poyet signed papers in 1923, 1924, and 1933 as Warrant Officer, Commanding. But a news item in 1930 listed him as Major (The Sheffield Standard, March 28, 1930).

bring students from Village Three and Village Two to school in Village One. The school was sort of an experimental thing with rest periods for the kids during the day.[6] Of course, we got out there in the fields and played ball and this sort of stuff. Ray Black was one of the principals here and later on he was the principal at Sheffield High School. Then I think that Mr. Black went back to school in Birmingham and got his Ph. D. in education. He died in Birmingham but he was fortunate enough to come back and attend one of the Sheffield High School reunions and he seemed to enjoy that very much.

I remember very distinctly the time that Sheffield High School burned.[7] It stood on Atlanta Avenue and the typing teacher was a lady by the name of Mrs. Marden. She stood out on a very narrow ledge and some of the students went into the typing room and were passing those typewriters out to her and she was handing them down to somebody else. And it looked like she might fall at any moment. She was a feisty little thing and she was determined to save her typewriters. And I recall that everybody that had brothers or sisters in the building was running around trying to find each other. It was quite a deal.

Chief Martin was talking about the old streetcar running out through here. The tracks went up just about where the Sheffield High School is now on down to what we called the Junction and on across the old bridge into Florence and on down to East Florence. Now, you would not know it because they came into Florence with the new highway and lots of construction work.

---

[6]Maurice F. Seay and William J. McGlothlin, "A Description of the Wilson Dam and Gilbertsville Schools," Bulletin of the Bureau of School Service (College of Education, University of Kentucky) XIV (#3), March 1943; Virginia W. James and Grace Tietje, "Going to School in an Officers' Barrack," Childhood Education XIV, (#1), 9-11 (Sept. 1927).

[7]Sheffield High School burned April 21, 1938.

A History of Nitrate Village One[1]

by John C. Mothershed

United States Nitrate Village No. 1, better known as Village One, has played an important role in the development of the Muscle Shoals area. It is highly significant for its association with the construction of Nitrate Plant No. 1 and the early days of the Tennessee Valley Authority (TVA), as an early 20th century planned community, for its distinctive "Liberty Bell" design, and as an excellent example of early prefabrication and standardization in housing construction.

On June 2, 1916, President Woodrow Wilson signed into law the National Defense Act. Section 124 of this act gave the President power to find the best and cheapest way to produce nitrates. The need for domestic nitrates evolved because the usual supply of nitrates from Chile was being interfered with by unrestricted German submarine warfare. The Act also provided for the government to use or buy all lands needed for the production of nitrates.[2]

Nitrate Plant No. 1 and a village to house the employees were built just west of the city of Sheffield. The plant was a modification of the German Haber process for extracting nitrates from the atmosphere. Information to help design the plant was obtained by U. S. Intelligence.[3] Construction on the project began on October 23, 1917. The contractor for the construction of the plant and village was the J. C. White Corporation of New York.[4]

---

[1] This paper was written in 1984 for Dr. Kenneth R. Johnson's History 300 class at the University of North Alabama.

[2] Muscle Shoals Commission, Muscle Shoals (Washington: U. S. Government Printing Office, 1931), p. 97.

[3] Earl H. Brown and Ronald D. Young, "History of U. S. Facilities at Muscle Shoals." Paper presented at Southeast Regional Meeting of the American Chemical Society, Gatlinburg, TN, 29 Oct. 1976.

[4] Report on the Fixation and Utilization of Nitrogen (Washington: U. S. War Department, GPO, 1922), pp. 268-270.

When the news got out that the Muscle Shoals area had been selected as the site for the nitrate plant, the people of the area celebrated with barbecues and bonfires.[5]

Village One was built about one mile southwest of the nitrate plant. The village consisted of 85 stucco houses, a school building, and an officers' barracks. The village was laid out in the shape of a giant Liberty Bell[6] This unique design was apparently picked to show patriotism during World War I.

Mr. Joe Long, a resident of Sheffield since 1905, remembers the area of Village One before construction begun. It was mainly flat with brush and scattered trees. Mr. Long remembers hunting birds and rabbits on the land, and he recalls that the area was very beautiful.[7]

Mr. Alfred McCroskey also remembers the Village One houses. He lived in a village house in 1918. Because of the large number of people coming into the area and the shortage of houses, finding a house was a hard thing to accomplish. Mr. McCroskey remembers moving into a village house before it was completed just to be able to claim it.[8]

The village houses were built for army officers and workers who had families. The three larger houses were built for higher ranking officers, and the houses around the "bell" itself were for lieutenants. The barracks were for single military men.[9]

The village was patrolled by military guards on horseback. Mr. McCroskey has fond memories of riding with the guards around the village as a boy.[10]

All of the village houses are basically of the bungalow type. Although the houses have similar interiors, the architects achieved an illusion of variety by using different window sashes and roof planes. All the houses, as well as the barracks and schoolhouse, have brick foundations with stucco walls. Most of the

---

[5] Marguerite Owens, The Tennessee Valley Authority (New York: Praeger Publishers, 1973), pp. 7-8.
[6] Historic Muscle Shoals (Sheffield, AL: Tennessee Valley Historical Society, 1983), p. 69.
[7] Interview with Joe Long, resident of Sheffield, AL since 1905, Sheffield, 21 Oct. 1984.
[8] Interview with Alfred McCroskey, resident of Village One in 1918, Sheffield, AL, 10 Nov. 1984.
[9] Interview with Mrs. D. O. Dugger, resident of Village One since 1934, Sheffield, AL, 6 Oct. 1984.
[10] Interview with Alfred McCroskey, 11 Nov. 1984.

houses today are white, with few exceptions. All the houses still have their original red tile roofs. But the barracks has been remodeled and no longer has its tile roof. The houses have wooden floors and all have common arched vents in the gables.

There are three basic categories of Village One houses. Category A consists of four types of houses. These were the smaller houses in the village. Category B consists of seven types of houses. They were the medium-size houses. Category C consists of only three houses, all of which are the same type. The three larger houses are located around the present Guntersville Circle and were built for the senior military officers.

This picture postcard from the 1920s gives a birds-eye view of Nitrate Village One. Although the card calls it a "Liberty Bell", other evidence suggests that the landscape designer used a handbell as his pattern.

The construction of Village One serves as a good example of the emergency wartime effort.

It utilized rapid construction and cost saving techniques. Ewing and Allen were the town planners. They used scale models to achieve their goal of a town laid out in the shape of the Liberty Bell. The Village is also an excellent example of prefabrication and standardization. In order to save time and money, all the hardware in the houses, light fixtures, and plumbing facilities were standardized. Money was saved by ordering large quantities of materials. And large crews of workmen were put on each project to save time. In Village One today, some of the original street lamps and fire hydrants of 1919 can still be seen.[11]

The social environment of the Village during this stage was a feeling of "oneness" due to the war effort. There was not a lot of time for actual social gatherings. Everyone was in a hurry. Another factor that deterred social activities was the great influenza epidemic of 1918. Although the Village was not hit as hard as other parts of the area, Mr. McCroskey said that the threat of flu stopped any attempt at socializing. He remembers that a whole family who lived next door to him died—all in one night.

Transportation to and from the Village was mainly by streetcar. Streetcars ran from Florence, Sheffield, Tuscumbia, and Nitrate Plant No. 2 to the outskirts of Village One.[12]

U. S. Nitrate Plant No. 1 was a technical failure and no ammonium nitrate was produced because the Americans did not have the necessary information and experience about the Haber process.[13]

When the First World War ended with the signing of the armistice on November 11, 1918, the construction and operation of both Nitrate Plants No. 1 and No. 2 were put on standby.[14] The houses, barracks, and school in Village One had just been completed and had seen little use. Prior to its closing, a number of improvements were made. In April and May 1919, the streets were graded, storm drains and sewers added, and a tennis court was built across the street from the barracks.[15]

The President was authorized before the armistice to sell war supplies and many buildings, plants or factories acquired since April 6, 1917, including the

---

[11] U. S. Department of the Interior, "National Register of Historic Places," 1984.
[12] Historic Muscle Shoals, pp. 153-154.
[13] Brown and Young, "History of U. S. Facilities at Muscle Shoals, p. 3.
[14] D. O. Dugger, unpublished manuscript on history of Village One.
[15] National Register of Historic Places.

land upon which they stood. But the Village along with the other United States facilities at Muscle Shoals were not included. Under Section 134 of the National Defense Act of 1916, "the plant or plants provided for under this act shall be constructed and opened solely by the government and not in conjunction of any other industry or enterprise carried on by private capital."[16] This put the Village and the nitrate plants in a state of suspended animation. That provision of the act would be the topic of heated debate between 1918 and 1933.

During those years, very few houses were occupied In fact, the Village was practically a ghost town. The only residents were a handful of Alabama Power Company employees who had permission from the government to operate the steam plant at Plant No. 1. The other houses stayed empty until TVA was established in 1933.[17]

Education has always played a big role in the Village. In the first stage, during the 1918 era, the U. S. government hired Miss Maud Lindsay to teach a kindergarten in the Village School. Miss Maud was nationally known as a writer of children's books and one of the best kindergarten teachers. She taught in the Village for about two years.[18]

The school building was erected in 1918 at a cost of $17,936.78. After TVA took over Village One in 1933, the agency opened the school for children of its employees.[19] Because the houses were on federal property, the children could not attend city schools. TVA made arrangements with the Sheffield School Board for the high school students to attend Sheffield High School with TVA providing transportation and tuition. Mr. Ray C. Roberts, a chemical engineer with a degree in education, served as the principal of the Village School and teacher of the 5th and 6th grades. Other teachers in 1933-34 were Miss Robinson and Miss Mary Grimes.[20]

In the fall of 1934, elementary classes were started in the renovated army barracks. Miss Virginia W. James, an outstanding progressive educator, was the

---

[16] Owens, The Tennessee Valley Authority, pp, 7, 8.
[17] Dugger manuscript.
[18] McCroskey interview, 11 Nov. 1984.

[19] Polly Worley, unpublished manuscript "History of C. M. Brewster School," 1976.
[20] Dugger manuscript.

principal.[21] In the basement of the barracks was a large open area with two huge fireplaces at each end. The fireplaces were used for pioneer cooking, popcorn popping during story time, and sometimes just as a place to relax and watch the flames.[22] The school day would start with a talk session. Anything from a "new camera" to national events were discussed. After this came work time which helped develop hand—eye coordination in early years and experimentation and research in higher grades. After lunch was sleep time and exploring time. The day ended with a story.[23]

The school had an average of 1,000 visitors per year who came to observe and learn about the new progressive education program.[24] During its last year, in 1940-1941, a 20-minute movie was produced about the school.

In 1949, the original schoolhouse, which had stood vacant for years except for occasional social events, was deeded to the City of Sheffield. It reopened in 1955 but closed the next year. Because of the new Rivermont subdivision, the school opened again in 1962. It was renamed C. M. Brewster School in 1974 in honor of a former Sheffield superintendent. Although the official name was changed, some residents still refer to it as the "Village School."[25]

The Village houses were reopened in 1933 shortly after the TVA was created for development of the Tennessee Valley. TVA was given the responsibility of using the Muscle Shoals facilities to produce fertilizer, generate and sell electric power, and control the Tennessee River for navigation and flooding problems. Senator George Norris, of Nebraska, had proposed this legislation under the administrations of Coolidge and Hoover but it failed to pass. After Franklin D. Roosevelt became president, Norris' proposal was quickly passed and signed into law by Roosevelt on May 18, 1933.[26]

---

[21] Worley manuscript; Virginia W. James and Grace Tietje, "Going to School in an Officers' Barracks," Childhood Education XIV (#1), (Sept. 1937), pp. 9-11.

[22] William J. McGlothlin and Maurice F. Seay, ed., "A Description of the Wilson Dam and Gilbertsville Schools, Bulletin of the Bureau School Services (College of Education, University of Kentucky) XIV (#3), March 1942, pp. 17, 18.

[23] Ibid. pp. 15, 16.

[24] North Callahan, TVA: Bridge over Troubled Waters (New York: A. S. Barns and Company, 1980), pp. 158, 159.

[25] Worley manuscript.

[26] Owens, The Tennessee Valley Authority, pp. 7, 8.

The property transferred to TVA included the 85 stucco dwellings in Village One plus the officers' barracks, the schoolhouse, and the streets, water, sewer and electric systems TVA renovated the houses for its expanding staff.[27] Two of the original dwellings near the schoolhouse are no longer in existence; one burned and the other was torn down because of termite infestation.[28]

Residents of Village One organized an association along the lines of a municipal commission government with a mayor and board of commissioners on Feb. 17, 1934, there was no intention, however, of establishing a separate city government. The officers were: N. D. Huff, mayor; Mrs. E. M. Jones, finance; C. H. Young, public safety; Mrs. A. M. Miller, recreation and social activity; R. M. Jones, judge; and D. Roy Virtue, clerk. The mayors of Florence, Sheffield, Tuscumbia, and Muscle Shoals directed the inaugural exercises, and then everyone celebrated with a big dance and party.[29]

Mrs. D. O. Dugger, a Village resident since 1934, recalls how scarce the houses were. She said that her husband had to live in "First Quarters" near Plant No. 2 for six months until he could get a Village house. Mrs. Dugger remembers all the dances and other social events that were held to get the residents acquainted with one another. "Most of the residents were from out of town and the gatherings helped everyone to get to know their neighbors," she said. Mrs. Dugger has this personal feeling about the Village: "It was nice, easy living. A nice experience." She said that people in the community felt safe and that no one needed to lock their doors. She also stated that "kids ran around all over the place, and it was a wonderful place to bring up children.[30]

Another social event was the lighting of Mr. Charlie Painter's Christmas tree in his front yard. The residents threw a party by helping decorate the tree, singing carols around it, and then having a supper in the schoolhouse. That event

---

[27] John H. Kyle, The Building of TVA (Baton Rouge: Louisiana State University Press, 1951), p. 11.
[28] Interview with Charles Painter, resident of Village One since 1934, Sheffield, AL, 11 Nov. 1984.
[29] Florence Times, 20 Jan. 1934; Florence Herald, 16 Feb. 1934; Sheffield Standard, 16 Feb. 1934.
[30] Interview with Mrs. D. O. Dugger, 6 Oct. 1934.

began in 1937[31] People came from all over the Tri-Cities to see the huge cedar tree decorated with as many as 750 lights.[32] The City of Sheffield provided power for the lights while the Village folks helped with the other finances of the project. Unfortunately, the Christmas tree tradition died out in 1976. Mr. Painter said that the main reason for this was lack of support.

Some Village residents kept horses at stables behind the old Village Store. This picture shows Charlie Young and daughter Nancy ready for a ride. Courtesy of Ida Young

TVA did the upkeep and maintenance of the houses and parks. Mrs. Ellen Fields, a Village resident since 1935, said that she recalls TVA workers mowing a vacant lot beside her home. And TVA fixed things that broke around the houses.[33] Mrs. Dugger remembers TVA doing all the upkeep of the houses and also

---

[31] Interview with Charles Painter, 11 Nov. 1984.
[32] "Beautiful Tree at Village One Noted," Sheffield Standard, 29 Dec. 1939.
[33] Interview with Mrs. Ellen Fields, resident since 1935, 30 Sept. 1984.

remembers a mounted guard who patrolled the Village. He came by every house. No one locked their doors because of the patrol.[34] TVA rented the houses to its employees from 1933 to 1949. The monthly rental charge was $15.00 for the smaller houses and $25.00 for the larger houses. TVA provided fire protection for the Village, too.

In 1949, TVA decided to get out of the housing business. The sale of the Nitrate Plant No. 1 property began at 10:00 A.M., May 10, with an auction held in the schoolhouse. The prices of the houses ranged from $4,200 to $9,800. Included in the sale was the barracks, 59 residential sites, 8 residential acreage tracts, 3 industrial tracts, one business tract, and three farm tracts[35]

Many residents purchased the houses that they were living in. They would make the minimum bid acceptable to TVA and usually no one bid against them. An exception to this was Mr. Painter. He was well-liked, but someone bid against him. Then the crowd shouted in protest until the bidder withdrew his offer and Mr. Painter got his house! This shows the closeness of the Village residents at that time.[36] Everything on the Plant No. 1 Reservation was sold at public auction except the school building, the bell-shaped park, and the playgrounds. Those properties plus the utilities and streets were deeded to the City of Sheffield on May 11, 1949.[37]

Village One was nominated to the National Register of Historic Places in the fall of 1984. In due time, it was accepted and placed on the National Register. Today, this unique and historic district is one of Sheffield's most charming and interesting neighborhoods.

---

[34] Mrs. Dugger interview.
[35] "Village One Houses Being Sold Today, Florence Times, 10 May 1949.
[36] Mrs. Dugger and Painter interviews.
[37] "Sale of TVA properties at Nitrate Plant One Reach $525,379," Florence Times, 12 May 1949.

Growing Up in Village One

by Stanley M. Elmore

Village One, seen in retrospect, was, more by accident than intention, a unique place in time and space. It was built to house the senior staff, engineers and executives of the team selected to build Nitrate Plant # 1 near Sheffield, Alabama in 1918. Its creation was attached to the construction of Wilson Dam, the first major hydro-electric dam on the, yet untamed, Tennessee River. Both were begun as necessary to America's involvement in WWI and the production of explosives. The Armistice in November 1918 cancelled the immediate need for gunpowder, therefore other uses of the inoperable projects were revised to complete Wilson Dam so as to harness the potential energy of the waters and enhance navigation through the rocky shoals, a natural impediment to boat transportation since Colonial days.

Notice the horse and wagon in this 1918 construction scene at Village One.   Courtesy of Bobby Carroll

The potential for development of the natural resources of water, minerals, and inhabitants of the area was recognized by the U.S, Government. Having already invested millions of dollars in the dam, chemical plants #1 and #2 to no benefit, they wisely steered the endeavor to produce electricity and chemical fertilizers. After 12 years of haggling Congress, led by Senator George Norris of Nebraska, created the TVA in 1933. It was part of President Franklin Roosevelt's New Deal program to create more jobs for citizens hurt by The Great Depression that began in 1929. The Tennessee Valley Authority was a quasi-independent corporation of the U.S. Government, in conflict with private corporate interests and remained so for many years.

Ownership of Wilson Dam, chemical plants #1 and #2, along with Villages #1 and #2 were transferred to the TVA. The idea was not to be in competition with private industry, but to create a demonstration project that would show how government could enhance the lives and economic conditions of a rural region by using and developing all of its local resources, heretofore largely ignored by private industry because of the inherent poverty of the area.

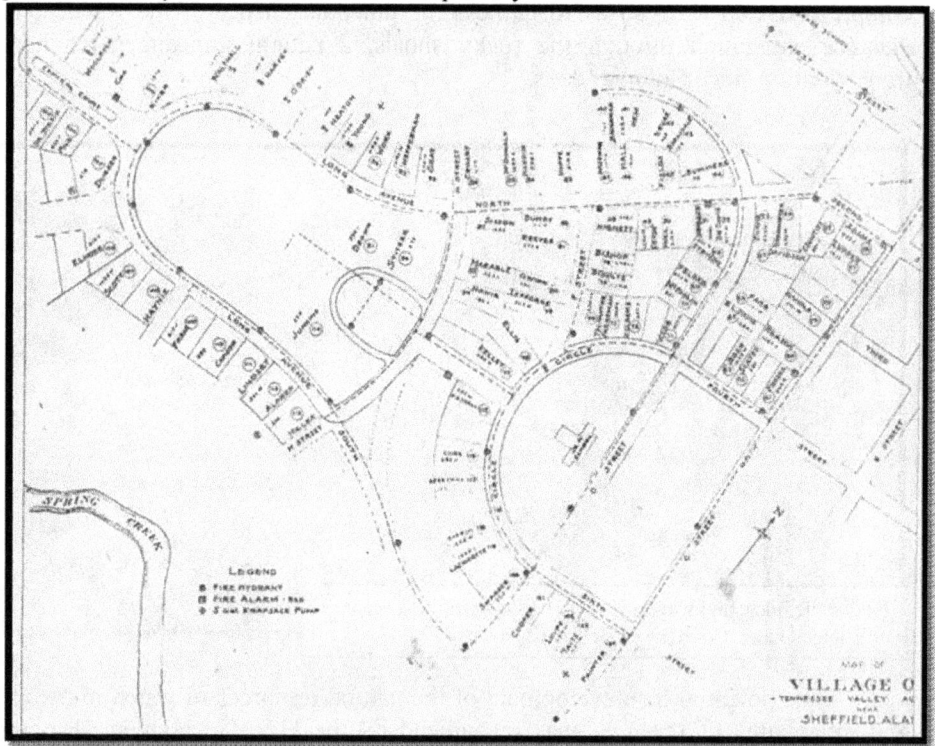

This Map of the bell-shaped Village One, made by TVA about 1950, gives the name and house numbers of the residents. The names of the street were changed after the village was annexed by Sheffield.

The two Villages were owned and maintained by the TVA and the housing was assigned by the TVA. In general, the houses were assigned to the professional and service staff of the chemical plants and dam and therefore subsidized to a degree under the TVA Corporate umbrella.

Landscape and Layout

Village One was located west of Nitrate plant #1 and Sheffield, inside the last U-turn of Spring Creek just before it empties into the Tennessee River, with limestone bluffs just east of its connection. A low elevation running from south to north marked the highest ground and approximate center of the village and the high end of a grassy field, which locals called "the big circle". Oak, black walnut and sweet gum trees were scattered along the edges of the field which followed a bell shaped road around the open field. The roads were laid out in the shape of a dinner bell, with the handle or loop road to the west and a semi-circle of a road formed the clapper of the bell to the east at the top of the rise, rimmed by the three largest houses in the village. Three-or two-car garages with gravel driveways were constructed intermittently behind every two or three houses, one space per house. Their construction was red brick foundation, ship–lap wooden siding, tin red roof, with storage room to spare. There was a heavily forested rim separating the lawns and houses from Spring Creek that was crisscrossed by foot and dog paths and was a perpetual heaven for hiding and childhood exploration. It was a natural sanctuary for foxes, raccoons, snakes and birds.

There were 85 two and three bedroom houses constructed of above ground red brick foundations, wood frame covered with white stucco and red tiled roofs. A colonnaded front porch, usually accommodating a swing or gliding sofa was a common gathering place on hot summer days. Most houses had a basement with a coal-fired hot air furnace and a bin for coal storage, and a walk-up attic that easily converted to a bedroom with a window. Each living room had a fireplace and hearth, framed by a mantel and some shelving encased with glass-paned doors. Original kitchens were equipped with a wood stove for cooking, but were converted to electric ranges with ovens when Wilson Dam began producing electricity, but block ice refrigeration persisted into the early 1940's and cardboard placards of 25 50 75 100 printed in large black letters were a common memento, found in many basements or garages. Each house had one bathroom with a four legged bathtub, shower with curtain, flush toilet and wash basin with hot and cold water spigots. The water pipes were galvanized iron and corroded with some frequency. There were sash windows with screens and glass paned front and back doors with a light outer screen door for warmer weather. Clothes lines were in every back yard and, although illegal in most neighborhoods today, were and are ecologically efficient and took good advantage of the clean air and abundant Alabama sunshine. Scrub boards and wringer washers were common in most homes until the 1950's.

Picture of Village School under construction in 1918. Courtesy of Bobby Carroll

Most telephone service was on a 'party line'. For the newly born, a party line meant that you shared the telephone wire to your house with someone else, not in your house, and could not call out nor receive a call until the other party hung–up their telephone. Furthermore, a telephone operator sitting at a switch board somewhere in town had to connect your call and could talk to you or monitor your call, if they wished. We enjoyed all the modern amenities of the time.

Other houses were located to the east and north of the "big circle" and were often referred to as 'the little circle" that formed a semicircle around the T-shaped school house which stood large in its middle. The school building had a naturally lighted basement, first floor had handsome classrooms with slate blackboards, a large auditorium with folding chairs and a balcony and stage; a second floor with a carbon arc slide projector, library and more classrooms. It too was constructed with a red brick foundation, white stucco walls and red roof tiles. There were swings, see-saw and monkey bars to one side and a natural ball diamond on the other.

TVA School

More houses were north of this out of service school building and bordered the main entrance road into the Village, later named Wilson Dam Avenue. At the periphery of this original housing was a three story rectangular building, built as Officers quarters in 1918 for personnel supervising the construction of Nitrate plant #1.

This was converted into the TVA Elementary School in the mid 30's. The school was organized and run as a Progressive School, similar to a Montessori school today. Classes were small with dedicated teachers who read classic stories and poems to us. Each class had hands-on pet and animal experiences. We grew vegetables in a garden and played outside in the honeysuckle thickets (our jungle) at least once daily. We learned manual skills such as carpentry, finger painting, candle dipping, and building with oversized blocks. We all had our personal bed roll for the mandatory nap after lunch that we brought from home in our lunch boxes. Those who lived in Village One walked to school and those who lived in Village #2 and Village #3 were bused across the town of Sheffield to attend the TVA school. Village #2 (about 186 families) was built to house those who worked near Nitrate-Fertilizer Plant #2 on the east side of Sheffield and Village #3 (about 12 houses) was on the North end of Wilson Dam and housed some who worked at the Dam. There was often a gold fish or guppy, guinea pig, kitten or cat to feed and plants to be watered. Each child was eager to be chosen to do any of these duties every day.

We were introduced to animal reproduction systematically by gathering tadpoles from a pond or creek and bringing them to a fish tank, with glass sides so we could watch their metamorphosis into frogs. We collected chrysalis from bushes and waited for the butterfly to emerge. Once we were taken to a chicken hatchery where we were given a tour of how eggs were selected and arrayed for incubation into chicks. I believe some of us were given newly hatched chicks to take either home or to school. These were the days when some chicks were dyed green, blue and red for the Easter season.

There was an annual Field Day in May toward the end of the school year. Competitive sack races, tug-of-war, and 'wheelbarrow races' where one student was the wheelbarrow (hands were the wheel and their legs were the handles) and the other student was the driver. There were swings, see-saw, monkey bars and two tennis courts with night lighting in the field across the road, in front of the school building. We also sang a lot of songs. It was a great time for group play and learning by doing and touching new things. Intellectual rigor of reading and writing was not emphasized in the lower grades. When we integrated into the Sheffield schools in 1942 I could not read at third grade level.

Students at the TVA School in the Barracks (now an apartment complex) enjoyed many outdoor games and activities. The taller girl inside the ring of children is identified as Kathryn Fields. Courtesy of TVA Library

Community

Walking and bicycles, using the common road in front of every house, tied families together and served the same purpose as sidewalks. These roads were topped with loose gravel until the late 1930's, then solidified with hot tar, which reduced the dust and bicycle skidding accidents. Concrete walks were constructed from front steps to the street edge about the same time and gave uniformity to the village curbside appearance. Electric street lamps with frosted globes were situated at regular intervals along the road system and were lighted each night. These lights added safety for night riding bicycles and walking couples or individuals as well as security. Serendipity was thus created whereas adults and children met in the evenings to play games, chat informally with neighbors or just look at the stars together. Lawn chairs and porches also invited adults to stay and talk after dark in this era before television. The distance around the "big circle" was approximately one mile and my father walked three times around, almost every day, until just before his death at 81. One cannot over estimate the salubrious social dynamic of this design and influence on this semi-rural community.

The School house in "the little circle" was really the community center for group activities. Over time it served for adult group singing, using "The Golden Book of Favorite Songs", 202 favorite songs, many carried over from the 19th century; men's volley ball; black and white two-reel movies; women-less weddings; elementary school costumed plays (costumes made by the actors); folding bandages (during WWII); small pox vaccinations and typhoid shots; and Boy Scout meetings. These were official sanctioned events and occurred regularly.

There was, however, surreptitious use of this building in other hours, usually in daylight, by us children of the Village. I can only testify to that which I participated. It was by modern terms 'breaking and entering'. It was easy to unlock a basement window during a sanctioned event or jam a door lock and return next day and roam the building, marveling at the broken carbon arc projector in the balcony or examine the electrical system behind the stage, or play hide-and-seek in the many rooms and closets throughout the building.

The most thrilling activity was playing hockey on roller skates on the smooth concrete floors of the basement rooms. No one could buy a hockey puck in any of the stores (remember this was Alabama and most of us had never seen a hockey game) so we used a crushed, from top to bottom, Campbell soup can. It was about the right size and weight and very durable. A few of the boys had 'store bought' hockey sticks, so we knew how to shape ours out of local woods (hickory, oak or ash). All the stick handles were appropriately wrapped with electrical or friction tape. We played without any padding, sometimes in short pants and sustained a collection of scrapes and bruises on our knees, elbows and shins.

Skate keys were as necessary as a pocket knife in order to remain competitive. I can still reproduce the unique sensation, like a chill, of sliding across a concrete floor on my knee or elbow by just recalling the experience. Only the best skaters completed a game without some blood loss. It was always a great adrenalin rush that we call a "high" today, and it strengthened the bonds among the boys who played. Adults knew we were in the building illegally but never called us on it. It is fair to add that there was never any vandalism. Theft would have required some heavy tools as there was little that was portable. Just walking around, in what seemed a vast empty space with its creaks and echoes, imagining its former use, was a trip into the past and gave a sense of its good service before we were born.

We played softball and baseball in the field south of the school building. The grassy area was below street level and home plate was backed by a small stand of pines. The Diamond was not of official dimensions but close enough to seem so. The bases were just a wider area of exposed red clay and the pitcher's mound was flat, not a mound, but it served us well. Gathering enough players to have scratch teams required that we include boys both older and younger (from eight to eighteen) and occasionally a girl when we were desperate to play. A team could be as few as seven or on best days eleven per side. Equipment was a collection of whatever any of us had. It was common to have to use the same gloves for both teams and not everyone owned a bat or ball and no one owned a catcher's mask. The older boys usually chose teams alternately from the collection of greenhorns and everyone knew who were the best pitchers and hitters, and they were chosen first. But we had all started at the bottom of the unproven ability ladder and had to perform if we were ever to rise in this sports hierarchy. It was in this milieu that I found out I batted better left handed, even though I was right handed, and that when allowed to pitch I could occasionally throw a strike, but never got close to the top of the selection process. God, it was fun to play with such a mixture of friends without any adult supervision or advice, and I can vouch that games were played, usually, honestly and fairly and every one learned how to arbitrate a dispute. Good training for later life.

One of the glories of growing up in Village One was the absolute freedom to do whatever you wanted to do on any given day after school and on weekends. Nobody had excess money to spend on frivolities. We had loving, caring parents whose fathers worked for the TVA; lived in a vibrant community of honest, mostly Church going citizens that favored education as the path to a secure future. There was no fear of theft, murder, abduction. or abuse, Sex was never discussed in our presence and pregnant mothers were not supposed to be seen publicly when they started to show a little tummy bulge, although this social custom was on its way out by the end of the War.

We had freedom to roam the grassy fields and forests behind our houses as long as we did not get too near Spring Creek, which of course, was always a major attraction. We would build secret huts or lean-tos out of native and near-by materials of sedge grass, fallen limbs and sticks. These structures became more sophisticated when we were allowed to use the hatchet and pocket knife. We experimented with matches, smoked rabbit tobacco and grape vine and occasionally caused a grass fire that required a visit from the nearby Fire Dept. No structures were ever torched on purpose and lessons were learned, mostly as how to use fire more safely and less obviously. Grass fires did occur occasionally without juvenile involvement and sometime during the War, 5-gallon backpack, hand-pumped fire extinguishers were placed at the back of garages for quick access to anyone nearby who could lift it and put it into service. Occasionally, they really did perform their intended purpose, but were frequently checked for their readiness by passing children who had never had such a powerful water gun before or since.

Most afternoon and weekend activities arose spontaneously. Sometimes they were organized in a moment of mutual agreement by the assembled majority and a game of touch football, softball, baseball, roller skate hockey or dig a hole in the woods. A critical number would evolve and likely attract others who might not have commitments elsewhere. An activity that may have been local or regional, were rubber-gun battles. One must recall that rubber was scarce during the war and car and bicycle tires all had inner tubes. Fixing a flat on either type of vehicle was something every boy could do. We all had patch kits with serrated tops, a tube of rubber glue and set of different sized patches.

When automobile inner tubes became unsalvageable, they could be converted into an arsenal of rubber missiles by cutting across the flabby tube with scissors or a razor. They were cut approximately ¼ to ½ inches in width and usually tied in the middle with an overhand knot, which helped increase its accuracy. One could use a "rubber gun" (an oxy-moron before the word was born) made from a flat 1 inch x 2 or 3 inch pine board 14 to 24 inches long with multiple notches cut into the top side or a simple stick with a Y shape or just string them on your thumb for quicker access. These rubber missiles when stretched and released could lay a nice red welt on someone's skin, usually accompanied by an audible reaction. We would choose –up sides and define a territory to defend. One half would then attack the other half. A circle of bicycles made rapid protection while the attackers circled and shot their rubber loops. Great fun!

Another skill and activity derived from unusable rubber inner tubes was the making of sling shots. First you had to find a branch of firm wood (oak, ash or hickory) that had a usable Y-shape or fork. Cut the grip and tines to suit your hand, notch a circular groove with your pocket knife near the ends of the two tines. Fashion a cradle for the sling out of scrap leather and attach two strips of rubber tubing, about ½ inch wide and 12 inches long. Tie the ends of the rubber strips to the tines with string secured in the notches and the other end to the leather cradle. Now it is ready to shoot well chosen stones, large ball bearings or marbles. It is amazing how accurate and powerful these custom made toy weapons could be. We also experimented with slings (such as David used against Goliath) made of rope and a larger cradle than in a sling-shot. Although we could demonstrate its increased power, we could not control its accuracy as well as a sling-shot or David.

In those days the most ubiquitous tool was the folding pocket knife. No wristwatches, cell phones, I-Pods or ball point pens. The pocket knife is still the most versatile tool that doesn't talk to you. Besides being available for any contingency, we learned a game of skill with it called mumbley-peg. Its origins are unknown, but is a game passed down through generations of boys that helps cement male bonding before we knew that dynamic existed. It requires each player to demonstrate his ability to begin each step with the knife point against some part of your anatomy and flip the knife onto the ground so that it sticks up at least one finger breadth at the free end of the knife. Anything less does not count.

Essentially one starts with a move called "scalp the Indian", the knife, blade open, is laid on top of the head, in the palm of one's hand and quickly, with a flick of the wrist delivers the blade into the ground. If it sticks up at least one finger breadth it counts as a point. This maneuver is repeated by launching it serially from the brow, then chin, shoulder, elbow, wrist, and from each finger tip of the free hand. And finally "jump the fence"; in which the blade is stuck in the ground at an angle and launched over the other hand, held at 90 degrees up (the fence), so as to again land with knife point in the ground, one finger breadth up. Whoever completes these serial steps successfully wins the round and the loser has to pull a wooden peg, driven into the ground by the winner, in only three blows of the open bladed knife (as a provisional hammer) with his teeth. This is called "rooting the peg" and remains a favorite metaphor for failure. It's a game a boy could practice alone so that he could surprise his competition later. It is a game played by any number group of boys, anytime, anywhere. It was a skill that had real cachet, but is no longer practiced in our politically correct culture.

Girls our age played hopscotch on the smooth sidewalks that connected our front porches with the street. White chalk was a common item in their pockets and they could draw out a hop-scotch lane quickly. They also played jump-rope there as well. They were practiced at double jump-rope and often invited boys to participate usually much to their amusement, for many of us got tangled in their rope webs, especially when they delivered a 'Hot' tempo. Again this illustrates the value of sidewalks in creating social interaction in a community. Walking stilts were something we could make out of scrap lumber. Stilts were fun and increased our balance skills and could be shared with girls as well

Simple tools could be utilized in different ways to enhance our fun and knowledge indirectly. Mirrors and magnifying glasses for example. In the summer especially, when the sun was the brightest and highest we sometimes borrowed our mother's hand mirrors or a wall mirror for a bigger and brighter flash. Taken outside and into the sunshine we would flash a beam of concentrated light into far away windows, trees, walls or anything that took our fancy. These beams easily crossed the big circle with great intensity. We never developed any code of communications, only nuisance value. Using magnifying glasses was a popular activity of directing the sun's rays so as to burn leaves, sticks, wood and start a fire when we wished; all innocent applications of natural light collection and several notches down from chasing rainbows, common at the end of summer showers.

Playing marbles was very popular, especially in areas of denuded grass like the playgrounds where red clay soil was exposed and hardened. One could draw a lag line or circle in a few strokes with a finger or stick and the game was set. We usually played for 'keeps' and hated to lose our favorites. Many games could be derived on the spot with a few marbles in your pocket. We had immyies, cat's eyes, shooters, solids, glassies and steelies. A bag of 10 to twenty colored marbles could be bought for ten or fifteen cents at the candy store and at a young age we valued these as precious jewels as a sign of individual wealth.

If you had a family dog at your side you were never alone. A boy and his dog gave more options and cemented friendships as nothing else. My first dog was a scruffy collie named Hilo, given as a puppy by a family friend from North Carolina. He was my constant companion and confidant. Moles were ubiquitous and their tunnels were easily tracked and Hilo had such a good nose he frequently cornered a mole and killed it, after digging yards of ruts in the grassy lawn. We shared the triumph with mutual admiration. Once when I was possibly six or seven years old, unable to swim (until I was 12), Hilo and I ambled down to the creek to a place we called the "rock chair", for obvious reasons. Somehow I got myself stranded below a vertical rock face and the water's edge. I recall a certain panic and Hilo began to bark which attracted the attention of some older girls who were strolling nearby who gave me a hand out of trouble. I did not ever tell my parents about this and avoided, at best, a tongue lashing.

I recall that many family dogs waited patiently for any evidence of human activity and would show up just for a pat or two. Others, loyal to their property would hide, or probably lounge, under a bush or shrub until you came near their property line and then suddenly charge you, barking vigorously, seldom biting. They all had individual characteristics that we recognized and accepted. One was "Snowball", a fairly small fuzzy white Spitz, belonging to the Youngs. When riding a bicycle by their house Snowball would suddenly charge from a bush near the road and bite the bike tires. It came as a surprise at first but we came to expect an assault every time we rode by.

Robert McManus lived in house #94 across the big circle for me (between the Youngs and Heffernans) for a short time, until 1948 or 1949. I earned some pocket money, fifty cents an hour, as a baby sitter for their children. They had a beautiful blonde female Collie dog that had puppies and they gave me one of her male pups whom I named "Laddie". He was the color of the Lassie of dog movie fame but had shorter hair. We were pals for about three years until he disappeared without a goodbye. Dogs were not fenced or leashed and ran loose in those days, though they usually stayed at or near their owners homes. My mother opined that he was "dog napped" for he was a handsome dog with a friendly disposition. It was to be psychologically my first death in the family.

My best friend and human confidant was Bill Lindsey who lived two doors up the street from me. He was a year older, but in the same class, because I had been allowed to begin Kindergarten at the TVA school at five. His grandfather was a physician, who practiced in Florence and his father had graduated from the U.S. Naval Academy before the War and was employed by TVA as Personnel Director. Bill was an only child and was allowed more latitude in his conduct than me. His parents bought him the comic books of the day. Superman, Captain Marvel, Bat Man, Spider Man, Flash Gordon, Big-Little Books, were all cutting edge culture of child and adolescent fantasy in the 1940's. A comic book cost ten cents, well beyond my means, and Bill had dozens of them. Bill Lindsey was the most generous and loyal friend I ever had. He shared everything with me and he had more toys and "things" than I did. He got a 25 cent, later 50 cent allowance a week, which put his purchasing ability well ahead of most of the rest of us, yet he always shared his good fortune. He had a beagle dog named "Butch" who palled around with the bunch of boys and their dogs.

The big circle provided a public green space that was used by everyone for a wide variety of group or individual activities without having to schedule or get approval from any authority. It was mowed regularly by TVA maintenance men, in the early 40's by mule power pulling a reciprocating blade that was about 8 to 10 feet long that could be raised by the driver when obstacles intruded. By War's end, Worthington riding tractors, painted black and white, pulled a trio of spinning mowers that did the job expeditiously. Adults might drive a bucket of balls from the edge across from their house, or ride a black horse around it.

Donald Heaton built a large Newtonian telescope and planted a steady pipe base in the big circle across from his house to support it and invited all to view what we had never seen before. The rings of Saturn, the "Canals" of Mars, a pocked marked Moon and the beauty of Orion's nebulae. What a gift to the child who knew nothing of other worlds and could later correlate this experience with his school books. In addition the Alabama skies were wide and clear of pollution and the constellations were almost touchable, lying on our backs in the grass of the big circle looking at infinity and wondering.

Friends and Neighbors

A cascade of names of villagers comes to mind, some fragmented, some barely remembered.

There was an excellent collection of compound or double names as; Mary Sue (Dugger), Donna Ann (Dugger), Patty Lee (Stout), Mary Jane (Hall), Paula Jean (Kelly), Febby Ann (Williams), Betty Lou (Scott), Mary Joyce (Barron), and best of all Gloria Dawn (Scates) said to be characteristic of Southern feminine culture. There were an equal number of single named girls as Audrey and Nancy Young, Martha Haynie, Ann Harvey, Dorothy Heffernan, Ethel and Ruth

Barksdale, Alice, Alberta, and Janet Brown, Evelyn Frear, Peggy Wade, Leslie Copson. Susanna Virtue, Susan Tschantre, Betty Reeves, Patsy Walthall. Of course these girls had middle names but did not use them informally. Boys usually used single names or name variants Bob or Bobby for Robert, Dick for Richard etc. Jim, Joe, John, James, Bill, Billy, Buddy, Lewis, Edward, Charles, Graham, Gordon, Roy. I recall in third or fourth grade I was teased that I had two last names and no first name. At the time I felt deprived for not having a simple and common first name and fancied the name Jim as giving me better acceptance in my peer group. After seeing the movie "Stanley and Livingston" I forgot this anxiety about my name. Of course we all had middle names which were used only by our parents and when it was used you knew you were in trouble. Think of what fun we would have made of the actor we knew as Cary Grant, who was born Aloysius Leach!

The big circle was a magnet for kite flying, bows and arrows, snow forts, touch football, star gazing and flying model airplanes. In those days most of our model planes were constructed of balsa wood, tissue paper, airplane glue and powered by rubber bands and a wooden propeller. Paper or paper and stick gliders were also popular. Don Crosby was an expert model builder and possessor of a gas powered model airplane motor. Those were the days of spark plugs, before glow plugs, and needed a lot of expertise to start, fly and retrieve a free flying gas powered model plane. The high pitch buzz of his engine was sure to attract a crowd and he always put on a good show if the engine would start. The propeller could sure bite your finger if it kicked back while cranking a cold start. And the big circle was clear of overhead obstructions. Of course he had more help than he needed but was always gracious to his gallery. He was an icon to us boys and helped us solve flying and control problems in our own models It was no surprise that he later learned to fly real airplanes and make a career of it.

One year several of us boys received bows and arrows for Christmas and suddenly the big circle sprouted hay backed targets or a discarded cardboard box. These were long bows made from lemon wood and had to be strung for use and unstrung for storage so as to preserve the flexible power in the wood. We learned to use beeswax on our bow strings and a leather wrist protector to prevent string abrasions. We learned how to notch and fledge an arrow. Our arrows were plastic tipped and remarkably durable considering all the targets we shot them into. The dumbest thing we did was try to shoot an arrow as straight up as we could and see how close it would fall to the shooter. They in fact came dangerously close and we soon disabused ourselves of that practice before anyone got seriously hurt. It was, to a degree, a passing fad however valuable skills and lessons were learned and in time translated into obtaining an archery merit badge from the Boy Scouts.

Sky gazing was a common pastime that one could do anytime day or night and the big circle was the finest of venues, just lie down in the grass and look up. In the daytime there was usually a variety of slow moving cumulus or cirrus clouds that gradually changed shapes so as to stimulate our imaginations. We saw ships with sails, peoples faces, animals, flowers, landscapes, all floating in the air and morphing into yet other earthly objects. It could be mesmerizing, though we had never heard such a word. It was freeing and expanding our imaginations, soothing to our psyche (another word that came later) and could be engaged for hours, but it took another person or more to share it with to make it work. I remember Martha Haynie and Bill Lindsey as excellent imaginers. One could do the same at night, substituting stars for clouds and trying to get a handle on the concept of infinity and the vastness of the Universe. Believe it or not there was at least one or two nights when the Northern Lights were visible in Alabama, though not as well defined, as those seen since at higher latitudes, they expanded our knowledge and imaginations.

Recalling rare events brings to mind those occasional winters that dumped several inches of snow, causing school closings and wintertime play. Even in Alabama, most families had a sled, homemade or store-bought, stashed away in the garage or attic for such occasions. I do recall several winters when there was enough snow to build snow forts high enough to give protection from snow balls hurled by the opposing side. Another unusual activity was the participation of adults using their cars to tow a large sled or a string of sleds behind their car to give us an additional winter thrill and it compensated, somewhat, for the lack of any nearby steep hills

Games

Games were almost always unscheduled and spontaneous. In the evenings 'Hide and Seek' and 'Kick the Can' were group games that always included girls and boys playing together. These games were played in summer evenings around someone's house, yard and garage. The geographical limits had to be defined in advance so whoever was "It" at least had a chance to tag someone. In these games size and age did not matter, only stealth and speed and the girls were very good at both. Table games such as ping-pong, Monopoly, Rook, Hearts, Slap Jack, Old Maids, Fish, Parcheesi, checkers and Canasta usually included girls (or was it other-way–round)? I recall the end of WWII in August 1945 while playing Monopoly at Bill Lindsey's house with Martha Haynie and Patsy Walthall, when the radio announced the dropping of the atomic bomb on Hiroshima.

There was one experience that could have ended fatally. As previously mentioned, first generation electric refrigerators were one of the marvelous, modern marvels that most residents had transitioned to in the early 1940's, often leaving a bulky true ice box unused in a garage. While playing 'hide and seek' with some of my neighbors, I squeezed into one of these ice boxes and closed the door on purpose or accidentally, I don't know. Nevertheless I quickly realized I had absolutely no way of opening that door from the inside and it was made air-tight. I started screaming and kicking in the little space available and panicked, realizing that if I was not rescued soon I would die for lack of air. Good fortune came in the persons of Bill Lindsey, Leslie Copson or Evelyn Frear. I don't think my parents ever found out about this episode of stupidity. I later read that these types of unused ice boxes were indeed lethal hazards to children in the United States, who did the same thing I was rescued from.

World War II

Now, I recall December 7, 1941 while playing in some pine woods next to my house on Sunday afternoon; Bill Lindsey came over to tell me his father had just heard on the radio that the Japanese had bombed Pearl Harbor, Hawaii. I was eight years old and had never heard of it.

Geography lessons came rapidly afterward and we learned much about the wider world after that day. From that day onward we became obsessed about airplanes (mostly), guns and warships. Lead soldiers and toy reproductions of war machines were collected and used to re-enact battles that we heard about on the radio. Propaganda encouraged us to hate the "Japs" and Germans and we did with enthusiasm. The war expanded our vocabulary and imaginations rapidly.

The War caused some families to move away and many of the young men to join. From the Village, I recall Gordon Heaton, who had graduated from West Point, was a successful Squadron Commander of B-17's in England. Bill Aldred joined the Marines and was wounded on Iwo Jima. Oscar Crosby joined the Army and served in Normandy. Charles and Bill Young, Fred Wedemeyer Jr., Raymond

Adams, John and Barney Heffernan were among the young men who were or came of age early in the war and did not come home until it was over. Bill Lindsey's father was recalled into the Navy, causing my best friend to disappear for a year or so. Bill returned to the Village for the remainder of the war in 1943. His father was beach master of Red Beach for the invasion of either Guam or Saipan and returned to his former job with TVA after the war.

The war came close to the Tri-Cities area due to its proximity to Courtland Air Base near Leighton. Crews were flying in B-24 Liberator bombers for their last stage of training before going overseas. Local families were asked to invite two, three or four crew members to Sunday dinner. Our family had several flyers on at least two occasions and I remember one fellow from Brooklyn, N.Y. who entertained us with his accordion. It was my first good look at that instrument and it intrigued me until I learned the price. Liberators were in the air night and day and occasionally crashed, but not near the Village. After the war was over, I salvaged an aluminum seat from a local junk yard which had picked up the broken planes. It helped me create some flights of my imagination.

Well after the war was over, about 1950 or '51 four pairs of giant B-36 bombers rendezvoused over Sheffield flying at about 1000 to 1500 feet. Each pair had come from the four points of the compass and crossed over the city. Each bomber had six engines at that time, so 48 turbo-engines turning at that altitude was a ROAR that can never be forgotten. Imagine seeing eight of the world's biggest bombers in one visual field coming together at slightly different, low altitudes at once.

A Coast Guard station was constructed near the mouth of Spring Creek, only a short distance from the TVA School building (former Officers quarters). It was officially there to mark safe channels in the rising level of Pickwick Lake, then under construction, with colored buoys. It was staffed by ten to twelve young men in Sailor uniforms, who lived on that small base for the duration of the War. They operated an all-steel trawler-type boat, about fifty feet long, rigged to hoist buoys and their concrete anchors. They were armed with small arms and the base was fenced with chain-link fence topped with barbed wire. It was supposed to be inaccessible to civilians but a bunch of boys on bicycles were occasionally allowed on the premises. Probably to relieve the boredom and monotony of such backwater duty as well as yield to the eager faces of boys who were attracted to anything military. Once they gave us a demonstration of a new type of .45 caliber machine gun. I still have some of the zinc casings.

There was a wide and deep erosion ditch running from the Stanford home #84 toward the Coast Guard station. Some of the older boys (Jimmy and Billy Worthington as I recall) rigged a steel cable through a two-wheeled traveler, with a knotted manila rope attached, across the chasm. The ditch was at least 20 feet deep and about 30 feet across. The fun and danger was being able to hold on to the rope without falling into the ditch. To a 10-year old it could be threatening but exciting and not something you told your mother about. Today it would be called a Zip-line, sold commercially.

Civil Defense regulations were highly regarded and practiced in the Village. We equipped our houses with blackout curtains and adhered to turning out all lights and adults allegedly stopped smoking their cigarettes during drills, which were usually done in the evenings. These were initiated by the sound of a siren and ended by two blasts. Civilian Defense arm bands and white colored metal helmets were provided to a select few, who were probably younger and most physically active, to be the observers, leaders and enforcers of the program. These were moments of heightened alertness and anxiety and lots of chatter about the enemy and what might happen if we were bombed. Select boys were chosen to be messengers on bicycles during an alert. Bill Lindsey and Bobby Reeves were among the chosen. I was not and was envious, for I thought I could ride as well as them and it was an early status symbol in the pecking order of young male culture.

Victory Gardens were created in many grassy open spaces or lots near a house. My father, who was raised on a farm, would have had a garden whether we were at war or not. It was at least a quarter of an acre in size, plowed and harrowed by mule power in the spring. He always sowed Bibb lattice, radishes, green peas, beans, yellow squash, cucumber, potatoes and several plantings of Golden Bantam corn: sometimes cabbage, watermelon and cantaloupe. Tomato plants were purchased in Tuscumbia at Mr. Hoskin's Seed Store near the Court House. I always wanted to go so I could see the live monkey Mr. Hoskins kept at the entrance to his store (an early advertising device). It was my first experience seeing an exotic animal up close. We were warned he would bite if we got too close, but his behavior was most interesting to watch.

Gardening was hard work, especially reworking the soil after the spring plowing with a hoe or shovel creating furrowed rows and learning how and when to plant a variety of vegetables is a valuable lesson in survivability. How many people today would know that each eye of a potato, if cut out of the larger whole will grow to be another potato plant with many new potatoes? Squashing bean and potato bugs with your fingers is the most efficient and ecologically safe way to preserve the crop. Messy but effective, just let your fingers do the walking through the beans and potatoes.

My mother canned much fruit (peaches) and vegetables (corn, pickles, beans, and tomatoes). These were preserved in Mason or Ball glass jars with rubber seals after boiling, steaming or cooking and provided many excellent meals in the winter. Our next door neighbor, Mr. Scott, built the first dehydrating oven in the neighborhood and could shrink many vegetables and fruits and preserve them in waxed paper bags, a real space saving technique.

More Adventures

Sometime after the end of the war fireworks became more available and were not saved for just the Fourth of July. M-50 and M-80 cherry bombs were the explosive of choice. We demonstrated their power in many ways. Initially we would ignite them under a variety of tin cans from the kitchen and they would rise into the sky proportionately, relative to the powder charge underneath. The cans typically expanded toward roundness until they split apart. We obviously took the experiment to the limit of available containers and can now tell you that an M-80 could lift a metal garbage can several feet into the air. After running the gamut of containers someone discovered we could lift the manhole covers of the sewer system, that were strategically located around the Village, with an M-80 dropped through the finger holes. These covers probably weighed about 20 pounds. By pure serendipity someone observed that we produced different degrees of lift from manhole to manhole. Again someone, with advanced knowledge, reckoned there was sewer gas (methane) in these holes in the ground and in different quantities. This explained the different results. One final test was to simply drop a lighted match into the finger hole and observe what happened. If we had not violated that manhole for several days there would be a notable BANG and the cover would rise or rock a little proving the power of sewer gas alone. No one ever got hurt and these trials entertained us for a season.

Let's face it, explosives fascinate children. So to continue these confessions I shall tell you about an extension of our experiments. To the east of the Village, the Southern Railroad operated a Round House locomotive repair shop just across the road from TVA property, maybe a half mile from the little circle. Some adventurous soul had discovered, in the cab of every engine sitting on a siding, awaiting repairs, housed some explosive tools of the Engineer's trade. These were kept out of view of the casual observer, in a space under the hinged driver's seat. Lift the seat and behold! A treasure of signal flares and warning rail torpedoes. Once word was out about these devices, it was too enticing not to participate in theft of these marvelous incendiaries and some of us helped ourselves over several weeks, until the Railroad realized what was going on and sent a message to TVA officials that if the thievery did not stop, there would be serious charges brought against any who were caught. It was over in less than a season but it gave us a certain pleasure in experimenting with some adult, real-world explosives. If you fit a rail torpedo into an 18-inch piece of plumbing pipe and throw it into the air so that it landed on a hard surface (the street) the torpedo would explode with a very loud BANG that was a different decibel from the M-80's, very satisfying to a boy.

During our early teen years most boys had a BB gun and/or a .22 Cal. rifle. We were instructed in gun safety by parents and older boys. More so by Bobby Reeve's father, Wesley Reeves, who organized our group of boys and girls into membership in the American Rifle Association and arranged target practice at the local National Guard Armory. We could go any day into the woods and hunt squirrels, shoot tin cans or mistletoe or just "plink" one into Spring Creek. We were never to shoot toward the Village or do anything that would cause loss of this privilege.

There was a sewerage pipe that crossed Spring Creek, just upstream of the Coast Guard Station, which carried Village sewerage to the Tennessee River. It was at least a 12-inch diameter steel pipe, suspended by a cable support system and was at least 15 to 20 feet above water level. Walking "The Pipe" was another rite of passage for admission to the brotherhood. It required balance and a steady nerve, for there was no hand support available. One had to cross on foot power alone. Fortunately I had a sling on my .22 rifle which left my hands free to grab the pipe if I fell. It was a true balancing act with inherent danger. I do not remember anyone falling off or being injured from this activity, yet not every boy actually tried it. I was warned by parents not to walk "the pipe" but did many times for there were open fields of corn and pristine woods to be explored on the other side of Spring Creek. Later some cows appeared in the open spaces and we had to be very judicious in choosing targets.

Related to these activities was the interaction of younger boys learning from their older brothers or friends how to catch, dress and cook cat and bream fish from the Creek and skin and dress a squirrel for frying. Cooking and eating a freshly dressed squirrel on the fly was a giant step toward maturity. This kind of hands-on learning experience was given freely by young men and older boys who wanted to pass valuable lessons to the next generation, much as they had received it. Today such experiences would come only at great expense, if at all.

Animals and Varmints

During the earlier years of the 40's, perhaps earlier, it was common for families to raise chickens and rabbits behind their garages in a wired pen or cage. Fresh rabbit was sometimes served on Sundays instead of chicken. The practice eventually ceased after foxes found a way to breech any security, even elevating the pens off the ground. Our family never kept any chickens or rabbits but did purchase rabbits from neighbors who raised them. Live chickens were sold at the A&P in Sheffield (no frozen foods in those days) and one had to prepare the chicken meal from step 1, kill the chicken, step 2, remove the feathers, step 3, remove the innards, step 4 divide the carcass, step 5 cook and serve. This would be called a "Range Chicken" today since it was not raised on wire in a massive chicken farm, where chicken feet never touch the ground and are sold at a premium.

Wilder varmints were about. Copperhead snakes were relatively frequent surprises among shrubs and ivy around the house or under a downed tree or rotting log. Water moccasin as well, because the village was in the big bend of Spring Creek. A hoe was the safest tool used to kill a snake. Snakes were wherever frogs and lizards hung out. Green snakes were frequent in the shrubs and bushes around the houses and we learned to protect these because they ate pesky insects. Even girls were not afraid to pick up these gentle snakes. Black widow spiders were also frequently encountered as well as writing spiders stringing their webs from bush to bush. I don't recall anyone being bitten by any of these critters, but we were instructed what to do if someone was bitten. In those days you were supposed to take your knife, clean or dirty, and incise the puncture sites and suck out the poison with your mouth and spit out the residue, after creating a tourniquet with a rope or belt or a strip of clothing. Stories of the painful death after such a bite were enough to keep you mindful of the possibility.

Paper wasps and yellow jackets were ubiquitous in the eves of garages and some shrubs. It was common to look for a nest if you were going fishing in the creek with a line and pole. Sometimes if there was nothing else to do we would just go looking for hornet nests just for the challenge and thrill of running away without getting stung. We would use the longest pole or stick we could find and prod the nest until it fell. The nascent grubs were an enticing morsel for the plentiful bream in Spring Creek. I think most every boy who played "catch me if you can" with hornets and yellow jackets suffered a sting from time to time. Local treatment and first aid was to apply fresh mud or a paste of baking soda on the sting. That emergency application still works today.

My brother Kelly was in the most senior last class of the TVA school before they transitioned to the new Art Deco Sheffield High School. The TVA school had maintained beehives as part of live demonstrations to educate children as to where honey came from. When the school was shut down he inherited the hives, bees and all the paraphernalia that came with beekeeping. He made a protective straw hat with a copper wire screen to shield his face from stings. He became a master beekeeper and could harvest honey every year. That is when I learned the difference between drones and worker bees and that drones don't sting, and the importance of the queen bee. Eventually the queen flew off to swarm in the wilds and that ended my bee and honey education. Kelly earned his beekeeper merit badge and later in life kept bees and harvested honey in Ohio.

Brown wild rabbits were common in the grassy areas between the houses and forests and were sometimes hunted for a free meal. But the tularemia microorganism was carried by some wild rabbits and I was warned not to touch any of them. Ticks were and still are a constant threat, because they may carry Rocky Mountain spotted fever organisms and now Deer Tick Disease both debilitating and lethal. Tick inspections of arms, legs and especially hairy area were productive.

After the Frears moved from house #109 in the mid 40's it was occupied for a few years by the Christensens, a couple with a young son. They were members of the Audubon Society and showed us how they caught birds and banded them with a little leg bracelet with a number in it, so the birds could be traced if netted again or were found dead. They moved on after the Village was sold.

I recall several lazy summer afternoons when someone got interested in tracking down a tree frog. We were all very good tree climbers and on those days one or two of us would climb trees nearest the sound of the tree frogs and on more than one occasion we captured one of these tiny creatures in the high branches for all the assembled to examine, then we let it go. Bats were also found occasionally in the darkest parts of garages or abandoned spaces and most unexpectedly in trees or bushes The bats we captured were usually lethargic in the heat and daylight and usually allowed us close scrutiny and rarely tried to fly, but they would bite, if not handled gently.

Mosquitoes were everywhere in the evenings when we would play 'kick the can' or lie in the field looking at the sky and malaria occurred frequently enough to keep us alert to their dangers. My brother, Kelly, had recurrent bouts of chills, high fever and shaking. He was treated with quinine, bed rest and cold towels. TVA had a mosquito and malaria laboratory near Village Two and I recall having a tour of it, being impressed by microscopes, glass dishes, blood cells, and large photographs and posters of mosquitoes, enough to make a believer of the menace. TVA also had a vigorous mosquito program that included spraying Paris green (an arsenic compound) on all standing water and the entire Spring Creek, using motor boats and airplanes. It was a common experience to be awakened at sunrise on a summer morning by a Stinson bi-plane diving down below the tree line following the curve of Spring Creek and the increased whine of the radial engine when climbing out from his dangerously low flight path. This was the equivalent of crop-dusting today without the cleared fields and straight furrows to follow. This job was really dangerous. The creek surface would be covered with a green scum for days afterward. These measures were effective in arresting the spread of malaria in the Tri-Cities.

Traditions

Holidays were welcome changes from routine activities. Christmas was time to go into the woods surrounding the Village and cut down some kind of evergreen, usually a red cedar. Scotch pine or firs were not native to Alabama. A homemade tree stand was easily fashioned from wooden crate lumber (common shipping containers in those days), or 1 inch by 2 inch white pine scrap and a few nails. One string of electric colored lights and a few colored glass ornaments were basic decoration. Faux icicles made from tin or aluminum foil and popcorn on a string finished the decorations. Mistletoe was either shot from its symbiotic relationship with an oak tree with a trusty .22 cal. rifle or knocked down with a long pole, if low enough to ground level. It always amazed how yielding high growing mistletoe was to a .22 bullet. I guess because it was so brittle. Compared to the excess of things given at Christmas today, Santa usually brought only one surprise gift. That gift always brought joy and had lasting value and was cared for and treasured for years afterward.

I never learned when or how the tradition of collecting discarded Christmas trees began, not for recycling but for burning. Boys began to gather these trees from homes about a week or two after Christmas and drag them to the open field across the street from the old school building in the little circle. Toward the end of January, when it was cold, word was circulated via the boy's grapevine that tonight the trees would be burned. On that night many families and children gathered after dark had settled and someone would light the fire. 40 to 50 dead cedar and pine trees make a big fire and we would dance around like a bunch of crazy Indians, occasionally running to the edge of the fire to grab an unburned end of a burning limb and throw it into the air as a flaming arrow or torch. There was no ceremony, just spontaneous socialization in sharing a common tradition.

This event was usually back-lighted by what appeared to be a giant outdoor Christmas tree in the side yard of Charles Painter's home #124, whose house was on the south side of this field. Mr. Painter was a master electrician for TVA. Every December before Christmas he would climb the TWO trees and array many strings of colored lights in the branches so that when lighted it appeared to all as one great tree. It was the apparent tallest and largest outdoor Christmas tree in the Tri-Cities and many city residents would drive out to Village One to view it. For its day it was a marvel and still well-remembered by many locals to this day.

Halloween was another boy's night out. In those days "trick or treat" was taken literally and in retrospect some of us neighborhood boys used this Halloween night to punish or get revenge on families they did not like. The most popular ticks were to either jam a pin into a front door bell or a stick in the steering wheel of an unlocked car to activate the car horn. Either trick caused an adult to come out of the house and un-stick whatever was tooting or buzzing, annoying yes, destructive no. Also removing porch furniture or garbage cans to another place or house was popular at Halloween.

During our High School years we began to have more interaction with girls. Among those was the summer ritual of surreptitiously swimming at "the Bluffs", on the Village side of Spring Creek that were about 10 to 15 foot high limestone embankment on the Tennessee River, just east of the confluence of

Spring Creek into the River. These were visibly secluded from the Village and any houses, but open to the wide River. The water was deep enough to dive into safely from any height. The girls usually had bathing suits under their outer clothing, if not they might just jump in, clothes and all. At this time of the year boys wore short pants and maybe a T-shirt, but developing a tan was de rigueur for most, so most were without shirts of any kind. If the venture was planned ahead then bathing suits were used, most of the time. Jumping off was easy but diving into those waters was intimidating and I thought the girls were slightly more venturesome than boys in this matter. In retrospect it was a dangerous activity, for the River had swift currents, but there were no major injuries or fatalities. Yes, there was some "skinny dipping" which was a new dimension in maturation, but never any sexual aggression or displays. It still fascinates me how controlled and relaxed the girls were about these shared experiences. It is fair to say, not every boy and girl who swam at the bluffs swam "au natural". There was an honest innocence in this activity that seems lost today.

The River

The Tennessee River was wide and swift and after Pickwick Dam was completed during the 40's it became Pickwick Lake, a lake that rose and fell at human command. Before this impoundment was completed, government archeologists hastily excavated known Indian mounds on both banks of the river and Seven Mile Island (an island truly seven miles in length on the north side of the river, now lake). Many Indian artifacts were gathered and taken to museums. Due to the rise and fall of the water of the flood control Pickwick Lake, soil was more rapidly washed by the waters and hydrolytically excavated and exposed more of these mounds. Bill and Johnny Aldred owned a wooden canoe and explored many of these mounds. Bill Aldred was my brother Kelly's good friend and they would explore these mounds and find many arrowheads, pot shards and other flint tools. These "mounds" were really chipping villages of the Native Indians who preceded white settlement of the river. They were marked by the accumulation of millions of discarded muscle shells that were eaten while making flint tools and arrowheads for a variety of uses. Seeing these many concentrated shell areas makes the name, Muscle Shoals, a valid name of genuine historical meaning.

One wonderful day after the War and Bill Aldred had healed his wounds, he included me with my brother Kelly, in a day long trip around Seven Mile Island, in his newly purchased Storm boat and 50 H.P. outboard Evinrude engine. On a stretch of beach on Seven Mile Island I found 95% of an Indian pot that had been missed by the archeologists. It remains a treasure that generated a profound respect and interest for the North American Indian Culture that no longer exists.

In either 1939 or 1940 a severe tornado hit Tupelo, Mississippi about 50 miles to the West of Tuscumbia. Northwest Alabama received some of the peripheral damage in the form of hundreds of mature trees blown down in the Village area. One serendipitous effect was that it provided numerous pine logs in a compact area that could be exploited. Dr. Earl Brown, a research chemist with TVA, was Scoutmaster of Troop 82 composed of boys from Village One. He conceived of using the logs from these downed trees to build a cabin. With mostly Scout labor under his direction, a full sized Adirondack cabin was built in the wooded area behind, but out of sight of the Aldred #112 and Haynie #113 houses and with a view of Spring Creek. This became a gathering place for campfires and the telling of ghost stories on scheduled nights and continued to be a regular stop or meeting place for anyone roaming the wooded area. This provided a genuine idyllic woodland venue for Cub and Boy Scouts for several years until the un-preserved wood rotted away.

Ordering wondrous magic tricks and gadgets from the Johnson-Smith Company catalogue that specialized in novelties tweaked our imaginations and took our pocket change. Trick handshake buzzers, Whoopee-cushions, instructions on how to become a ventriloquist were only a few of the items in that catalogue. Every boy had a catalogue and never enough money to buy what one wanted the most.

Stamp collecting, especially during the War, was a popular activity and it really helped us learn about the larger world. Mr. Ed Woolrych #102 was an avid collector and gave us good advice about the value of stamps we might buy or trade. We spent a lot of our spare money on "blocks of four' newly issued stamps and/or ordering a packet of 100 stamps for about 25 cents from the Jamestown Stamp Company. Trading stamps cost nothing and increased our sensitivity to compare values through bargaining and barter.

Each family had their own rules about raising children and allowing privileges. Though not widely different it did lead to some inequalities among child groups. Most children were expected to perform regular household chores that were truly sexist in those days. Most boys were expected to mow their lawns with a push lawn mower (motorized lawnmowers were not available until about 1948 and were expensive) about once every week or ten days and were give a minimal allowance for their effort. This also allowed them to purchase whatever they could afford. Some families, like mine, believed that providing each child with ample food, shelter, clothing and medical care and basic toys or bicycle, was enough and whatever else you might want would have to await Christmas or a birthday. But you could use the family push lawn mower to earn some pocket money at your own discretion. Fortunately for me, there were kindly neighbors who either had no children or no male children at home who let me cut their lawns for about one to two dollars per lawn every two weeks, depending on size of the lawn. In time, over a summer I earned enough to buy a five shot clip bolt action Winchester .22 cal. rifle for $30.00. I still have this gun and it still shoots straight after 58 years.

Bill Lindsey and I worked Saturdays, for about a year, at the Liberty Super Market, the first in Sheffield, for 50 cents an hour, working 14 hours on Saturdays, doing carry-out, stocking and mopping the entire floor after closing time. To have about $7 in your pocket was real money, the most I had ever earned in one day.

Such was life in Village One in the 1940s. Death, always lurking in the background, took its toll, but fortunately rare in a population of young and middle aged adults. There were two deaths which would probably not have happened, if their illness had occurred ten years later. Mr. Roy Heaton, house #96 and Mr. Rhodes, house #104 died from a ruptured appendix. Prompt surgical intervention could have prevented both. Della Gwynn Rhodes, his wife, was my excellent fourth grade teacher and Mr. Heaton is the man who gave me my first ride in a sailboat. He built his sailboat, named "MY TOY', by hand and sailed it on Wilson Lake. This experience left a desire to own a sailboat and learn to sail, which I did 25 years later. And George Stanford, still in his teens, was killed while water skiing at night when he struck a submerged log.

The Village was for sale in 1949. Resident owners were given first option to buy and most decided to stay in this marvelous location. Nevertheless, many new families, not directly affiliated with TVA moved into the neighborhood. The streets were renamed and the houses renumbered. I had lived at 106 Village One for 14 years and then 105 Wheeler Avenue for the next four years.

In 1949 Mr. James Russell, house #84, was the Scoutmaster of Troop #82. He had two sons James Jr. and Roy who were in our troop as well. Mr. Russell conceived a plan to raise money to send members of our troop to the Boy Scout National Jamboree in Valley Forge, Pennsylvania in July 1950. The Village had been recently resurveyed to reestablish the legal property lines of the now privately owned homes and the metal corner markers were still fairly prominent and easy to locate without a transit. His idea was to offer to set these metal stakes permanently in cement for about $2.00 per stake. We scouts were to save tall 32 oz. tin cans (grapefruit juice was sold in that size in those days). We would dig a hole around the metal stake to a depth of about 18 inches not moving the stake, center the can round the stake, and fill it with cement. Viola! A permanent property marker. We made several hundred dollars that helped send Mr. Russell, me and about 10 other boys from our Troop to the Jamboree attended by 45,000 Boy Scouts and their leaders. We were visited by President Harry Truman and General Dwight Eisenhower who gave speeches to our assembly. I feel confident those metal markers remain secure and well-preserved.

Rounding the Circle

Recalling experiences and events of over fifty years ago is a common human trait. Recorded history began as oral history finally recorded as tales of giants and magical things and sagas of hardship and survival, heroes and villains. Recalling them with precision and pure accuracy is unlikely however there is pleasure and amazement in doing so. It is as if we are reviewing our own tree rings before our demise. Some years were broad, filled with light, learning and success and others narrow, dark and paltry. It is interesting that we tend to remember the good and happy times and forget or repress the bad and embarrassing events of our personal history. For me it proves the brain is designed to preserve the best of ourselves that will tie us to a future we shall never know.

Village One was just a place, a space in time inhabited by some fortunate people who made a good life for themselves and their children. It was well used and its users were well rewarded in many different ways, yet it could not have left a record without people interacting with each other. Without its story it could be just another Nasca line in the dirt. One memory may bring up another by association, released by peeling off the layers stored of unused neuronal circuitry or a folded protein that had not been called to duty in fifty years. How does our brain retain so much data? Or better, why does our brain retain so much data? As we age we tend to remember fifty or sixty-year old events in our lives better than events that occurred yesterday. It is a puzzlement, yet what a trove of memories that belongs to us individually, like DNA we are exclusive in our memories as well as our genes, one of a kind, never to return. In the long run it is the people who are the institutions, not the bricks and ivy: the people are the story not the locale.

Writing these recollections of Village One seems to evoke one memory on top of another and could conceivably go on for awhile, but now enough has been documented to establish that it was special in time and place. Nevertheless this coda may be a final layer of unfolded memory.

This is the time to recognize the influence of siblings in our lives. Some, like Bill Lindsey, were only children and did not have the opportunity for intra family dynamics. Sibling rivalry and favoritism happens in every family and can be constructive and destructive. Most of us emerge better adults and maybe better parents as a result. Being the youngest surely gave me advantages my older brother and sister did not have, yet they showed me the path to a better person than some primitive instincts would have allowed.

My brother Kelly Jr. or "Sonny" as he was called at home was a paragon of virtue and ability. He took me fishing and taught me how to set up a fishing line and bait a hook with earthworms or wasp larvae: how to remove a fish without getting barbed and to scale and dress a bream for frying. He made beautiful, colorful kites which he flew in the big circle. He made a variety of kite designs and demonstrated their efficiencies and deficiencies. Once he made a large box kite that carried a Kodak box camera that took a picture of the big circle from above. His most memorable was Chinese dragon kite that had a painted dragon face and a long multiple articulated tail of smaller kites making an impressive tail. He won some blue ribbons for his designs and craftsmanship. He climbed the ladder of Scouting to Eagle rank with palms that gave me incentive to follow in his footsteps. We learned survival skills that have proven invaluable in our life time and are sadly deficient in too many of today's youth.

My sister Isabel gave me some insight into the female mind and habits that could be construed as survival skills for later life. After my brother graduated from Sheffield High School in 1944 and entered the NROTC program to become a Navy flyer I became old enough to share in some inside household chores as well as begin learning and practicing some table manners. Isabel did her best to indoctrinate me in correct protocols of socialization, hygiene and manners. I am sure such tasks drive some people into Zoology, as wild animals would seem smarter and easier than little brothers. In as much as my mother did all the preparation and cooking of meals, my sister and I were charged with clean up. She taught me the proper order of dish washing: glassware first, china second, silverware, then cooking pans and skillet last. Never leave a knife or sharp object invisible in dishwater. Then wipe all flat surfaces with the dish rag. One of us would wash and the other dry. Then I was instructed in the proper way to set a table and the protocol of serving, sitting, or standing and use of the napkin. I am still trying to get it right, but it is not her fault for primitive instincts continue to intervene.

We were served by regular delivery of fresh milk and cream in glass bottles to our back door. The milk was not homogenized then and some winter mornings the milk froze and pushed the bottle cap up by expanding frozen milk and cream. We also subscribed to the Birmingham News paper every morning and the Tri-Cities Daily every evening. These services were provided by Donald Painter, son of Charles Painter, House # 124. Deliveries were made by bicycle and were faithfully delivered for many years. From time to time Don would let some of us boys deliver part of his route and pay us for our services. We learned how to fold a newspaper and tuck the final fold to make it more aerodynamic so that we could fling it from the street on our bikes to the porches or front steps or the subscribing houses. It was a learned skill that challenged the simultaneous riding and throwing abilities of many young teenage boys and had "cache" among the brotherhood. Of course if you missed your target and landed it in the bushes and failed to make it right, you were severely chastised if you had to confront the recipients when you made your collection rounds at the end of the week. For many of us, Donald Painter gave us our first taste of serving the public in a responsible way and it put a little change in our pockets as well.

Money was a scarce commodity among all of us boys and girls in the 40's. This being so led us into bartering, which in retrospect, came naturally without instruction from adults. Some like James Farneman made things (replicas of military guns and other weapons) from scrap wood which was desirable to boys. Some had toys, comic books or stamps they no longer wanted and were willing to trade for something someone else had who was willing to trade dissimilar items, not necessarily of equal value. Nevertheless that's the way many items were exchanged without parental approval or sometimes knowledge. Some of us were scavengers of things found without apparent or known owner. This was especially true after households left a pile of "things" to be collected as garbage when they moved away from the Village. Rummaging through these discards proved that one person's garbage is another's treasure. I was a good scavenger and still have a propensity to save obsolescent things because they have intrinsic value possibly useful if or when an appropriate occasion might arise.

Village One was surrounded by a forest of trees including pine, cedar and hard woods. Tree climbing was an inherent skill in all Village children, girls included. If branches were low enough to reach by jumping they were climbable. If the branches were not low enough to reach from the ground level and if the trunk was not too big we could shinny up to the lowest branch and then climb to the top in most cases. It was a quick way to an elevated view of the landscape. Most of us learned the best trees to climb and some were used frequently to hide, get a view or just climb for the fun of it. Somewhere during these escapades one of us found we could "ride" a smaller tree. It would have probably been a young hardwood rather than a pine. Nevertheless the way it worked was to climb as high as we could so as to bend the crown of the tree over and downward without breaking the trunk. In some cases the tree could be ridden like a bouncing hobby horse or a see-saw with one rider. Some trees were broken and ruined. Sometimes the tree would break unexpectedly and could dump you hard to the ground, causing a few bruises and scratches.

During the War we were encouraged to collect scrap metal and Bill Lindsey and I scoured the Village and environs for anything we could carry. Over time we collected nearly a truck load of discarded metal which made us feel we had made a contribution to the War effort. We had "meatless Tuesdays" when no one was supposed to eat any meat, meaning beef, pork or lamb. I believe chickens and fish were exempted. It was the first time I learned about religious practices related to foods, approved and prohibited. All families were allotted ration coupons for sugar, meat, gasoline and tires. Long after the War I learned there was no serious shortage of gasoline in the U.S. but by limiting gasoline, the degradation of tires was indirectly slowed, thereby saving rubber which was in short supply.

Ambiance

Recalling those lazy, hazy days and nights in Village One is to see a sylvan landscape where Nature dominates with fresh air and natural light. It is to smell cut and growing grasses, hear the sounds of crows and Bob Whites (quail) in back yards in the early morning: tree frogs and locust buzzing in the afternoon heat: bull frogs, whippoorwills and hoot owls, with their distinctive songs, at night. These simple symphonies occasionally punctuated by a steam train's toot or a box car coupling or uncoupling. The clear night sky filled with a parade of mythical starry arrangements to suggest eternity and infinity. Wonderment enough to last a lifetime and more.

Finally I would like to make a connection, of a sort, with today's obsession with celebrity and the concept of 'six degrees of separation', that theoretically connects all of us through common, possibly unrecognized, associations.

As best I can remember, Mrs. Fred Gray house # 92, who lived on the "big circle" hosted her nephew from Birmingham for about two weeks during two summers during the War years (1943-44). He brought a bicycle with him that had a speedometer on it, the first I had ever seen, and he let me ride it. I remember going up to about 25 MPH (probably downhill). His name was Wayne Rogers, later to star with Alan Alda in the television series M*A*S*H* as "Trapper John" during the 1970's, later to become a financial analyst and advisor to the Hollywood Stars. Wayne's father was a Federal Judge in the Birmingham District., brother of Mrs. Gray.

To summarize my growing up in Village One is to recall halcyon days when almost all play was outdoors, free, unstructured, unsupervised, spontaneous, adventurous, and FUN, shared with best friends, neighbors and dogs. Summers were lived barefoot, in short pants, and developing a deep dark tan. My only regret is that I can only relive them on paper and alone. This was a time in Alabama that was my Camelot.

The above narrative is equivalent to a transcript of a verbal history, nothing more.

Manuscript completed March 23, 2006

McWilliams Pure Milk Company[1]

by Robert Lee McWilliams

I was born and reared on the dairy farm experiencing all work involved in running the family business. As I grew older, I helped my father supervise and manage the milk company. Because of my long experience in the milk business, for much of my life, I worked in the distribution of milk from house to house and store to store in the Quad Cities area.

The McWilliams milk business began before World War I. My grandparents, James McWilliams (born September 22, 1866) and Mary Lou Willingham McWilliams (born March 8, 1871) and their children--Andy, William, Floyd, Alvie, Elizabeth, Julia Bell and Lillian--lived at the Fairview Farm located north of Second Street in Muscle Shoals, Alabama. This area was called South Florence. They farmed, sold vegetables, milk, butter and cream. Milk was carried in buckets to the customers in a horse drawn wagon. Customers met the wagon with their containers where the milk was poured from buckets.

My father, Andy L. McWilliams, oldest of the seven children, and his brother William C. (Uncle Bill) helped manage the farm and worked at Martin Stove Foundry in Sheffield. They rode their motorcycles to work every day. Colbert County's first tractor was sold to my dad and Uncle Bill in 1912 by T.T. Rowland & Son, an International Harvester dealer in Tuscumbia.

In 1917, upon entry of the United States into World War I it became necessary for the government to build plants for the production of nitrate for use as military explosives. President Woodrow Wilson selected Muscle Shoals as the site of a huge nitrate plant and a dam to supply the electric power needed for its operation. The Fairview farm was part of the property sold to the War Department and the McWilliams family moved.

My dad and Uncle Bill, as partners, bought the Christian family house and land in Tuscumbia from their great uncle, John Alexander McWilliams. The family moved to Tuscumbia. This property is presently known as the Tennessee Valley Country Club and Golf Course.

---

[1] This is a revision of a paper presented before the Colbert County Historical Landmarks Foundation, Tuscumbia, AL, Nov. 16, 2003

In 1917 Andy and Bill enlisted in the U S. Army. They were discharged and returned home March 1919. Their farming operation consisted of a team of horses, some farm equipment and a few cows. My dad managed the farm and Uncle Bill worked at Martin Stove Foundry to help finance their farm program. The family continued to sell milk from buckets and cans.

My dad and Uncle Bill married sisters Ellen and Ida Foster in a double wedding ceremony on October 8, 1919, at the Foster family home in the Red Rock community, which is located thirteen miles west of Tuscumbia. Ellen and Ida attended Florence Normal and had been teaching school for several years before they married the brothers. The two couples settled in their home in Tuscumbia, but three years later, in 1922, Andy and Bill sold the property to a doctor in Tuscumbia who had commented that it would make a great golf course.

John Hubert McWilliams and Jimmy Ruthland drove their milk truck in the TVA Jubilee Parade, July 4, 1935.   Courtesy of Robert Lee McWilliams

The two brothers again bought property together in January 1923. This time is was the Foster home place from Ellen and Ida's parents, George W. and

Martha Ellen Foster where the girls had grown up. They bought more cows and a truck and sold dairy products in Tuscumbia. They sold milk also to Mrs. Charles Polk who operated the bottling plant in Sheffield. There was no electricity in Red Rock. A Delco system was installed on the farm so that electric milking machines could be used.

With growing families, it became necessary for the brothers to find separate home places. In 1923 Andy bought Uncle Bill's share of the Red Rock home place and Uncle Bill bought the Sherrill home place located west of Barton.

McWilliams Pure Milk Co. advertised its "Grade A Pasteurized Milk" in a 1947 railroad celebration booklet.
Courtesy of Helen Keller Public Library

Mrs. Charlie Polk owned a herd of milk cows that were pastured in the area where Sheffield High School is located today. The city passed an ordinance that no livestock could be kept within the city limits so Mrs. Polk sold her dairy business to my dad and Uncle Bill bought her cows. Our family then moved to 1300 Annapolis Avenue in Sheffield and the dairy business became McWilliams Pure Milk Company. The business grew and deliveries were made in Sheffield and Tuscumbia.

Daddy and Mama raised and educated eight children: John Hubert, Robert Lee, Charles, George and William (twins), Walter, Mary Jo McWilliams Carter and Martha McWilliams Ladd. You may have already guessed, but they taught all of us how to work by their examples. Dad's wakeup call was 2:30 A.M. every morning and the workday started on the farm. Daddy died October 15, 1974 and was buried beside Mama in the Barton Cemetery in Barton Alabama.

My dad, his brother and wife Lillian Taylor McWilliams moved to the house in Red Rock and managed the farm. Dad had plans to move the processing plant to the farm in Red Rock but there was no telephone or electric service and improved roads were needed. The first telephone line was obtained in 1927 by my dad and his two brothers-in-law Joe Foster and Owen Foster. They leased the line that had been built along Memphis Pike (the Lee Highway) from the telephone company located in Sheffield. They had to build their own phone line from the highway. In the late 1920's Alabama Power Company extended a power line 1-1/2 miles from the one on Memphis Pike. Then electricity was made available to the farm. By 1933, Highway 72 west was paved so Dad moved his family and the dairy business from Sheffield to the farm in Red Rock.

All food establishments were required to have a food permit. The dairy was inspected and milk samples taken regularly by the Health Department. All employees were required to have a health card.

There are several stories I remember about my dad and the milk business. The first diet I remember was one Dr. Littlepage prescribed using skim milk and bananas for a few of his patients. Daddy supplied the skim milk for some of those patients. Another memory is that my daddy always gave the preacher in Tuscumbia and Sheffield a half pint of whipping cream every Sunday morning. Lewis Cottrell told this story many times. A woman, one of Daddy's customers had developed a little rash of some kind and the doctor prescribed a milk bathe. Daddy asked the husband if he wanted "pasteurized" and the husband said, "No, only to her waist!" Probably my favorite memory reflected Daddy's patriotic spirit. Having served in the army himself, he was very patriotic. During World War II when food, gasoline, tires, etc. were rationed, a call would be made to my dad that the troop train would be coming through Sheffield and milk was needed for the soldiers. Milk was delivered to the train at any hour-often in the middle of the night! We would ask Daddy how we would deliver milk to our regular customer the next day. He would answer, "Well, we'll ration our customers. If they usually get two quarts of milk, we'll leave them one quart. The soldiers come first."

When Pickwick Dam was being built during 1935 and 1936, dairy milk contracts were bid. Daddy received the contract. The milk was delivered in ten-gallon cans to the commissary. Roads at that time were paved with gravel all the way from Barton to Pickwick, Tennessee. He fulfilled that contract. At a later date, Daddy received the contract to deliver bottled milk to the commissary and to the Village houses (about 130). One of our drivers at the time moved into the house with us and could not understand why we went to bed at 7:30 to 8:00 each night. In less than a week, he understood. We were getting up at 2:30 every morning to start our day on the dairy farm!

Improvements made over a period of time included a new refrigeration plant, an enlarged boiler room, a new 200 gallon pasteurizer, new bottle washer, new bottling machine, modern dairy barn, two new silos, feeding barn, tool building, electric hay drying barn, new trucks, milking machines, and various modern farming equipment. In later years new health department regulations required a milk refrigeration tank. Milk was delivered twice a day, 365 days per year, until gasoline was rationed during World War II. In the early 1940's, the price of milk was 14 cents per quart.

Then tragedy struck our family! Mother died September 21, 1946, while on vacation in Hot Springs, Arkansas. She had always been an active partner in the business and she loved the farm.

When industry opened up after the war, all of our good help got jobs and moved to town. So, in 1955 we closed the McWilliams Pure Milk Company and retired. My dad married Nila James Willis from Russellville, Alabama in December, 1955. My wife, Alma and I bought 120 acres of the farm land where we live. My brothers, George and Walter rented the farm and continued to milk cows and sell the milk to a local dairy until 1972. Walter bought the remainder of the farm that same year. The family home had burned in October 1969.

Some lessons about cows were learned by all of us. One lesson was that cows had personalities just like people: bossy, nosy, timid, shy, pleasant, pleasing, gentle, and nervous and loners. Names of some of our cows were: Spot, Blaze, Star, Sunshine, Red, Brownie, High Pocket, Whitey, Blackie, Thunder, Lightning, and we had one milk cow named Hell.

Some of the employees I remember were Ralph Owen, F.W. Perkins, Sr, Ace Perkins, Bazzle Brooks, Mrs. Solomon and family, Ruby Davis, James Rutland, Wallace Rutland, Carl Posey and family, Ozzie Newsome and mother, Gabe Newsome, Crawford Barnes, Obbie Landers, Amos Page, aunt Winnie Page, Wilson Page and Cynthia Annie, Neal Page, Humphrey Thompson, Ambus Thompson, Freddie Thompson. Jim Lee and Ethel, Roy Mize and Mildred, Orbert Mize, Garnie Mize, Leroy Mize, Lloyd Blankenship, Uncle Floyd McWilliams., Floyd McWilliams, Jr., Mr. Raines and Zora Belle, Charles Darby and Katie, Forrest Goodloe and Wyomia, Raze Page, Tracy Page, Ruby Garner, Roy Garner, James (Doodley) Goodloe and Connie Mae, Jim Smith, Buster Goodloe, James Earl Lee, Rossie Lee, J.C. Kimbrough and Williams Harold Kimbrough.

Other Colbert County dairies that bottled milk were Tom McCollum (also made ice cream and ran a cafe); Jim Lewcy; A. D. Cornelius; McGuire (on Sixth

Street); Dall McGuire (on River Drive); Rosedale; John and Myles Carton (on Cook Lane); Glenview (I. M. Glenn, Hwy 20); Streit (Sheffield); U. S. Nitrate Plant; Crescent (Nashville Ave., Sheffield, ice cream); Polk (1300 Annapolis Ave., Sheffield); McGavock (at Pride); Al Blackburn (Tuscumbia).

Colbert County milk producers who sold their milk to McWilliams Pure Milk Company and Streit Milk Company were Joe King, Elbert Smith, Odes Ponders, Fred Rutland, Jimmy McWilliams, Jack McWilliams, Walter and George McWilliams, Bob McWilliams, Robert Huston, Crawford Barnes, Floyd McWilliams, David Streit, Owen Whitlock, Dr. Griffith, Bridge Rutland, Willie Olive, and Bob Clingan

Tuscumbia Ice Company and Sheffield Ice Company provided ice for the trucks because there were no refrigerated trucks at that time.

Some Sheffield Businesses that I Remember

The Southern Cotton Oil Mill was located in Sheffield, west of Martin Stove and Range Company, north of the railroad tracks, and north of Shop Pike. The mill processed cottonseeds by taking off the hull and cooking the seeds. After the cottonseeds were cooked, they were pressed to remove the oil. The products that the cottonseeds produced were cottonseed hulls, cottonseed cakes, cottonseed meal, and cottonseed oil (for making Wesson Oil). The mill products were shipped by rail in tank cars and box cars. In the fall, when the mill was running, it created an aroma like bacon cooking. It smelled so good to me when we were delivering milk house to house in Sheffield.

The Ball Field and Fairground were located on Old Jackson Highway behind Bank Independent off Second Street, Jackson Highway and 27th street.

Thompson Barbecue located at 5th Street and Montgomery Avenue in Sheffield had the best barbecue. It was cooked over hickory wood on an open pit. The customers were able to order outside meat, inside meat, or mixed. Their sandwich was served with a handful of potato chips and a Coca Cola.

The Sheffield Hotel was the show place of the Shoals. It was located at 5th Street and Alabama Avenue. It was the largest building in the area at the time. The hotel was four stories high and opened for business in February, 1893. The hotel had 163 guest rooms and the dining room occupied the entire north side of the second floor. The hotel had revolving doors to the lobby area and people came from everywhere to see and walk through them. It was the center of social and cultural life in Sheffield and a gathering place for all classes of people, industrialists, and loan sharks. Famous people who were entertained in the hotel included General "Fighting Joe" Wheeler, General "Black Jack Pershing, Thomas Edison, and Helen Keller. I remember the hotel served the very best roast beef sandwich you could buy anywhere in the world. It burned June 14, 1948. At that time the hotel was owned and operated by Robert Martin.

Martin Stove and Range foundry, owned by W. H. Martin, chose on occasion to make its payroll with silver dollars to see the effect and where the silver dollars would show up. Certainly those silver dollars found their way to grocery stores, barber shops gas stations, clothing stores and throughout the city of Sheffield.

J. F. Moore Grocery on Furnace Hill. Early in the morning when we were delivering milk in this section of Sheffield, the fishermen would be bringing in their fish from the Tennessee River on their backs. I remember on one special day a fisherman had a good string of fish. As he walked up the street, he yelled "Bugle mouth bass, bugle mouth bass, bugle mouth bass." There was only one thing wrong—the fish weren't "Bugle Mouth Bass" but really carp.

The Grab was a Southern Railway store located off Shop Pike between 11th and 12th Streets across the railroad tracks in Southwest Sheffield. The Grab sold all kinds of supplies, gloves, shoes, and clothing - things people needed. They sold all kinds of food items, too. Milk was sold in glass bottles with a deposit charge on the bottles but they still lost many bottles because people would carry milk with them in their lunches. Later The Grab moved to South Montgomery Avenue near the railroad where the Economy Carpet building was located.

Hot Tamales. I remember a black man who made hot tamales and put them in a copper bucket to keep them hot. He walked up and down the street shouting "Hot tamales, hot tamales – so good! Ten cents or three for a quarter."(I believe that was the price but I am not sure).

Sheffield Ice Company. John B. Lagomarsino's office was in the 100 block of North Montgomery Avenue. The ice plant itself was located down on the river off Alabama Street and Mr. Lagomarsino kept mules in a barn behind his office. In the early 1930's the ice company delivered ice with a team of big black mules that sported all the harnesses with a big red tassel on each mule's headdress.

The mules began the delivery route in the 100 block of Montgomery Avenue and continued up Montgomery Avenue. The ice customers all had number cards with 25#, 50#, 75# and 100#. On the day of ice delivery, the customer placed the appropriate card in the window to order his ice for the day. Everybody used ice. They had ice boxes to keep drinks, ice boxes to keep food, and ice water coolers.

Crescent Milk and Ice Cream was located in the 100 block on Nashville Avenue and was operated by W.W. Grizzard. The Company sold milk and ice cream. Many times when I would go on the milk route with my dad, we would go by their business because they made and sold Eskimo pies (vanilla ice cream bar covered with chocolate). I still remember how good they were.

Dad's Oatmeal Cookies. This cookie was sold everywhere in grocery stores. The cookies were packed in a big three-gallon jar. On another counter next to the cash register, you could find a pack of Tom's Peanuts to go with a bottle of Coca Cola.

Streit Milk Company[1]

by Charlie "Bud" Streit

Streit milk was delivered to schools in individual half pint bottles. Courtesy of J. Harold Parker

No one knows when people first used animal milk for food, but we have learned that as early as 4000 B.C. the people of Egypt and India raised dairy cattle. In our country, the milk business began in a very small way. Farm families used as much milk as they needed and traded or sold the rest to neighbors. This is how the Streit Milk Company began.

My grandfather, Christian Streit (1865-1957), emigrated from Bern, Switzerland, and eventually moved to Colbert County and settled near Leighton where he bought approximately 500 acres of land and began farming. In 1932, my father, Charlie Streit (1901-1988), began his milk business on this farm. After the cows were milked by hand, my parents would filter the raw milk into 10-gallon cans and then bottle it. At that time, the bottles were washed by hand using a bottle brush. They sold milk to neighbors and others in our area and their business grew. My father then mounted two electric motors with bottle brushes in an open vat with three compartments, which

---

[1]The paper was presented before the Colbert County Historical Landmarks Foundation, Tuscumbia, AL, Nov. 16, 2003.

washed, rinsed, and sanitized the bottles.

In the summer of 1934, the Streit Milk Company opened a plant in downtown Sheffield on Nashville Avenue to render a complete service with quality products.[2] In that building, we began to pasteurize the milk, which is a heating process that destroys bacteria as well as other organisms that may cause milk to spoil.

A year later, my father told <u>The Sheffield Standard</u> newspaper that "the Tennessee Valley Authority has done much to help our business and our customers in this district" by creating a larger market for Grade A pasteurized milk and milk products.[3] We were then selling milk to TVA for people working at Wheeler Dam with daily deliveries being made direct from our Sheffield plant. The newspaper reported also that Streit was "among the most modernly equipped milk plants in the district. Recently, it has installed quite a bit of the newest machinery."

From Nashville Avenue, we moved to a building on Raleigh Avenue, and our family lived on the second floor above the milk plant. I was about eight years old at that time. Then, in 1940, my father bought the lot on South Montgomery Avenue lying between Ashe Street and the American Legion home and erected the final Streit Milk Company building.

We were a processing plant and had both wholesale and home delivery. We contracted with local farmers for milk; later, when we needed more milk, we began hauling from dairy farms in Tennessee, mainly Giles County. When local farmers increased their herds of dairy cattle, we cut off the out of state supply. I remember a number of times when we ran short of milk, and mother would get me out of school to go with her to Tennessee to pick up milk. Daddy would take my sister to the local dairies to pick up the late milking. Then the four of us would go to the plant and bottle enough for the next day's sales.

In the thirties, forties, and fifties, the farm milk was poured up in 10-gallon cans and brought to our plant where it was transferred to storage tanks. I remember when we first began to homogenize milk. That is a process which forces pasteurized milk through a machine under pressure of about 2500 pounds per square inch at a temperature of 140 to 175 degrees. This breaks down the fat

---

[2] <u>The Sheffield Standard</u>, July 13, 1934.
[3] <u>The Sheffield Standard</u>, June 28, 1935.

molecules so the fat does not separate from the milk. We had a machine—a separator—to remove all, part, or none of the fat from the milk The milk also went through a clarifier that prevented sediment from forming in homogenized milk and removed white blood cells, debris, and some bacteria. We made buttermilk and also sold cream, coffee cream, and chocolate milk, and at one time, my father made butter which he churned by hand. Butter was made from 100% pure cream and a little salt. When the cream is churned, it separates into butter and buttermilk. We bought cottage cheese from Purity Dairy when it was independently owned. Before the days of sour cream being a popular item, I will never forget the day a lady came into our plant and asked to buy some sour cream. That was the first time that I had heard of such a thing. I went into the back, found a bottle of cream that had gone bad and sold it to her. It was really sour! I have often wondered if she used it.

Charlie Streit posed with his milk delivery truck in 1933.
Courtesy of Charlie "Bud" Streit

In the sixties, we bought an insulated tank truck to pick up milk on the farms and deliver it to our plant. This eliminated lifting the heavy cans. The milk was visually inspected by the milk truck driver for quality, volume, and temperature and a sample was taken to test the sanitary quality and fat content in our lab. If the milk did not meet our specifications; it was sold to a cheese plant.

The Health Department checked our plant every month. Besides checking on sanitary conditions, milk was checked to make certain no water had been added or any cream removed from it. Our plant was well-supervised to protect the public health.

From the beginning, Streit Milk Company had home delivery. We began by delivering seven days a week and later reduced delivery to three days a week. Customers would put out the number of empty bottles to indicate the number of filled bottles to be left. If the customers wanted buttermilk or cream, they would leave a note in the bottle. Customers were billed the first of each month with the milk delivery. When paper cartons came into use, customers set up a monthly schedule with the secretary in the office and the milkmen left the milk according to their route books. Our milkmen reported to work at 3:00 A.M. to begin home delivery. During very cold weather, they had to start later to keep the milk from freezing. After home delivery, they worked the grocery stores and restaurants.

In late 1949, we installed a wax-coated-paper packaging machine, which would bottle quart, pint, and half-pint cartons. The machine melted the wax, dipped the paper carton into the wax, cooled it, filled the container, and sealed it all in one operation. In later years, the wax carton was replaced with plastic coated cartons, both inside and out. In 1962, we installed a new Poly-Pak machine which packaged milk in half-gallon plastic cartons.[4] My mother would not use the cartons. She still preferred the sterilized glass bottles for her personal use and would pour her milk into her own glass bottles.

Colbert County was good to Streit Milk Company for 40 years. We had a very good business. Until the large chain companies came to our area, we furnished most of the schools, restaurants, and plants. We provided clocks to most of the Sheffield schoolrooms and grocery stores. We grew with the community. I remember each year a large number of school children toured the plant while I explained the process of bottling and pasteurizing milk after it leaves the farm.

During our last five years in business, we saw the change from local processing plants to the large national chains. Of the four local plants, we were the last one to sell out. We sold our company to Pet Milk Company in 1972. Today, there are no home deliveries and the large chain grocery stores have their own private label milk. Today, Purity is the only milk company competing against chain store milk, and it is no longer privately owned. I don't know of any local

---

[4] Tri-Cities Daily, section 2, page 2, Nov. 6, 1962.

dairy farms left in Colbert County and I know of only one in Lauderdale County. Meadow Gold pulled out of Alabama the last of October. The days of the small independent milk processing plants are gone, but it provided my family a good living.

Sheffield Once Had Thriving Coffee Manufacturing Plant[1]

by Richard C. Sheridan

Old Gold Coffee, "every drop as good as gold," was roasted and distributed by the Alabama Coffee Company during the 1930s and 1940s. This Sheffield firm was incorporated by Philip Olim and his wife in 1930 for the purpose of manufacturing and selling coffee in the wholesale and retail markets. Under the supervision of its manager, Lawson Haynes Blanton, Sr., the business thrived in the 1930s. He had formerly worked in the coffee industry at Huntsville, Alabama, and in the state of Louisiana.

The "Old Gold" brand of vacuum-packed, roaster-fresh coffee was packed in fancy gold-colored tin cans with red and blue lettering. Courtesy of Mike Jones

By 1935, the firm was producing six new brands of coffee in its modern plant. One million pounds of coffee were roasted, packed, and sold by the Alabama Coffee Company in 1938. Six hundred thousand one-pound packages went out from this plant that year. Some contained larger amounts of coffee. Each package was printed with the slogan "Roasted and Packed at Muscle Shoals, Sheffield, Alabama." The Old Gold Coffee was packed under high vacuum to retain its freshness and pleasing aroma.

The company continued to specialize in Old Gold and three other brands—Muscle Shoals, Alabama Yellow Hammer, and Drinkers Delight.

---

[1] Reprinted from the **Times Daily** (Florence, AL), August 24, 2008

Another brand, Miss Florence, showed a stylishly dressed young lady on the side of the can. In 1938, the firm was using three trucks to distribute its products in North Alabama, Southern Tennessee, and Eastern Mississippi.

In 1939, the company reorganized and the scope of its business was expanded to include teas, rice, cocoa, spices, extracts, prepared mustard, salad dressing, and vinegar. The company did process and sell teas and Blanton had little copper teapots made to give to his best customers. But it is unknown if the company actually engaged in the manufacturing and sale of all the above items.

During the reorganization, Blanton took over the company as its major stockholder, treasurer, and business manager. The other officers for the first year were R. L. Sterling, president, and A. O. Blanton, secretary. For several years, Mrs. Alice O. Blanton was employed as the bookkeeper for the firm. The Blanton children, Lawson, Jr. and Joyce, helped out when a big order arrived.

During World War II, when coffee was in short supply, Blanton developed and marketed a "coffee stretcher." One-half pound of the coffee stretcher could be added to one pound of coffee to make it go further. Blanton was also interested in opening a coffee shop on Montgomery Avenue, but never found the right opportunity.

For many years, the firm was located at 209 Frankfort Avenue, Sheffield. About 1951, the plant moved to 420 Austin Avenue. The company went out of business about 1953 as it was not listed in the 1954 City Directory. Blanton's health was declining and he died about 1955. He was buried in Huntsville, his former home.

Old timers who grew up in Sheffield still recall the fragrant odor of roasting coffee as it drifted over the west side of town. And the old coffee cans and jars are highly prized today by local collectors.

Alabama Coffee Company used this roaster to prepare its different brands of coffee.
Courtesy of Alice Blanton Haddock

Boyhood Days in Sheffield 1937-1943[1]

by Robert H. Meadows

Editor's Note: Robert H. Meadows spent the first ten years of his life on farms in Limestone County AL and Lawrence County, TN where his father was a sharecropper. In 1937, the Meadows family moved to Sheffield when the father began delivering syrup for his cousin W. L. Craft, owner of Dixie Syrup Company on West 20th Avenue.

A New Beginning, December 1937

I do not remember the specifics about the moving. What stands out in my mind about my first impression of city living is the bright electric lights and the stench of coal smoke being burned to heat the homes.

Each room of our house had only one light bulb hanging down in the middle of the room from the wire dropped from the ceiling—a 100 watt bulb compared to a coal oil lamp was almost blinding. It was December '37, the weather cold enough to have heat in the house. My dad had bought a new "cold morning" coal-burning heater. Just outside the back door a pile of 1 ton of lump coal as black as midnight. It was like broken rocks (hard and jagged). We would fill a coal scuttle (bucket) and set it beside the heater in the living room, then add a lump at a time when needed to keep the fire going in the heater. I feel sure this was the order in which the move took place. My dad owned a two-door, two-seated Model A Ford at that time. I figured he drove to Sheffield (only 45 miles), left the Model A, and came back in Craft Syrup Co.'s truck (a 1-1/2 ton Ford flat bed with a cattle stake bed). He probably got all of our stuff for the house and brought us on that load. Maybe same or next day he went back for a load of hay to store in the barn at the Syrup Co. to feed the two cows and mare, which he brought on the last load. I'm not sure of the order. I am sure we moved, brought two cows and a horse and lots of hay to feed to the animals. I do remember Mom and I had to stay by ourselves for a few days, as Dad's oldest brother in Athens was very sick. His brother died just before Christmas.

---

[1] This article is reprinted from Papa's Journal: A Pilgrimage of Priceless Memories by Bob Meadows (Copyright 2006) with permission of Kathy M. Green, 329 Robert Avenue, White House, TN 37188.

Dad made it home for Christmas. I had my heart set on an eight-string mandolin from Santa. But Mom had practically assured me that day that I would not get the mandolin because Dad had to be out of town and might not be home, etc. Dad did come home late Christmas Eve, and early Christmas morning there was my eight-string mandolin. I virtually knew for certain all about Santa then.

The house we moved into could not have been more convenient to Dad's work. It was exactly 1/2-block from the syrup plant. Only a lumberyard was between the plant and the house. The man (Bryce Garner) who owned the house lived in two rooms. He had his own front entrance. We lived in three rooms with our own front and rear entrance. Even though we had running water in the kitchen, we still had an outdoor toilet. But this one was a city toilet.

The syrup plant was the biggest building I had ever seen in my life. While it was not new, it was in perfect repair. It was three stories tall with a full basement, beautiful red brick trimmed in white, and lots of big windows on every floor.

The lot around the plant must have been an acre and was completely closed in by an eight-foot high solid wood fence. To the back of the lot was a very nice barn with three stalls, two cribs, and a loft. This is where we kept the animals. The barn, the fence, and the interior of the plant were painted the same color—a sort of golden yellow.

The plant and our house were much nearer to downtown Sheffield than my school was from where we lived in Tennessee. There has never been a kid more excited that I was. Our next door neighbor was Buford Garner, the brother of Boyce. He had what seemed to me a passle of kids—Buford, Jr. my age, Julia just under, Rosalie, then Betty. Buford and I became good friends and playmates very quickly.

The main reason Dad moved the two cows was there was a good place they could be kept. Also Mom was attached to her cows since she had milked them for several years. Most important they would produce milk and butter for our table. It didn't take long to realize the two cows produced much more than we could use, so Mom began to sell raw milk to neighbors—that called for a refrigerator to store the milk. So, Mom bought a fridge and paid for it with milk money. That milk money also allowed me to buy my lunch in the school cafeteria instead of peanut butter/jelly sandwiches. I could buy a big bowl of homemade soup for 5¢. Milk was free, and 10¢ would buy a hot lunch.

School

Right after New Years 1938, I started to school at the Alabama Avenue Grammar School—no more than a mile from home. The school ran from first through sixth grades. I have never seen so many squeally kids in my life. There were hundreds of them it seemed. I was half way through the fifth grade at that point. I continued there through the sixth grade. It didn't take long for me to adjust to my new world. Soon I was acquainted with a lot of kids that lived all over the city. The Garners were quite religious. Mrs. Garner taught a Sunday School class at the little Baptist church in the same block we lived in. I would attend Sunday School with them frequently even though Mom and Dad did not go. Rosalie, younger than me, could recite every book in the New Testament. I thought that was really neat.

Syrup Plant

When we lived in the country, on occasion, Dad would strum the guitar, and he, Mom, and I would sing old folk ballads as well as religious songs. We were pretty good because neighbors would invite us to their house to play and sing for them. The first summer in Sheffield as soon as school was out, Mom wanted me to attend the Vaughn's singing school in Lawrenceburg. They made arrangements with the Oscar Bassaham family for me to stay with them and attend the school. I probably had the talent and certainly the interest in song and music to pursue it, but Dad did not seem to care and Mom didn't have the means financially—so it just fizzled out. I never really learned to read music, let alone play an instrument.

The syrup plant building and operation was such an interesting experience for me. Mr. Craft had been producing "Pride of Dixie" honey flavor syrup for years in a limited facility in Florence. Moving to Sheffield, he not only modernized, but had room for expansion. So he added two or three more new labels—by the brand "Crafts". These new syrups called for a corn syrup base. A huge 20,000-gallon tank was installed in the basement of the plant. The reason it was so big was to hold and store a railroad tank carload of corn syrup. The railroad had a spur line right beside the plant, and when a car came in they would park it on the track outside the building, run steam through the tanker to thin the syrup, then it would drain right into the 20,000-gallon tank.

They needed lots of steam to cook and operate the plant, so a boiler room was added to the back end of the building. The big boiler was sorta scary to me. A hot fire going in the boiler to raise a lot of steam pressure. If the pressure got too much, a pop off valve would open, shooting steam high into the air making a terrible noise. I had a fear it would blow up, so I'd usually run to some safe area.

Watching the motors working on the various tanks throughout the building was mind boggling for a country kid. Then the automatic filling machine was really something. The syrup was never allowed to cool down once it was cooked until it was put into buckets—either 1/2-gallon or 1-gallon tin buckets. The filling machine was set to whatever size container to be filled. When the container reached exactly the right amount, the weight would trigger a cut off and shut the hot syrup off. The operator, wearing gloves, slid the bucket under a capping machine where the lid was sealed on. The bucket traveled down a conveyer where a person glued a label to the bucket. Traveling down the line another person placed the bucket into a cardboard case or box. When the box was full, he sealed the box and slid it down a chute to the basement where it was stored. When Dad made a delivery he would drive the truck into the basement and load the orders.

My Dad worked for the syrup company about two years when he quit in 1939 to take a better job with the local Coast Guard. The Coast Guard patrolled the Tennessee River and maintained buoys and light houses from Cairo, Ill., to Guntersville, Ala., and to Chattanooga, TN. However, during the two years at the syrup plant, he traveled a lot and was gone from home a lot. He made frequent trips to Wewahitchka, Florida (we called it Wewau) to pick up a load of strained honey in 55-gallon wooden barrels, used in the syrup. Wewau is just north of Port St. Joe in western Florida. Today, it would take about six to seven hours to drive there. Back then with narrow and crooked roads it took Dad a full day and night—about 24 hours, and he never stopped except for gas and to eat.

On one trip, Mom and I went with him—never again. I'd just as soon be locked in a doghouse as three people in that truck cab, and it rode like a truck. To make bad matters worse, when we crossed into Florida, suddenly the water smelled and tasted like pure sulfur. I got sick as a dog, was starving for a drink and would throw up at the smell of the water. It was awful. However, the bee farms there were educational, seeing how they robbed the hives and strained the honey and put it into the barrels. Dad would load 16 barrels of honey each weighing 800 lbs. on to the stake bed of that 1-1/2 ton truck. The overload springs would be bent in the opposite direction over the axle housing, under almost six tons of weight. That was simply crazy. There was no way to get from there to Sheffield but to come over Red Mountain south of Birmingham. The roads were two lanes, narrow, and crooked. When he topped the mountain at the statue of the Vulcan (Iron Man), it was usually in the wee hours of the night and the traffic was light. He would put the transmission in what we called super low (1st gear). As he went off the mountain, he would have one hand on the steering wheel, the other holding onto the emergency brake lever, his door open and his left foot on the running board ready to jump in case the brakes failed or a drive shaft broke. His right foot would be pumping the brake pedal. Needless to say he had his hands and feet full to get the load off the mountain. The engine would be screaming as if it would fly apart under the force of that six-ton load. There was a traffic light at Five Points, almost down the mountain and coming into Birmingham. If the light per chance was red, too bad. No way could he stop that truck. Like I said, crazy, and I never wanted to go back to Florida.

Furnace Hill

The area of town we lived in was called "Furnace Hill". Back in World War I, there were huge iron furnaces in the area nearby and a nitrate plant. Though the furnaces were gone, there were huge mountains of slag above the river as a result of dumping molten rock and earth when the iron was removed. Also foundations of concrete still stood that once supported the factories—between where we lived and the river (Tennessee), which was no more than a mile, all this area was located. It truly was a kid's paradise to explore and play in. My friend Buford. and spent hours and hours and days exploring all the ruins, and of course the river.

Being a country boy, having already proven that I could pretty well take care of myself, Mom was not too strict about where I went. Buford and I went fishing just about every day during the summer vacation. I remember an experience that happened one day, probably in March because the weather was still cold. Buford. and I were down at the pipeline dock. That's where barges of gasoline would unload and pump gasoline to the Texaco storage tanks just up the street from where we lived. There were several flat bottom wooden fishing boats tied to the bank side by side. (In 1938 about all fishing boats were flat bottom, wood and homemade of yellow poplar boards 12 to 14 inches wide.) The water was literally covered in thick green algae floating on the surface. I was standing up on the seat of one of the boats. Buford was in about the 2nd or 3rd boat over when I decided to join him. Seemed to me that the simplest thing to do would be to step or jump from one boat to the other—wrong! When I went into the motion to step out of the boat I was in to the other beside it, the boat shot out from under my foot, leaving a gap of 2' between me and the next boat of nothing but moss and water. Kurplunk, I went into the cold water head and ears. When I came up and crawled out on the bank, green slimy algae coated my head and clothing, changing me into some lake monster-looking thing. I was freezing and took off running to the house as hard as I could go. When I arrived home my teeth were chattering and I looked a fright—soaking wet, coated in green algae, and freezing. My mom absolutely broke up. She knew I had fallen into the lake.

    I used to hang around the old Sheffield ice plant a lot. It was on the river, just down the hollow and railroad tracks from the syrup plant, probably no more than 1/2-mile. The Tenn. Valley Sand and Gravel Co. was also there. Boats and barges would dredge the channel and bring up sand and gravel and store it there in huge mountain piles. There was always a lot of activity going on there, and it was a good place to fish. There was a huge spring that gushed out of a rock cliff where the ice plant got its pure water to make the ice. The spring formed a clear eddy or slough. Quite large and aquatic weeds grew in it. You could see large bream and bass lazing in the clear water. They would never bite a hook because it was too clear, but when the river got up, it pushed muddy water back into the slough and improved fishing. One day I was fishing from the roadside, directly in the discharge of the spring, beside a large sycamore tree. The river was high and water muddy. In fact water was nearly up to the road that went to the ice plant. I was catching nice bream like crazy on grasshoppers. I ran out of hoppers, would run to the end of slough, catch a few more, then another bream as fast as I could pull them out. A man in a nice car saw me and stopped. He came up and started a conversation. Back then there was a size limit on almost all game fish. It was 4" on bream. I had a whopping string of very nice bream the man had already seen. Then I caught a smaller one, too small for the size limit. I was about to throw him back in when the man said, "Hey, I'm the game warden. Big fish for big boys, little fish for little boys. String him up if you want to." So I did.

    It didn't take long for me to learn all about the Saturday movies. The Ritz Theater was on the street going from our house to main drag, which was Montgomery Avenue. Until a kid was 12 years old, he could get in the movies for 10¢. In other words, we needed 25-35¢ to take in the movie, have a drink, a bag of popcorn, and maybe an ice cream at the drug store after the movie. After Mom had given me 10-15¢ every day for lunch at school, I knew better than to hit her up for too much on Saturday. Buford's folks weren't in any better financial condition than we were either, so Buford. and I through necessity became enterprising young men. There was a scrap iron yard just south of town. Today they are called recycling centers. The scrap yard would buy any amount of iron, copper, brass, and aluminum. Not far from our house there were a number of old junk cars, dumped in a field near the city dump. I can't imagine why anyone would abandon an old car when it could be sold for junk, but they were there none the less. Buford and I built ourselves a neat two-wheel cart using a couple of old coaster wheels and axle. Guess we could haul and pull 50 lbs. of scrap in our cart. Every afternoon we had free, we would comb the area for scrap iron. Where the old furnaces once were we would find a lot of iron in the slag piles. Also we'd take the copper wiring from the old junk cars, remove any aluminum trim and the speedometers and gauges. We'd collect our booty and store it in the shed behind our house, then Saturday morning we would load up and head for the scrap yard. Normally, we'd have 50-70¢ to divide and that would satisfy our needs for the day.

Saturday was always a Western Movie (we called Shootum up) of the hero of the day. Gene Autry, Hoot Gibson, Tex Ritter, Lone Ranger, then Roy Rogers were the cowboy heroes of the day. Also, a serial we called a continued movie. Tarzan was really big in 1938-39. Unlike today, then the stars would tour the country making appearances at theaters. I remember Gene Autry and his side kick Frog Millhouse (Smiley Burnette), also Tex Ritter, coming to the Ritz Theater. It would cost a quarter when someone made a personal appearance.

I never told the manager of the Ritz when I reached 12, so kept buying a ticket for 10¢. The manager took up tickets so he knew about all the kids. One day after I had reached twelve, he took my ticket and said to me, "Boy, how old are you?" "Eleven," I replied. "What year were you born in?" Knowing my answer had to be a year off from the real year—1926, I quickly responded, "1925." He took me by the shoulder, marched me out of the lobby and said, "You are 13 years old. Buy an adult ticket." I was so embarrassed and humiliated, plus it took my last 15¢ to get a 25¢ ticket. From that day forward I had to buy an adult ticket. That's about when I became Bob instead of Bobby.

Skating

There were a lot of kids on the block where we lived even though there was only seven houses. There was the Richardson Lumber Yard and syrup plant, two churches, a grocery store, and a vacant strip - all this in one city block. There was Myrtle and Mary Morris across the street, also Jimmy Moore across the street. His folks owned the grocery, and they lived up stairs over the store. The four Garner kids next door, Goober Koonch third door up, and two Tidwells (Mary and Jim), lots more out of our block.

One of the first things I learned to do was roller skate. All the streets in town that were paved were smooth as a table top. They really made good and lasting asphalt back in those days. All kids skated in the streets and sidewalks. Even little Betty and Rosalie could skate like a pro. I simply had to have a pair of skates, and so it came to pass. Every night under the streetlights we would skate until bedtime. We'd play hockey by using a tin can and a stick. It was much fun, and sometimes got a little rough but it made very good skaters out of us. We'd get a group together and skate all over town. There were several favorite hills we'd love to skate down. One was on North Montgomery Avenue, leading up to the standpipe (water tank). The hill from standpipe down to level area was three or four blocks.

We'd start at the pipe and roll all way down, quite fast I might say. Another spot was the hill near the Alabama Avenue School. It was only a block long but very steep. We would fly down it. Since there was no way we could stop should a car be coming, on the cross street at the bottom we always had another person as a lookout to tell us when it was clear to come down the hill. I skated for the next four or five years until I was in high school.

One night in late spring, the weather was warm and skating made you even warmer. We had a big hockey game going. Now the thing then to prove you were tough was to chew tobacco. Several of the boys from the slum area chewed. Nothing to do but for me to give it a try. I put a chunk of Days Work or Red Apple, not sure which, into my jaw. Pretty soon it juiced up, and I was spitting tobacco juice as big as the next one. Next thing I knew, while skating I swallowed some of the juice. Then I begin to feel woozy. I knew I'd better head for home. When I got in front of the lumberyard, almost home, I hit the grass and threw up everything I had eaten for the last week. I have never been so sick in my life. I lay there on the ground, head swimming, and stomach aching. I gagged until I was sore all over. Finally, I made it home. You can bet I never told Mom or to this day I never had another piece of chewing tobacco in my mouth.

The All Important Bicycle

A bicycle had become as important to a 12-year-old as a car is today to a 16-year-old. Buford had a bike, Jimmy had a bike, Goober had a bike. In other words, anybody who was anybody had a bike. I'm sure my folks decided they would not be out done. Dad was making a delivery to Lawrenceburg one day and took me with him. Likely it was on a Saturday or I would have been in school. (People worked on Saturday, six days a week then.) He parked the truck on the square, and we walked to a hardware store nearby. Standing there admiring the display of bikes parked on the sidewalk for display, Dad says to me, "Which one would you buy?" I pointed to a red one. Next thing I knew, Dad had purchased that 26" balloon tired bicycle. I was ecstatic. Nothing to do but ride it right then. around the courthouse square I wobbled about two or three times. I think the bike cost $16 or $18. I can tell you, I was one more happy kid. I don't know what the occasion was, if there was one. Maybe it was for my birthday, or it could have been a peace offering Dad was making for being bad. He had begun to drink and run around a lot.

Having a bike opened up a whole new world for me. I could go places and see things I'd not been able to do before. I could meet new people and go long distances to see and play with them. But the first order of accessories for my bike was a basket. A basket fastened to the handlebars, went out over the front fender, and was supported by two rods that attached to the front axle. It was for carrying books, groceries, supplies, and even small kids. My mom readily supplied me a basket. Oh, I had my share of skinned elbows, burns, and bruises as a result of wrecks. But the bike became a very important part of my life. The bike made the movie or downtown only five minutes away. I could now be at school in five or ten minutes.

When we went toward town, as we passed in front of the syrup plant, immediately we crossed a railroad overpass. The track in the gorge under the bridge went down the valley to the river, docks, ice plant, Tenn. Valley Sand and Gravel Co., etc., etc. There was a lot of activity down there and switch engines were on the tracks almost daily. I had never seen a real train until we moved to Sheffield. Across the trestle or overpass, 20th Avenue ended and 3rd Street began and only eight or ten blocks away was downtown. Half way between was Tri City Produce Co. This place became our banana supplier. Here's why: Bananas were hung in stores on their original stalks, and they were ripe when sold to the store. They were not cut off and green as they are today. Bananas were shipped to the Tri City Produce Co. by a railroad car called Refer. A Refer was an insulated box car packed with lots of ice inside to keep the vegetables cool while in transit. The car load of bananas, green and intact on their stalks and packed in straw, would be parked on a spur track at the rear dock of the produce house to be unloaded. As the workers would carry (tote) the stalks from car to warehouse, some green bananas would fall off the stalk. The produce workers would never pick up the strays. It was OK by them for us kids to get the loose bananas. Sometimes I've gotten as many as a bushel from the floor of the empty boxcar. Mom would place the green bananas in a dark closet until they were ripe. We always had plenty of bananas. Sometimes we'd find apples, oranges, and lettuce where they would spill some and never picked it up. Another use for the basket on my bike.

Dad was on the road a lot making deliveries or going to Florida for honey. He would leave the Model A parked in our front yard. Mom really couldn't drive, and Dad would have had a fit if he knew she even tried. One day she says to me, "Let's get the car out on the street. I believe I can drive it." Our street was very wide and not much traffic. She cranked the Model A. I was sitting beside her. "Now what do I do?" she asked of a 12-year-old. I had watched Dad enough till I felt I could drive. I told her where reverse was and what to do. I also had to tell her which way to turn the steering wheel to back up in the right direction—Whew! We finally got on the street. She would start off in lunges or jerks. Finally she got the feel of the thing and could drive pretty good. We never told Dad. Thereafter she only would drive when it was very necessary.

Our first year in town was the first year in our lives we didn't have a garden or grew our food. It was easier going to the grocery, but not nearly as good and a lot more expensive.

Mischief

I have been reluctant to mention this subject because my opinion and attitude has changed 180 degrees since growing up and realizing the importance of all forms of life. Also, the misuse of guns has become fearful. I am strongly against young people (kids) having toy or real guns in any form. But the truth is the truth. Yes, I owned a Daisy B.B. gun while on the farm. I shot anything I could, especially birds—pretty birds, songbirds, insect-eating birds—I didn't care. I shot them just to see them fall. I am now so ashamed of that act. When we lived in Sheffield I got a Daisy Pump Air Rifle (B.B. gun), and there the hunting and killing continued. At about 14 I owned my first really dangerous gun—a .22 semi-automatic. The killing became even more deadly. Hunting for sport and food went out 50 years ago. There is no other reason to kill.

On 20th Street a bunch of us would play every night outside. The weather would have to be quite bad to keep us inside. Next door to Buford lived an old man and his wife. He was cantankerous and didn't like kids at all. Nothing was more fun than to aggravate this old man. Sometimes we'd knock on his front door and run or throw firecrackers near his house. The most fun was the China berry trick. There was a large China berry tree in the Garner's yard. Late summer the tree would be loaded with hard, green berries, about the size of a small marble. Buford and I would climb this tree and pick pockets full of China berries for ammo. Now, Mr. Sampson Call's roof on his house was tin, and when three or four fist full of China berries were unleashed and rained down on his roof it sounded like a hail storm. Old Man Call would run out with his shotgun and run around the house. Of course, we would be long gone. Depending on how mean we felt we might cut loose with another round when he got settled down.

All the while I lived in the country, I never knew anything about trick or treat. In fact I never knew anything about Halloween until moving to the city. Oh, I'd heard wild tales from adults about turning over someone's toilet or taking a buggy apart, then assembling it on the peak of some barn. The big deal in Sheffield was to parade up and down the streets in town soaping store windows with a 5¢ bar of green OK soap or a cake of white Ivory. Sometimes a few of us would let the air out of a person's car tires we didn't like. We would always give Mr. Call's house a work over with China berries. Later on the schools started having big Halloween parties and entertainment in the football stadium to get kids off the streets—it worked pretty well.

Hobby Planes and Dime Stores

At about 13, I became interested in aviation and airplanes. I started fooling around with small balsa wood kits purchased at the 10¢ store from 25-50¢. The first models I built were about 12" wing span and turned out quite well. I was encouraged so by compliments that I got into modeling quite serious. I was building large models at age 16 and 17. Though I belonged to the Muscle Shoals Model Airplane club, I never built a gasoline-powered model. I owned two or three engines, but felt I could never afford the complete package. I built several 6' wing span planes and several 4' models powered by rubber bands that were great flyers. At that time, radio controls had not come on the scene—only free flights. By the time I was 15, I must have had at least two dozen planes of all sizes hanging from the ceiling in my room.

Stores

Would you believe when I was a kid we had J.J. Newberry and Woolworth's 5-10¢ and 25¢ stores? We called them dime stores. The merchandise was displayed on top of counters or tables. Strips of glass forming compartments for the items on the tables. Merchandise was piled loose in the compartments. They had just about everything—eye glasses, Bobbie pins, thread, lipstick—you name it, they had it—all for 5, 10, or 25¢.

You could go to the meat department of a grocery store and buy a nickel's worth of cheese and crackers—enough for lunch. If you bought a roast, steak, pork chops, or a pound of bacon, the butcher would show you a quarter of beef or chunk of meat. You picked out what you wanted. He would cut it to your order. He would slice your bacon while you waited, then wrap it in white paper. None of this precut junk already wrapped in plastic and displayed in a meat case.

My first job at age 13 was at Mason's Grocery. I was stock boy, and I also carried the grocery basket for customers as they shopped for their groceries. There were no carts with rollers. Stock boys carried their baskets and helped them find what they were looking for. Most customers would simply call in their list, and the store would deliver the groceries to their home.

Another important store to me was the Webster and Long Paint Store. Why was a paint store important to a kid? Because every Christmas season this was the place to buy fireworks. Back then there were no controls on firecrackers. Golly, a person could blow up just about anything. The "ZEBRA" brand firecracker was what we would shoot. They were about the size of a cigarette and about half as long. Very powerful and very loud. If that wasn't big enough for you, there was the cherry bomb—round 1" waterproof fuse, would explode under water. Once, someone flushed a cherry bomb down the commode in the rest room at school, and it blew the plumbing apart. Then there was the two-incher—and the four-incher. All very powerful and dangerous. We'd blow up everything from the outhouse to the garbage can. A favorite trick was to light a big one, drop it down in the pit or hole of an outdoor toilet and hear the muffled sound when it exploded.

Drug stores were every kid's favorite place. Every drug store in town had a soda fountain. They were often sort of a hang out place for kids. We could buy a "big" dip in a cone for a nickel. A dime cone was a whopper.

The gasoline stations, called service stations, were different than today. A person drove up to the pump for gas, an attendant would come out to serve the customer's car. Even $2 worth of gas would deserve a windshield cleaned, oil checked, and "FREE" (it was called) air in his tires.

Green's Shoe Shop was a busy place, as people had their shoes repaired with new heels and soles as long as the upper leather remained good. The Greens were wonderful people and loved young folks. There was Milborne (Mr. Green) and Ruth (Mrs. Green). Mrs. Green was a pretty lady and several years younger than Mr. Green. The Greens lived in a house or an apartment to the back of the shoe repair shop. During business hours, you could go from the shop into their house. On Sundays, a back door opened from their back porch to the alley. Their back yard was small but private. It was enclosed by a tall wood board fence. They had two boys, Ray and Roy, and a girl, Zelma. She was my age with the boys being older. The Greens became like second parents to some of us kids, and their home became a gathering place.

Winter '39

I guess my Dad only worked at the syrup plant for a year, because I remember the winter of '39 was the worst on record for Sheffield. Also thinking back, the awful cold spell had to have come in January or February of '39, and Dad was already working with the Coast Guard traveling up and down the river on their boat. It came a big snow, about a foot deep, then the temperature plunged below zero and lasted about two weeks. The water main coming from the standpipe down Montgomery Avenue that supplied water to the city froze. The line was two or three feet deep in the ground. I don't remember how long we were without water or what we did for it, but I do remember the school system shut down for two weeks. Not only was there no water, consequently no heat because of no water.

Kids had a ball. We spent hours and days with sleds, ladders, garbage can lids, and anything that would slide on the wooded hills between our house and the river. We also crashed into a number of trees. We would put about six kids on a ladder and down the steep slope we'd go. Half would fall off and tumble to the bottom. The job was getting the sliding equipment back up to the top of the hill. Buford and I would go down to the river, and all the calm sloughs would be frozen 5" or 6" deep. We would walk, run, and then slide on the ice.

My Dad told a tale about Pickwick Lake being frozen. Their crew was down stream when the cold spell hit. Several days later they were on their way home. When they locked through the boat locks at Pickwick Dam, the lake was solid ice. Their boat was a 40-ton, steel hull cutter with a big powerful diesel engine. The captain decided they could lunge into the ice and break their way through. Dad said they had spent half day backing up and plunging into the ice and had only broken up about 100 yards. They decided it was hopeless and tied up to the dock at Pickwick Dam. Dad said that the following week there was miserable. The boat, being steel and in water, had a tendency to freeze up into the ice. They could not allow that to happen, so with a chopping ax, would have to keep the ice from freezing to the boat. They would have to keep the boat's engine running to supply heat to the cabins, gallery, etc., in the cold steel boat. They could not run the engines for 24 hours a day for fear they would run out of fuel. I can imagine their predicament—no transportation, so they couldn't go anywhere. After about a week, the weather warmed up, the thaw began, and they were able to plow their way home.

They told of another sorta funny story that happened on the boat. It might have been this same time. Anyway, occasionally he would carry my .22 rifle on the boat. This time they were plowing up the lake where there was a lot of ice. Suddenly, he saw what he thought was a bunch of ducks sitting on the ice some distance away. The boat got closer and closer. The ducks had not flown. Dad just knew he was going to have ducks for dinner. Out with my Springfield Semi-Auto, he took aim and spat, spat, spat. The ducks did not fly. Another half dozen rounds then he knew something was afoul. The skipper turned the boat toward the ducks and when close enough to see what it was, much to their surprise, here's what had happened. At some time, they had roosted on the ice and melted out a little indention. Then where their tail was, droppings piled up and at a distance it looked like a duck head. He was shooting at duck doo.

The 2nd Move

When school was out for summer of 1939, I finished the 6th grade at Alabama Avenue. The Junior High (7th and 8th) was some distance away on Atlanta Avenue and 10th Street. Then we moved to a better and bigger house on 10th Street, just one block from the Junior High School, also two blocks from the City Park and even closer to the river where I spent so much time anyway. The house was 'A' frame, five rooms, with a closed in back porch, and a bathroom— for the first time in my life, a bathroom. We still had to use the coal burning stove for heat, and Mom was still cooking on her wood stove. We did have hot and cold water in the house. But the house and area (neighborhood) was a great improvement over the 20th Avenue place. We even had a nice garden space in the back yard and an unattached garage beside the house which became my shop, storage house, office, and museum.

This house was about 4' off the ground at the lower side and a door opening to an under-house storage area. I quickly turned that space into my private house where I built model airplanes. I could make a mess and leave parts out, and they would not bother Mom or be in anybody's way in the house. My bicycle had gotten stolen right off our front porch one night just before we moved. I was on foot again or on roller skates.

The Coast Guard station where Dad worked was in Village One on Spring Creek, probably three miles from home. Tuscumbia was another two or three miles from there. I cannot remember how I got to Tuscumbia. I may have skated. I went to the Western Auto Store and saw the most beautiful bicycle I had ever seen in my life— 26" white sidewall tires, luggage carrier, front headlight, a battery case between the bars of the frame, maroon and yellow. Oh, Lordy, I would have killed for it if someone said that's what I'd have to do. It was a "Western Flyer". The bike was $26.50, I think, and it could be bought on credit for so much a month—like $5 or something. I had to have that bike. I must have had a down payment, and all I needed was a parent signature on the papers. I rode that bike to the Coast Guard station or the back way, which was a muddy dirt road, to get Dad to sign the papers. He pitched a fit, but after assuring him I would pay for the bike, he signed. I rode back over the muddy road to Tuscumbia to deliver the signed paper. My bike was a mess of mud, but again I was one more happy kid. I was so proud of this bike, I went everywhere to everyone I knew to show it off.

Now I had always been pretty much of an enterprising young fellow from scrounging up scrap for show fare. I even sold Grit papers for a time to win prizes such as knives or watches. Now I had just landed an afternoon paper route delivering the <u>Birmingham Post</u>. This was hard for the few dollars a week it paid, but I managed to pay for my bike. The paper route took me into parts of "Baptist Bottom", as it was called, then out to the north end of town, several miles for a few customers. Collecting was the hardest part. Sometimes people would not answer the door, probably because they didn't have 50¢ for a week's paper bill. The paper route taught me a lot about people and business.

Soon school started again, and I entered the 7th grade at the new Jr. High just up the street. This was in the fall of 1939. I met so many more new people at this school. New people were moving to town. The economy was getting better. Lots of construction was beginning. Reynolds Metals Co. was starting a huge aluminum plant at Lister Hill, near Muscle Shoals. Jobs were plentiful and salaries were getting better. Things were happening in Sheffield, too. We had a new Colbert Theater (movie), and Liberty Super Market (grocery), and a Belk Hudson dry goods store.

My First Real Date

It seemed I've sorta liked the girls all my life and had taken sort of a shine to some, but I never had what might be considered a date. I had taken a shine to a cute girl named Agnes McCluskey, and I thought she liked me, too. The movie "Gone With the Wind" was the rage at the new Colbert movie. I asked Mom if I could take Agnes to see the movie. Mom gave me permission, and I asked Agnes if she would go with me to the movie. She agreed and there became my first date. I think we might have rode our bicycles to see the show. After that I considered her my girlfriend for a time. Mostly because of her, I started attending a Presbyterian Church just four blocks from our house. I really enjoyed the group in my Sunday School class. They were very active in outings, etc. They (we) would have wiener roasts, parties, and things often.

Through the City Park and down the valley about 1/2-mile was the river. I continued to spend many days fishing as well as swimming. The cove at the end of the valley was called Whippoorwill Hollow—the best and most favored swimming place on the river. All the kids and young adults would swim there everyday during the summer. There was shallow, gravel bottom water for the kids, tapering off to deep as one would want. Thirty-five foot cliffs surrounded the cove. A steel ladder fastened to the cliff, making it easy to climb to the top and dive off if you had the guts. I could never force myself to dive any higher than 10'. It truly was a great place, and it was free.

One day tragedy struck. An older boy was there with a new Thompson boat and outboard motor. Outboards were few and far between, so he was showing off. He would give guys a ride in his boat. "Porky", we called him, took a ride. Porky sat out on the bow of the boat. The boy was running fast in a circle, splashing in his own waves. The front end of the boat was bouncing up and down. All Porky could do was hang on. Suddenly Porky fell into the water on the outside of the boat as it turned. The motor ran over Porky and sheered a pin. We knew immediately Porky was in trouble. He did not come up. The boy running the boat panicked. Several older boys who were good swimmers swam to the boat. They found Porky and brought him to the bank. His face and leg was VERY bloody, big open gashes were cut down across his face through his lips and chin, and two big cuts were just above the knee cap and one just below. Six or eight of us carried Porky up the hill where someone had parked their car, and Porky was rushed to the hospital. He was to be okay. Later, he had a lifetime scar on his face. His front teeth were knocked out. Two big scars were on his leg. He was lucky to be alive.

I was about 14 now and thought I was 23. We continued to gather at the Greens. Zelma was very popular. Ray had joined the National Guard that was forming in Sheffield. There was a new hangout place for teens and young people. It was "Thompson's Bar B Que", a very popular place. We called them cafés then, but this was a drive-in café as well as a sit-in restaurant. A drive-in then was exactly that. You would drive into a lot, usually on the back of the building, sit in your car, and a "curb hop" would come take your order. A curb hop was usually a cute girl dressed in shorts or a short skirt. When the order was ready, she would return with your food on a tray that would hook to the door. If you had a date, you could eat in the privacy of your car. If a guy had no date, he would flirt with the "curb" girls, which was the reason for hiring cute girls. Thompson's was the meeting place and the eating place. My Western Flyer bike continued to take me everywhere I wanted to go.

Trouble

I guess it was about 1940 when Dad went to work at Reynolds as a painter. He joined the union and had no trouble getting on construction. He was making more and more money, drinking more, running around and laying out more, and becoming much more abusive to Mom and me. He seemed to resent every penny he had to give us. I needed tires for my bike. They cost about $2 each. He threw a fit. He raised hell to give me money for school (books, supplies, and lunch). It became necessary that I go find a job after school.

I went to work at H. G. Hill store as stock boy and basket carrier, as I had done at Mason's. The pay was only $7 or $8 a week, but more than I previously had. I would work on Saturdays and afternoons after school.

My new friend Buck and I became very close. His name was Vernon (Buck) Sanders. Everybody called him Buck. We had so much in common. He built model airplanes, as did I. We would work together and share our knowledge. He loved to shoot a gun and be on the river. He collected postage stamps, and I became a stamp collector. He was a year older than I. His dad was a salesman for a coffee company in Sheffield and owned a 1939 Nash car. Buck wasn't driving yet, so we went everywhere on our bikes.

A favorite place we would go was to Seven-Mile Island, on the north side of the river. The head of the island was across from the old furnace slag pits and it was truly seven miles long. Nobody lived on the island. I've heard there were moonshine stills there. Once someone grazed cattle on the island and would transport them on and off by a barge-like boat.

Anyway, the island was quiet, lots of strange birds. Carp would wallow in the shallow waters, and their top fins would be out of the water—perfect targets for a .22. We could shoot all we desired, and no one would bother us.

We would rent a boat from an old couple who lived in a house boat tied to a cove near the water works plant. A paddle boat would cost us $1 for all day. One day we rented a boat. It was a very small flat bottom, narrow and only about 10' long. We figured it would be fine and would paddle easier. We took out for the island and spent most of the day. Coming back was rougher than we guessed. We were paddling against a pretty good current coming up stream. Too, the wind had gotten up a little.

This was probably in March. The sun was warm, but wind still quite cool. We were hungry and tired, but kept struggling with the home-made paddles. Then a motor boat with two men in it came up the river. They pulled up near us and asked if we'd like a tow. Oh me, they must be from heaven we thought. Not having a tow or anchor rope in the boat, the only thing we could do was pull along side their boat and hold on to their boat side. This we did, and they throttled up their motor. Their boat was bigger (higher sides) than ours. Not only were we straining to hold on, I noticed their boat was kicking their wake over into our boat, filling our boat full of water. Buck was seated in the front of our boat and not aware of what was happening. I knew we were about to sink. I yelled to him to let go their boat. He did, and the men in the motor boat never slowed up. I'll never know if they were aware of our dilemma or didn't give a hoot, but they never looked back. No sooner had we released their boat when my end of the boat filled with water and slowly went down under the surface of the cold river. I could see the front end going down and the water coming up around Buck's seat. He had his rifle in his hand sitting there as if waiting for the boat to stop sinking.

Buck always wore a cap that resembled a Navy captain's cap or a Western Union cap. He had his cap on that day. God gave me a talent to keep cool in an emergency, so I never panicked. I knew the boat was wood. While it would fill full of water, it would not sink. The thing to do was hang on to the boat. I was so busy hanging on to my rifle, making sure the boat didn't get away from me, and rounding up the paddle which was floating away, I didn't have a chance to see about Buck. I assumed he would have the good sense to stay with the boat. We were probably 300 or more feet from the bank up above the ice plant and a quarter mile from where the boat needed to go. To make things worse, we had on heavy jackets on top of our clothes.

I got the paddle, laid it in the boat, laid my rifle in the now full of water but floating boat, then looked around to see about Buck. All I could see about half way to the bank was a cap. I knew he was about to give up. I yelled, "Don't give up now. You're almost there." Buck will tell you today my yelling for him to not give up saved his life. He was exhausted and had about quit paddling, but he continued. I was paddling with one hand, swimming along beside the boat, and holding onto it and pulling it along in the water with the other hand. I got to the bank with the boat just about the time he made it. We crawled out on the bank.

The bank was 4' or 5' high and riprapped with huge limestone rocks to prevent waves and currents from eroding the banks. The rocks were warm from the sun, and we began to remove our clothing to dry out a bit. At that point, we were safe and our ordeal was getting funny as we reviewed what we had just experienced. Even though we were mad at the motor boat for ignoring us, we were laughing at our ordeal. I had dared Buck to go swimming earlier down on the island, and he said it was too cold. He said to me, "Well, Buddy we got the swim after all."

Buck pulled his soaked wallet from his hip pocket to take his money and papers out to dry. When he zipped his wallet open, the silver dollar he had carried for years with the date (year) he was born rolled out, plinked on a limestone rock, and plunk into the river. I thought that was really funny.

We dried out pretty good, bailed the water out of the boat, crawled back into it, and paddled on up the river to turn it in where we had rented it. This was only one of a number of scrapes Buck and I got ourselves into.

During 1940, I went from 13 to 14 in May. Dad continued to make big money by working lots of overtime. The country was preparing for war. Germany was invading much of Europe. Defense plants were springing up all over Alabama. Dad owned a 1937 Terraplane Hudson car at this time. We continued to visit our folks in Tennessee and my grandparents in Athens. We were only 45 miles from Lawrence County and about the same to Athens—only minutes in a good car. My first real experience of getting the feel of the wheel, as they say, was one Sunday Dad let me drive the Hudson from Uncle Fagin's house to Florence. Of course, I was sitting in his lap in case I got into trouble and he had to take over, but I did pretty good. Good enough that he would let me take the car and run errands occasionally by myself. There were times when I would ride to Reynolds with him, bring the car back, do something, then pick him up at 4 o'clock when he got off from work. I began to drive quite a bit and, frankly, drove for two years until I was 16 without a license.

Smoking

It must have been somewhere around this time and age when I began to smoke. At that time we did not have the knowledge to know of the harm and danger to one's health caused by smoking. Had we known, I can assure you I would have never laid my hands on a cigarette. Instead, it seemed the thing to do to be grown up.

I cannot remember how long I slipped around before my folks knew I was smoking. I'm sure Mom knew because of the horrible odor a person has who smokes. The one who smokes becomes oblivious to the odor.

There were no long or king-size cigarettes then. Neither were there filters—only regular, plain cigarettes—and, seems to me, they were around 15¢ a pack. I smoked Lucky Strike—LSMFT was their advertising slogan—"Lucky Strike Means Fine Tobacco". It continued, so round, so firm, so fully packed, so free and easy on the draw. One day I realized I was hooked on cigarettes, and quitting became impossible.

1941 – A Very Good Year

The year 1941 was the best year of my life so far. I was really into model planes. Buck and I continued to be good friends. I would be 15 in May. I started to high school that fall. I got interested in photography and became a shutterbug. Dad would let me take the Hudson out alone. My grandparents were still living. My dad went to Childersburg, Alabama, to work on a DuPont plant. Japan invaded Pearl Harbor December 7th. That plunged us into World War II. I tried to be popular with the girls and succeeded pretty well. I was becoming my own man. Buck was 16, and his dad let him take the car and date. Late in the year, my dad traded for a new 1942 Pontiac, and we would move again before the year was over.

Sheffield was building a new high school to be completed early in 1941. It was state of the arts for that time. A very modern and beautiful building on several acres, complete with a nice football stadium. In Sheffield or all of Alabama, it was football. Basketball wasn't played much. The high school was just three blocks further from our house on 10th Street than Jr. High, which made it awful nice walking to and from school. Sometimes I rode my bike, but mostly I walked. The school ground was a perfect place to fly my model airplanes on Saturdays and Sunday afternoons. Sometimes I would draw a crowd of onlookers who stopped to watch the planes fly. I guess I had at least a dozen planes by now.

Since I had a job after school and Saturdays, I did not always go with Mom and Dad to visit folks in Athens and Tennessee. I was getting older and big enough to take care of myself. Mom and Dad were planning a trip to Athens to be gone overnight on a Saturday. Buck would spend the night with me. We would be fine. As Buck and I made big plans for that coming weekend to be home all alone, he revealed to me he had found a pint of whiskey under the seat of his dad's car sometime ago and had hid it around their house. He would bring that pint, and we would have a party. Neither one of us had done enough drinking to even hardly know what it tasted like. Finally the moment came. I came home from work, and Buck rode his bike over to the house. This might be a good place to tell you that we never had a telephone in the house during all these past years and didn't for several more. Buck brought the pint of booze. We couldn't wait to get into that stuff. I've sipped on things that taste much better, but we were having a time with our coke and bourbon. I cannot tell you how long it took for our heads to start floating on the ceiling, but I do remember we were hungry and drunk. We decided to walk to Thompson's Bar B Q Café and eat. Figured we were too drunk to ride our bike and were. Thompson's was 7-1/2 blocks from our house. We were putting one foot in front of the other, staggering, trying to stay on our feet. Then our shoulders would bump against the other, and I would stumble to the right and Buck to the left. We were having such a wonderful time, I thought we would never get to Thompson's. We were drunker than "Cootie Brown". I don't know how long we were there or what we ate. I only remember being back at our house and sick as a dog—thought both of us would vomit our toenails. Neither of us had ever been that sick in our lives. Buck was even sicker than I. We got to sleep sometime during the night, and when we woke up Sunday it was way up in the day. Oh Lordy, how terrible the hangover was. Buck finally got himself together enough to make it home. When Mom and Dad came home late that afternoon, I wasn't feeling very perky. I think I explained our sickness away by insisting we ate something that made both of us sick.

By the time I was 15, I was driving the old Hudson quite a bit. I drove Mom to many places she needed to go as well as making trips alone to run errands, etc. Dad was working long days and often seven days a week with lots of overtime. He didn't have time to tend to local things, so I had to do it. Dad often rotated driving to the plant. He would carry riders when it was his week to drive, then ride with someone else and leave the car at home. I got the chance to drive a lot, yet I wasn't old enough to get a driver's license. I drove without one. When I was 15, I was 6' tall and looked every bit of 16 or 17, so no one questioned my age. I would drive to Athens to see my grandparents and to Lawrence County to visit relatives.

The Third Move

For some reason, we moved again. I think the person owning the house on 10th Street sold it. Whatever it was, we had to move. Dad found this place at 201 Atlanta Avenue. It was actually half of the house. For some reason, most houses built in the early 1900's that were two rooms wide had two front doors. This house was a good-sized six room house, every room exactly the same size. A front porch went all way across front of the house. With this plan, it was easy to make houses into what we now call duplexes. The Barbers lived in the half next to 2nd Street, and we took the other half. We each had a front or living room. The middle room was the bed room, big enough for two beds if needed. Then the kitchen. In all the homes back then, unless high society, one ate in the kitchen. There were two back doors going out on a covered back porch. On Barber's side of the back porch, there was a large closet, actually a storage room. A door led from their kitchen into this room. On our side of the porch, there was another room the same size. A door led from our kitchen into this room, but there was another door that opened out onto the back porch. In this room was the bath room—a commode and bath tub only. The men who shaved would do so in the kitchen sink. Both families shared this one bathroom. It wasn't bad because soon after the move, Dad took a job in Childersburg, Alabama, and he was seldom at home, only on an occasional weekend. Mr. Barber worked days and seemed to be gone at night, so he was never there much. There were only three people in the Barber family, Mr. and Mrs., and she was sorta weird, and a daughter, Ethylene. Ethylene was a year older than I and a grade higher in school.

This house at 201 Atlanta Avenue was on the corner of 2nd and Atlanta, the second busiest intersection in the city. It was entertaining just to sit in the front porch swing and watch the traffic go by. There was a stoplight at the intersection.

Financially, things were not that good with Mom and me and the household money. Oh, it wasn't because Dad wasn't making good money. He was and had been for a year. Some weeks he would make over a hundred dollars. Our rent was $15 a month, lights about $5, water $1.50, groceries about $15 a week or less, no phone, very little if any deductions (FICA or Income Tax). Compared to the years of 1930 to 1938, Dad was rich. Where did his money go? In the wind, on himself. He gave us as little as he could and would cuss about that. I've known him to go off for three or four days, drunk, and spend $600.

Anyway, it was necessary that I work to keep myself in school. Soon after I became 15, a break for a good job came my way. Remember "Porky" who got injured at the swimming hole? He got well and dropped out of school. He was delivering telegrams for Western Union during the day. Western Union had an opening for a delivery boy in the afternoon and evening (until 9 pm). Porky and I remained friends, and he knew I needed a good job. The Hills store wasn't much. So Porky told me about this opening. He said you gotta be 16 years old, but they don't check. You can tell them you are 16. I went to see the manager, Mr. Kirkpatrick, filled out their application, lied about my age, and got the job. I was so happy and so proud of that job.

I went to work afternoons after school, Saturday, and Sunday afternoons—about two hours on Saturday and Sunday. During the week, the office closed at 9 pm. Part of my job was to mop the office, back room floors, and the lobby floor at night before we left the office. I say "we" since the Teletype machines were operated by young women. There was one woman on duty after 5:00 pm and me, unless I was out delivering a telegram.

Oh, Lordy, did I ever ride a lot of miles! I put a speedometer on my bike, and one Easter I rode 32 miles delivering telegrams. Easter, Mother's Day, and Christmas were big days at Western Union. Still, few people had telephones, so they sent telegrams for special occasions. Once I had a "singoram" for a birthday. I had to sing Happy Birthday to this person. I got a 50¢ tip. I would frequently get a tip.

Most important part of the Western Union job was the salary. I would earn from $12 to $15 a week, and that put me on top of the world. I had money in my pocket, I could help Mom when she needed, and I paid all my school needs (books, supplies, fees, etc.). The "Western Flyer" bike became my lifesaver.

Bobby Meadows standing by the Western Union sign and again on his bicycle. Pictures are courtesy of Kathy Meadows Green

Atlanta Avenue, like 20th Avenue, was wide, paved, and as smooth as could be. A bunch of guys and girls would hold skating parties at night and skate mostly on Atlanta Avenue. From 201 to the standpipe was about 15 blocks. There was no shortage of good streets to skate on. We wouldn't call it dating, but all the girls and boys who were sorta courting would turnout and skate as well as just single and all friends. Some of the regular skaters were myself, my girlfriend Agnes, Zelma Green, Junior Higdon, Buck and his girlfriend Corelia, and a slew of others.

We wouldn't play skate hockey or anything rough. We'd just skate and have a good time. It would be sorta like now when kids park their cars at a certain place where everybody drives in or by. Sometimes on a Sunday afternoon, we would get a group together and skate to Tuscumbia and even to Florence. On other times the same gang would ride bicycles for miles on a Sunday. I remember riding bikes across Wilson Dam to go to Florence was a breeze (five miles away) to Tuscumbia (only three miles). The Muscle Shoals airport or to Muscle Shoals City was no problem for a biker.

Our house on Atlanta Avenue became sorta the gathering place for teenagers. Ethylene had lots of friends, but her Mom was strange. She wouldn't let Ethylene go anyplace unless I was along with the group. Her Mom trusted my judgment and me. If I said it was okay, it was okay. So our friends would meet at our house so Mrs. Barber could see there were no horns sticking out the head of the boys, then we were off to wherever.

Would you believe I was still sleeping on the little iron coil springed, half-bed we moved from the country. I started sleeping on this bed in 1933 when Fagin married and I began to sleep alone. We set my bed up in the front room (normally living room) along with some living room furniture. When more people were in the room than places to sit, my bed was used as a sofa. There was a small fireplace (grate it was called) in this room. When I had company and it was real cold, we would build a fire in the grate. Otherwise, the old coal burning warm-morning heater in Mom's bedroom (the middle room) heated the entire house. Even at Atlanta Avenue, Mom still had her wood-burning cook stove; however, since Dad was gone most of the time it was foolish to fire up the stove for just Mom and I. She bought a two-eye oil burning portable stove (like a hot plate). She could make breakfast and light meals on the oil stove.

High School

School was soon to start. Everybody was busy registering and gathering books and supplies. Getting schedules, homeroom assignments, and a hundred other things centered around starting high school. It was exciting, yet sorta fearful.

High school for me was kinda hard. Mom could not help me much anymore. I had advanced beyond subjects she had when she was in school. Too, I worked at Western Union until nearly 10:00 every night. Not only did I not have much time to study; I really didn't have much time to be a kid. Had I more time to study, I probably wouldn't have hated school as much as I did. All I liked about school was the girls. I think I was becoming a womanizer. The band was super. We had a director that had won prizes all over north Alabama for his 100-piece band and performances. The football team was even greater. Coached by Walton Wright, SHS was usually the champion of Tri Cities. To attend the football games was a great thrill and made the drudgery of school worthwhile. Most of the time when I went to a ball game or needed off from Western Union, I would find someone to deliver telegrams in my place. Sometimes Porky would double over and pull my shift. Our pay was figured on 50¢ an hour, so when I was off six hours, I was $3 short at payday, etc. Of course, there was no income tax. May have been a small amount like 1/2 of a percent FICA.

My friend Buck was courting Corelia Stanfield heavy. They were called the "love birds" in school. Buck would now take his dad's car out on a date. One Saturday night in the fall of 1941, Buck asked me and Agnes to go with them— probably to a movie. It was a rainy night I remember so well. After the movie, the thing to do was drive to some dark, secluded place and park for a little "kissy face". That's about all that took place in those days. Buck drove up to the standpipe and took a dirt lane down into the woods. The lane was narrow, and it became necessary to turn the car around to be able to drive out when we were ready. We parked, oh, for an hour maybe, and then we decided it was time to go. Buck cranked the Nash, backed the rear end sorta downward on a light hill so he could pull back into the lane he thought. What he didn't consider—the ground was wet and muddy. The leaves were slick. The grade was upward. There was no traction. The rear wheels did not move the car one inch. They only spun and buried quickly in the soft top soil of the woods. No use buzzing any more, we were stuck but good. Now to decide what to do. We certainly could not just sit there in the rain. Buck and I got out of the car and reviewed the situation. We decided some gravel and rock might do it. We took the carpet-covered plywood from over the spare tire in the trunk and walked several hundred feet to the standpipe. With bare hands, we scooped up a pile of crushed rock from the shoulder of the road and brought the rock back to the stuck car piled up on the spare tire cover. Distributing the rock equally under both wheels to give each some traction, we were ready to try once more to pull the car out. I felt I was a better driver than Buck. In fact, had I been driving, I'd had more sense than to drive down where he did in the first place. Since he was there, I would have backed the car up on the high side of the lane instead of the low side as he did. I felt now he should give the car just a little gas to prevent the wheels from spinning as much as possible. Well, he did exactly as I had feared. He cranked the engine and socked his foot to the floor on the accelerator. The engine hummed, wheels spinning, mud and rocks flying like bullets—the car did not move.

Only one thing left to do now—swallow my pride and go some place to find a phone and call a wrecker. Wet and muddy, I set out to the fine homes on North Montgomery Avenue only a couple blocks away. I picked one where I sorta knew the people. Knocking on their door, I was so embarrassed to explain my predicament and why I was calling at their house. The good people helped me find a wrecker service and sent one on its way to rescue us. It was only a few minutes until we saw the red and amber lights of the wrecker coming to us. Oh, what a great sight that wrecker was as he hooked a cable to the front end of Buck's car and began to slowly ease us out of the mud. I can't be certain, but I think it cost us $15 for the wrecker service.

December 7th, 1941, came on Sunday. Dad was home for the weekend from Childersburg in his new 1942 Pontiac. When Dad was good, he was wonderful. When bad or drinking, he was horrible. This was his good weekend and he offered me his car for the afternoon. I was 10' tall driving that new, sleek, stream-lined Pontiac up and down the streets. Most of us, not having phones, simply dropped by the house of a friend if we wanted to see them. I had picked up a girl I knew to ride around with me. We then picked up another couple. It was a beautiful, mild, and sunny day. We had driven all over the Tri City area—from Wilson Dam to Lovers Leap. We drove down Alabama Avenue to the river, past the ice plant, up the hill to Furnace Hill. As we were almost to 20th Avenue, where I once lived, the radio program we were listening to was interrupted for this message. It was probably around 1:00 pm, the President of the United States (F. D. Roosevelt) came on the air and announced, "Japan has attacked Pearl Harbor". Then he started giving the details, the gruesome details of death and destruction. We kids could not possibly understand or comprehend what was happening.

Before the Christmas holidays began, I had a good idea of what war was all about. My Latin teacher lost her only son. My cousin, Tillman Roberts of Tuscumbia, was killed later in the war. A number of other people we knew lost loved ones. A state of war was declared on Japan and Germany, and this country began changes that would affect our lives for years to come.

1942-A Very Trying Year

The war effect was really rolling—young men volunteering as well as being drafted into military service. Defense plants were springing up all over the area. People were coming from everywhere to work in Defense plants. Old hotels and rooming houses were being revived into sleeping rooms and meals for defense workers. Food ration stamps were being issued, as was gasoline and new auto tires were becoming almost impossible to buy. Shoes were rationed.

The speed limit became 35 mph on all of America's highways. Can you imagine going any distance, if you had the gas, at 35 mph? I think four gallons of gas was the standard allowance. The 35 mile speed was to conserve gas and tires. Technology finally developed a synthetic rubber, and one could get his old tires recapped. I kept riding my Western Flyer and delivering telegrams for Western Union. My Uncle W.J. (Mom's brother just two years older than me) had joined the National Guard and was now in the Army Engineers. I had built my biggest airplane yet, a 6' wing span Stinson 105. Actually, I redrew and enlarged the plans from a smaller model and purchased the material (Balsa wood) to build the plane. It was a beautiful model.

I had become good friends with Bobby Wilson, also a year older than me. We began to double date together. I sorta gave up on Agnes. Actually, I was about half scared of her Dad. I never did go into their house.

By now, the government was building prefab houses at a very fast rate. Near Village One, the houses were moved by truck in two sections to their location. The government was buying every lot available and putting a house on it for people to live in who were coming to our area. Muscle Shoals was almost solid with Defense houses, we called them.

I had met Rozanne Harbin, a newcomer to Sheffield High. She was a rough tomboy, and I really liked her parents. I called her Rosie. Junior Higdon was still dating Zelma Green. Junior was a good bit older than the rest of us. He was not in school and had a good job. He had bought an old Model A Ford van. We called it a panel truck or delivery truck. It had two bucket seats, then nothing but a floor. There were no windows in the side panels, so Junior put an old mattress back there and made room for four more people. It got to be sorta standard procedure that once a month at least, about six of us (three couples) would go to Lawrence County, Tennessee, "Honkey Tonking". That's what beer joints were called back then. We'd go mostly to Lawrenceburg where beer was legal. Sheffield was dry.

One Saturday night, Junior, Zelma, Bobby Wilson, Lois McCullum, myself and Rosie piled in the Model A and went to a Honkey Tonk in Lawrenceburg. I think the legal age then was 21, and I guess Junior must have been 21 because all it took was one person in the group to be of age to buy beer then no questions asked. We stayed there two or three hours drinking beer and enjoying country music. We all were getting pretty well hit in the tail, and Rosie was as high as a Georgia Pine. We started back home, which was about an hour and half at 35 mph. Soon as we hit the road, Rosie passed out — dead out. I couldn't wake her. When we got to Sheffield, she was still out. We couldn't take her home like this, so Junior drove down to the river. We took her shoes off, drug her out of the car, and held her up while we walked her in the edge of the water hoping this would wake her up. It didn't seem to be doing a very good job. It was now after midnight, and we all had to get home. We dropped Lois off, took Bobby home, and Junior drove to Muscle Shoals City to Rosie's house and pulled in the driveway beside the house. Rosie was awake enough to know where she was and could stand up on her feet. I walked Rosie to the door. Back then nobody hardly ever locked the doors, especially if someone was due in late. I bid Rosie a goodnight and left. What Rosie did not know was the family had company to arrive and spend the night. Her Mom and Dad had thrown a mattress on the floor in the living room and were asleep on the bed in middle of the floor. Rosie gently opened her front door, still bare-footed from the wading in the river and shoes in her hand, crept gently into the front room, stumbled over the mattress in the floor and fell into the bed with her Mom and Dad. At that point, Rosie must have smelled like a beer brewery. Sunday afternoon, I went to Bobby's house and called Rosie. Her mom answered the phone and said Rosie was not feeling well. She also told me what happened. I was expecting her to light in on my case at that point. Then she said she did not blame me, Rosie was old enough to know better.

I'm sure Dad was still working at Childersburg, at least the first part of '42. I know he was never home except for some weekends. There was a couple from Mississippi that moved into half the house next door. Their name was Aubrey and Edith Foote. For some reason his nickname was Goober Jack. They called him Goober. They were super people, and we liked them a lot. One week, a beautiful girl showed up at their house. Turned out she was Goober's sister, Ruby. I simply went bananas over her. She was from Iuka, Mississippi, and was maybe a year older than me. When she would come up on weekends to visit Goober and Edith, I would bust my tail trying to entertain her.

I guess it was because I was an only child, maybe because Dad was gone so much and I sorta had more responsibility, but I always had friends that were older than me—the boys especially; and most girls I dated were older. Seems I couldn't stand the silly kids that were my age. Consequently, I was buddies with the young men who worked at the service station across the street from our house. Just before I turned 16, one of the guys told me he had an uncle in Booneville, Mississippi, that had an old 1923 Model T Roadster for sale for $15. The old car would run, but had been sitting up for a long time. My friend said if I wanted it, he and his buddies would go down and tow the "T" back. I jumped at the deal, giving him $15 for the car and $5 for gas to go after it.

I've wished a hundred times I had taken a picture of the "T" the day they brought it to me. Everything about it was original. Though the cloth top was rotten, the frame was solid. The leather seats were good. The old 21" wooden wheels were solid, and the very old clincher rim tires appeared to be original. I was now the proud owner of a car. Even though it needed a lot of work, I was proud of it. It would be a while before I could drive it anyway, so I had time to get her in shape. In our back yard was a one-car garage nobody ever used except for junk. I cleaned out the building, got the double doors to working, and parked my Lizzy in the garage. At that point, most of the money I earned at Western Union was mine to do with how I pleased. Dad was still paying the bills.

When I turned 16, I could now take the drivers test for a license, but there was no car available I could use. Dad was working out of town. Mom made arrangements with a friend of theirs, and they let me borrow their practically new 1941 Ford five passenger coupe to go to Tuscumbia and take my drivers test. I could drive pretty good. After all, I had been driving since I was 14 without a license. I took the written test in the courthouse, and now for the road test with the patrol person. I drove around in the city doing all the numbers he commanded—parking, backing up, hand signals, etc. Suddenly he said make an emergency stop. My reflexes responded to his command. My foot slammed down on the brake pedal, bringing the car to a screeching halt. The patrolman was slammed almost into the windshield. Actually, what he wanted me to do was pull up the emergency brake (that's what the parking brake was called then) and bring the car to a stop. He looked at me and asked, "Is this the way you make an emergency stop?" I knew at that point exactly what he expected me to do. Not to be outdone, I replied, "Yes sir." Then added, "If a child darts in front of my car, this is exactly how I will come to an emergency stop, and sir, I likely won't take the time to roll down my window and give a hand signal sign either." He said, "Go on," and did not mark any points off my test. In fact, he gave me a hundred, and I got my license. I could not wait to get started working on my "T". About the only time I had to spare was after work during the week, which was usually 9:30 to 10:00 pm, and Saturdays. I took the old top completely off and made it an open convertible. It had no battery so had to be cranked on and run on magneto. I put in new plugs, points, and the piddley stuff. The transmission linings were worn out. The thing had no low or reverse. I pulled the transmission cover, removed the bands, installed new lining, and replaced. Having never seen a Model T transmission before, I thought I did right well. It worked perfectly. I could not afford a battery just yet, so had to crank or push the car off to start. Actually, it would start better if pushed off. There were times when I felt I pushed it about as far as I drove it. Finally, I managed for a battery, probably a used one, and could start the car by starter. It did have an electric starter that worked. Having a battery, the headlights would burn—sometimes. I now could go a few places at night. Occasionally, I would go to Muscle Shoals City to see Rosie but would go the "short cut". The short cut was a pig trail through fields and woods. I went this way in case my lights went out. They were accustomed to doing just that.

When my money would be tight, I would dump a gallon or two of kerosene in the tank. She would run just fine on kerosene, once you got it started. It was hard to crank on kerosene. Too, after it got hot and cut the switch off, the motor would keep running. I would stall or choke it down to kill the engine. Tires were a big problem. The 21X400" clincher rims were almost impossible to find, and the old tires were rotten. They would blow along the rim, but I managed somehow to keep shoes on her. Now I had her running pretty good, a new paint job was in order. First, I removed the dinky trunk. That left a flat floor behind the cab about 2' or 2-1/2' wide and probably that long. At least two or three people could then sit on the floor and hang their feet off, facing backwards, like in a pickup truck bed. I painted the fenders black and the body a powder blue. The old "T" was tough as nails, and I thought I was Mr. Rockafellow behind the wheel. I would drive my "T" to school, and suddenly I had loads of friends. I have had as many as ten kids in and on the Lizzy going down the street.

My friend, Bobby Wilson, worked part time at the Mutual Service Station on South Montgomery Avenue. On Sundays, he would be there alone catching the gas pumps. Then, no one pumped their own gas. I often would go out and spend the afternoon helping Bobby pump gas. That was an interesting experience for me. Bobby's house was sorta like the Greens. It was gathering place for Bobby's friends. (Bobby, too, was an only child.) Red and Boots Wilson were his parents. They loved to have young people around, and we spent lots of time at their home with other kids. Ruby came to see her brother often and I was always glad to see her. On one of her trips, her young brother (Boots he was called) came with her. He was two or three years younger, but I liked him from the beginning. He was a funny guy and usually the life of the party. When we both were together, we were a riot. When school started back in '42, Boots came to live with Goober. Then we became very good friends in 1943.

By the middle of the Summer '42, I can't remember the details about Dad since we didn't see him much. Only a picture of him and Mom in front of a 1938 Oldsmobile brings up some memories. I don't know if he wrecked the new Pontiac (probably did). I don't know if he was still working in Childersburg, probably not. I do remember driving the Olds to Iuka to see Ruby. What I remember most vividly is the following pages.

Dad

Dad got progressively worse with his booze and women. He would come home drinking and start a fight with Mom just to have an excuse to leave and lay out a couple of days. He pulled that stunt one more time and was gone for three or four days. Mom and I happened to be in Florence for some reason standing on the corner waiting for the light to change so we could walk across, when, my dad passed right by us with another woman in the car with him. He knew we saw him, too. That night he came home drinking heavy. I was home from Western Union already when all hell broke loose. Mom ordered him out of the house and to take his clothes with him. He left, and we never saw him again for a year or more. She sued and got her divorce even though we had no idea where he was. Actually, he deserted us, and this was grounds for her divorce. We found later, he had gone to Arkansas and got married out there.

Well, some tight times were in store for Mom and me for the next six or eight months. Our rent was $15 a month. School starting, I would be a junior. Our food bill wasn't much, maybe $8 or $10 a week. But our only income was my Western Union job of about $15 a week.

Mom had never worked for someone else. She had no experience even though she was very intelligent and could do anything. She began to apply everywhere for work. Through desperation, she took a job in a downtown rooming house helping prepare and serve meals to a bunch of defense workers who were living there. Mom worked the breakfast and lunch meals for $5 a week, plus two meals a day for the both of us—usually lunch and dinner (evening meal) for me. We were poor but proud and happy. There was no more fussing or fighting, only peace, at our house, and it was really so nice.

I realized I did not need the Model "T". It was great expense, and it took me no place I could not go on my bike. So, I sold her for $50 to an old man in Ford City. I continued to be in the crowd of Junior and Zelma, and they had a certain bunch who would still gather at the Greens. Also, Bobby and I had our little group who hung out at his house. Then I got pretty chummy with Peggy Azbell and a bunch sorta gathered at Ethylene's house—so, I was a busy kid. More and more newcomers came to school because of the Defense plants. Things were really popping in the Muscle Shoals area. By now, Sheffield had a big Walgreen's Drug Store, that sold just about everything. We also had a new and big grocery, the Liberty Super Market.

Editor's note: At age 17, Bobby Meadows fell in love and married Miss Evelyn White, of Lawrenceburg, Tn. In 1944, he was drafted into the U.S. Army and rose to the rank of Staff Sergeant. After his discharge in 1946, he lived in Sheffield with his family until 1955. After a successful career as a salesman, Bob eventually settled in Robertson County, TN where he passed away September 4, 2005.

Dr. George Washington Carver's Lecture Attracted Big Crowd[1]

by Richard C. Sheridan

Dr. George Washington Carver, noted black educator and scientist at Tuskegee Institute, was the guest speaker at the first meeting of the newly organized Wilson Dam Section of the American Chemical Society on June 10, 1937. Dr. Carver, who spoke on the utilization of the peanut, attracted a large crowd which filled the auditorium of the Sheffield High School.

Born in slavery, Dr. Carver came to Tuskegee in 1896 and after years of dedicated work became one of the country's leading black educators and also one of America's best-known scientists, being noted for his work with raw materials of the South, especially farm products.

On May 5, 1937, George L. Frear, a TVA chemist and secretary of the Wilson Dam Section, wrote to Dr. Carver and invited him to speak at the first meeting of the Section on a topic that would be of interest to both chemists and the general public.

Dr. Carver, who was director of the Research and Experiment Section at Tuskegee, replied that he appreciated the honor and would accept the invitation but wrote that "because of my advanced age, my physical strength is rather uncertain and I have to be exceedingly careful."

He went on to say that, "I do not charge anything for my demonstration. The only expense would be for gas for a small car which would bring the exhibit, my assistant and my secretary. In fact, the expense of the trip is all that we would expect."

When Dr. Carver and his party arrived in Sheffield in the afternoon of June 14, they were met by Dr. Max Bond, head of TVA's training section and adjuster for colored employees, who had made arrangements for their entertainment and accommodations.

---

[1] Reprinted from Times Daily (Florence, AL), March 6, 1997.

Dr. Carver and his assistants were invited to an informal dinner in his honor with members of the Section.. The dinner was to be held on the TVA Reservation. But in a letter to Frear, dated June 4, the professor doubted "if it would be possible for me to attend any social functions, as I have to conserved my strength very carefully." He indicated that his assistant, A. W. Curtis, Jr., could attend and tell the members about the work at Tuskegee.

George Washington Carver, renowned agricultural chemist, is shown here in his laboratory at Tuskegee Institute.
Source: Http://www.nal.usda.gov/speccoll/collect/history/imagines/carvergw.jpg

The audience heard "an interesting and highly instructive lecture" on June 15. Dr. Carver concentrated his talk mainly on the many uses he had discovered for the peanut. He displayed several of his products, including baby food made from peanut oil and orange juice, products resembling milk cereals, paints, varnishes, and wood fillers. He also displayed some paper made from the stems and leaves of the peanut. Dr. Carver discussed briefly his experiments with the sweet potato, and displayed a product then on the market—a candy made from sweet potatoes.

Three days later, the professor wrote to "let you know that we arrived home safely after one of the most pleasant and instructive trips that I have made." He went on to say that "I appreciate the courtesies extended me much more than I have words to express."

Despite his declining health, Dr. Carver remained at Tuskegee Institute until his death in 1943 at age 79. Today, the Carver Museum on the Tuskegee campus tells the story of his life and preserves his apparatus, discoveries, and collections.

The Wilson Dam Section of the American Chemical Society continues to sponsor educational programs such as college scholarships, high school chemistry contests, awards and technical lectures. But probably none of its other meetings has generated the interest created by Dr. George Washington Carver's visit and lecture.

My Greatest Mission in World War II

By Laverne Mills

Editor's Notes: Laverne Mills, of Sheffield, attained the rank of Tech Sergeant in the U.S. Air Force during World War II. He enlisted May 19, 1942 at Decatur, AL and served until May 31, 1945. His decorations included the Good Conduct Medal, Air Medal w/3 Oak Leaf Clusters, and European-African-Middle Eastern Theater Ribbon w/4 Bronze Stars. He was a flight engineer and gunner on a B-24 Liberator heavy bomber.

Flight engineer and waist gunner Laverne Mills posed in his flying uniform prior to a bombing mission in World War II.
Courtesy of Laverne Mills

This will relate my most exciting mission. It took place during my tour of duty with the 744th Squadron of the 456th Bomb group in Stornara, Italy. I had already flown several missions with the crew that I had come to Italy with.

I went on a short leave to visit my brother A.C. Mills in Rome. He was in the 34th Infantry and had been wounded in action. I went to see him in the hospital. While I was away, my crew made a flight. Their plane was severely damaged and had to make a crash landing in the Adriatic Sea. There were only three survivors.

I was transferred, as a substitute engineer, to a different crew to finish up my tour of duty. On the date of

December 2, 1944, I was to fly with Lt. Scarborough's crew.

The squadron orderly woke me up at 3:30 a.m.. I dressed, half awake, and made my way to the mess hall. We had toast, thick bacon, and powdered eggs that had been scrambled.

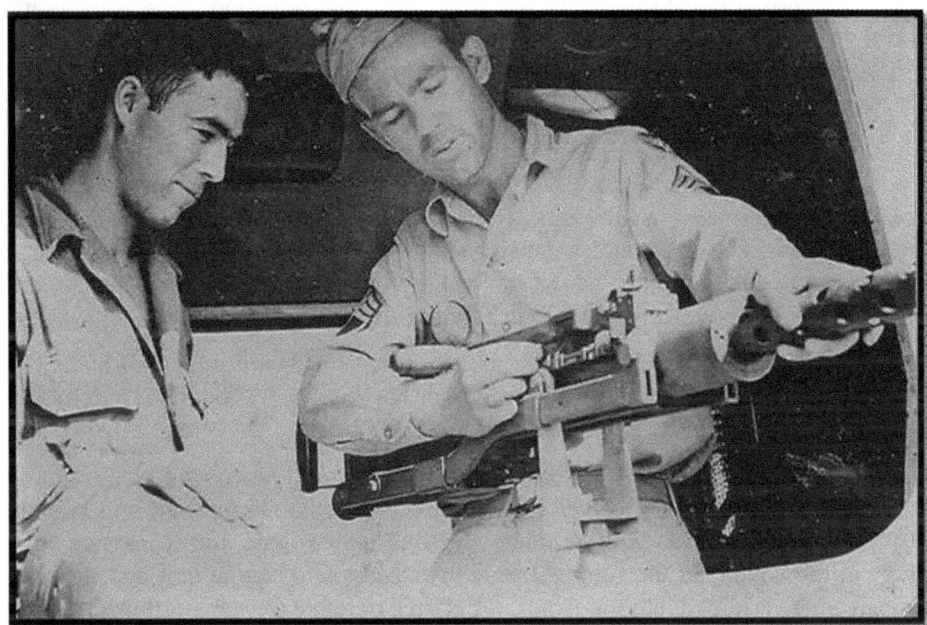

A.C. Mills watches and listens as his brother Laverne Mills described the .50 caliber machine gun that Laverne operated on a B-24 Liberator heavy bomber.
Courtesy of Laverne Mills

I gathered up my flight gear and joined the crew's enlisted men. We waited for our ride out to the flight line. Our crew had been assigned aircraft number 4441208. The crew helped me make the preflight inspections.

The officers arrived and proceeded to tell us about our mission. Our target would be the Odertal Oil Refinery. The location was close to the German and Czechoslovakian border. They told us that we would encounter heavy anti-aircraft fire, or flak, and perhaps enemy fighter planes.

I helped the pilot and copilot get their flight gear on. I then proceeded to get myself ready. I put on my electrically heated suit, my coveralls or outside jacket and pants, my Mae West (life jacket), and then my parachute harness. Next came oxygen mask by my battle station.

The 744th was flying with the lead squadron for this mission. We were in position number 4 in the flight. This meant that we were the fourth plane to take off. The group circled the field while getting into formation. We were going north, toward the Adriatic Sea, and we were gaining altitude as we traveled. Our course was set so we would miss the coastal anti-aircraft guns.

I had performed my duties as flight engineer, redistributing fuel and arming the bombs. This had to be done prior to reaching an altitude of 10,000 feet. I then proceeded to my waist gun position which was in the rear of the plane. Donning my oxygen mask, I checked my chute harness, flak jacket, and machine gun. The pilot made a crew check on the intercom. The flight continued and we were still climbing. So far we had seen no enemy fighters or anti-aircraft fire. Nor had we seen any sign of our fighter escort.

We were approaching the target and were now flying at 27,000 feet. The initial point was reached and we were on our bombing run. The plane had to stay in this pattern, no matter what was happening around us.

Flak bursts were being seen everywhere. I could hear small pieces hitting the plane. Wham! We received a shell hit between the number one and number two engines. God was with us. The shell did not explode, but there was a big hole in the wing, and the fuel tank was damaged. The engine quit and the prop was feathered (turned into the wind). I put on a portable oxygen bottle and looked in the bomb bay for damage. The bombs had been salvoed (dropped).

The pilot had radioed the lead plane and reported that we had been hit, but would try to keep up. I transferred the remaining fuel from the damaged area to the other tanks. The pilots were using a lot of trim to keep us under control. We still could not keep up with the group formation. Our craft was slowly falling behind. We had two good engines, but the third engine was running rough and the fourth engine was dead. The entire crew tensed up. We had no fighter escort. The German fighters would seize the change to go after a crippled Liberator.

The navigator and I told the pilot that we did not have enough fuel to reach Italy. We had lost fuel and were using more fuel than normal due to the way the plane was flying. A decision was made to look for Partisan held territory, instead of trying for Italy. We were near Kijaci, Yugoslavia.

The pilot told the crew to prepare to abandon the plane. I pulled off my flying boots, put on my high top shoes and snapped my chute into place. I was reciting the 23rd Psalm as the alarm bell sounded. The bomb bay door opened and I jumped out. The slipstream caught me. I think that I counted to ten before I pulled the ripcord. First the pilot chute sprang out, than I received quite a yank from the harness when the main chute opened. The fall seemed to be slow, but when I got to the horizon line it looked to be a lot faster. I hit the ground quite hard, but rolled with the fall, and I was undoing my chute as I stood up.

I landed in a clearing. A man pointing a machine gun at me was standing close by. I raised my hands and started calling out, "American, American." I saw that he had on Partisan I.D. markers. He waved the gun, motioning me to go in front of him. I gathered up my chute and did so.

We made our way to a farmhouse that was not too far away. There I found Lt. Bill Banister, copilot; Jake Rose, bombardier; Harry Moore, navigator; and Ralph Dexter, radio operator. We were short five of our crew members. I had not been able to count all of the chutes, so I did not know if everyone had made it out of the plane.

Moore's landing had been rough, and he had injured his head. Lt. Banister had managed to hang onto a first-aid kit. He bandaged Moore's head. The two of them destroyed the documents taken from the plane.

A little bit later a couple of Partisans came toward our group. They had a two-wheeled, horse drawn cart that was loaded with hay. They motioned for us to get in it. We climbed onto the cart, covered up with the chutes and they piled the hay on top of us.

A short time later we came to a small village. A group of people had gathered to see the American airmen. They were all armed with machine guns, even the young boys. Several of them were firing the guns in the air, but I did not feel threatened in any way. They seemed very hospitable to us. I asked for water. One man offered me wine, indicating that the water was bad.

I was standing by a tree, thinking about the situation that I was in. I noticed that one of the Partisans had killed a goat. They soon had the meat cooking over a fire. They were preparing a meal for us as quickly as possible. They were anxious for us to move on. Our parachutes had been seen over a larger area.

We had roasted goat and black bread with wine. I had never eaten goat meat before, but I was hungry. I had not eaten since breakfast which was at 4:00 a.m. We ate the goat and drank the wine. I could still smell the goat. We were joined at dinner by Rollen Johnson and Richard Helgoth, two gunners from our crew. They said that two chutes went over the mountain.

The Partisan group was given our thanks for the meal. We did not want to offend them. Due to the Nazi patrols, the Partisans did not want to move us until dark. They arrived with two more of the two-wheeled carts. I joined the rest of the crew and we were covered up in the wagons. The Partisans started off in a northerly direction.

A sentry challenged the drivers. He talked to the drivers and was told that the airmen were being moved. Our group traveled on. I had lost track of time by the time the drivers finally stopped in front of a large house. One of the drivers knocked on the door. He had us get down from the carts. I brushed the hay off and gathered up my chute. The driver had a short conversation and then we were invited inside.

The room was big with a large oval table in the center. An odd-looking vessel, with a handle like dipper, was in the center of the table. There was a large group of people assembled inside of the room.

A Partisan, the leader, stepped forwarded. He began to speak in fluent English. He had been notified by their underground about the American airmen. He told us that he had lived in the USA for a number of years. The Big Depression came on, and his family moved back and bought this farm.

We were motioned to sit down around the table with them. The vessel in the center of the table was filled with wine and passed around. The leader started asking questions about the USA. He wanted to know about the movies. We told him that a lot of the stars had entered the military. I bypassed the jug on several of its trips around the table. They started to sing. We recognized "Pistol Packin Mama." They sang one or two more and then our group joined in.

I told Lt. Bannister that we needed to hit the sack. It had been a long day. The leader understood and motioned to one of the Partisans. This one signaled that we should follow him. He led us to a large barn which had horses inside. One more Partisan joined the group. They approached the wall and began to pull away some of the boards. This exposed a set of steps. Our group followed the man up the stairs and another Partisan fell in behind us. The room had one bed, which the officers claimed. I still had my chute so I made a pallet on the floor.

I was tired and soon fell asleep. I was awakened by footsteps on the stairway. We tensed up, afraid that the Germans had found our hideaway. We had no weapons to defend ourselves. The door opened and a man with a lantern entered the room. He was followed by Roger Pauls and Samuel Sellers, two more of our crew members. I was concerned now about Lt. Scarborough, our pilot. He was supposed to be the last one out. Nine of us had been accounted for. I was afraid that he had gone down with the plane.

The Partisans got us out early. We were handed some odd tasting coffee and toasted brown bread. The people had turned out to see the American Airmen. There were several women in the group. They were looking at and handling our chutes. I gave them my chute and the other men followed my example. They all had broad smiles on their faces.

While we were standing around an old Ford truck came rolling up. The driver could speak English, so he could be our interpreter as well. Our crew climbed abroad the truck. Before starting off, our guide pointed to a boy that was about 12 years old. He said that the youngster had killed three Germans and expected to kill several more. The guide warned us not to wave at the people. We could be mistaken for Germans.

The truck rolled along. The area began to have more hills. We soon drove past an area with a lot of wrecked military equipment. I saw several German bodies. The guide said that the bodies had been left as a warning to the Nazis. The Partisans were very good at hiding from Nazis.

We climbed over the mountains and entered a small town called Knin. The driver stopped in front of a large building. He told us that it was the Partisan Headquarters. The guide motioned for us to enter. They had a large table set up for breakfast. I had hoped for some water. They brought us some cups of hot tea laced with some kind of hard liquor. Our breakfast was British rations of bully beef and brown bread.

The General came in and we stood at attention. He settled down and we introduced ourselves to him. He asked about our bombing mission, then he directly asked us if we had ever bombed Yugoslavia. We all spoke up to say that our targets had been in North Italy, Austria, Hungary, Romania, Czechoslovakia and Germany. He complimented us on being so young to fly such a large airplane. He said that most of their pilots were over 27 years old and we were in our early 20's. He finished breakfast with us and said that he was off to inspect his troops.

We boarded the truck once more. The guide said that we were headed for the Port of Sebinik, on the coast. The town had just been liberated from the Germans. We talked while he drove.. I had not been flying with this crew before so we exchanged information. We were also concerned about our families receiving Missing in Action telegrams.

We soon arrived in the Port of Sebinik and stopped by a large building. The driver went inside. When he came back, he said that we would have to spend three weeks in this area. He told us goodbye, saying that he had to get the truck back.

We now had a new guide. He led us to a warehouse. We were offered cans of anchovies, wine and bread. I had never eaten them before, but was hungry enough to try them. We remained in the warehouse while Lt. Bannister and Lt. Moore went in search of the military hospital to have Moore's head injuries checked out. They came back with good news. They had encountered three British sailors from British mine sweepers that had just cleared the harbor of German mines. We were invited to come down to the docks where the three mine sweepers were tied up.

The sentry invited us aboard and the commander welcomed us. He had heard about the bomber crew that the Partisans had arrived with. It was tea time and the captain asked that we be seated. A steward came in with cups followed by another steward with tea and another with shots of rum for the tea. All of us asked if we could have a drink of water. I had not had a drink of water since leaving Italy. The sailor instantly supplied us with mugs of good water. I drank water before tasting the tea. Lt. Banister asked the Captain if he could send the 15th Air Force a message about us. We did not want an MIA message to be sent to our families.

The Skipper told us that the crews had flown to Canada and then from there to Washington. They then boarded the new mine sweepers and traveled down through the Panama canal and across the Atlantic to the Adriatic Sea.

We were assigned three to each sweeper. They prepared a good meal for us. Afterwards the British sailors and our group went to the town square. The townspeople were celebrating their victory over the Germans. They were all smiling and dancing. The sailors and airmen added to their celebration. Returning to the ships, we were told that we would leave for Italy in the morning. Bedding was made up for us and we hit the sack. I finally felt safe.

The ships were underway when I woke up. We had slept in our clothes. The sea was very smooth. We had hot coffee, bully beef and brown bread. We all felt better.

We arrived at the Italian Port of Ancona. The harbor had been bombed. It had been rebuilt and the British were using it.

The British had notified Air Force Headquarters that they had arrived with nine rescued airmen. A truck arrived a short time later to pick us up. We thanked the British for our rescue and their hospitality, and climbed aboard the truck. We entered the town on a small, narrow street. I noticed that the color of the street had changed. The driver said that the Germans had lined men, woman and children up and shot them. Their blood had flowed into the mud staining the street.

The driver stopped in front of Headquarters. A Captain came out to greet us. We asked them again to check on the MIA telegrams. The Captain told us that it was chow time. He said that their "Thanksgiving Dinner" was late in arriving. Our crew joined the mess line. While in the line, we were telling the other men about our travels. We were almost there when the Mess Officer came out and wanted to know who we were and where we were from. He ordered us out of the line and we ended up eating sea rations for supper.

We spent the night in tents. At breakfast Lt. Bannister expressed his feelings on the treatment that we had received at the mess hall.

A plane from Bari arrived around noon and took us back to the base. At Bari, there was a truck waiting to take us to the hospital. Lt. Scarborough met us there. He had made it back with a "great group of Partisans." He had joined another crew that had come back the same day as we did. We took our first hot shower since the crash, and a corpsman dusted us down from head to foot with DDT to kill the lice. We all looked like old men. The doctors gave us a quick checkup. Our clothes had been cleaned and were waiting for us.

The officers were waiting to question us about our journey and about the treatment that we had received by the Partisans, I heard a Major ask the copilot what had happened to our plane. No mention was made about the crew. He was told that "the XXX thing quit flying" and we walked back.

The officer in charge told us that a plane from the 456th Group was on the way to pick us up. The plane reached our base and we were put in a holding pattern. A group was returning from a mission. When we landed there was more debriefing and then a stop at the flight Surgeons Office. We were offered a shot of liquor. The crew chief of our maintenance met us. They had waited for our return to the flight line, but gave up on us when it got dark.

I made my way to my tent. My belongings had not been packed up. All was well.

The next morning our Commanding Officer told us that we were back on flying status. I was anxious to finish my tour. I only had a few flights till I could go home. The Commanding Officer said that he would arrange "Rest & Relaxation" on the Isle of Capri. That trip came true the week of Christmas.

Reynolds Ventured into Space[1]

By Richard C. Sheridan

When America's first satellite, Explorer I, went into orbit around the earth, on January 31, 1958, it was spinning like a rifle bullet thanks to its complex spin-launcher built by Reynolds Metals Company in its Sheffield Missile Plant. And Reynolds Metals built the entire ballistic shell of the Jupiter-C rocket which carried this country's second satellite into orbit on March 28, 1958.

Technicians fabricated the tail section, the center section containing the huge fuel tanks, the nose section to house the guidance and control systems, and the spin-launcher for the upper stages at the Reynolds facility located in old U. S. Nitrate Plant No. 1 (acquired by the company in 1946). Reynolds Metals Company had began working with the U. S. Army in 1952 to improve the shell of the Redstone ballistic missile. Training programs were set up in the local union hall to teach selected employees the necessary skills for this highly specialized assignment.

The Jupiter C-3 rockets, built by Reynolds Metals Company at its Sheffield plant, were transported by truck to Detroit, MI where the engines were installed. Courtesy of Joe McAnally.

---

[1] Reprinted from the Times Daily (Florence, AL), Feb. 8, 2009.

Reynolds was soon able to assist the Army by reducing the amount of welding required to produce the Redstone rocket's aluminum fuel tanks. After successfully demonstrating its skill and capability in this field, Reynolds was selected by the Army to fabricate the complex shell for the Jupiter-C rockets. That rocket was a modified version of the liquid fueled Redstone missile; both of those rockets were designed by Dr. Wernher von Braun and his staff at the rocket center in Huntsville.

The Jupiter-C required far more rigorous standards than the Redstone missile, which itself demanded an extremely high degree of precision. For example, every inch of the 13,500 inches of welded joints in the Jupiter-C shell had to be x-rayed to make sure there were no weak spots. Furthermore, 24,500 spot welds were made on the shell to hold stiffener rings and braces. The entire plant was kept very clean to prevent a tiny speck of dirt from ruining the welding job. The spin-launcher, designed to give gyroscopic stability to the upper stages when the Jupiter-C was fired, was built to especially high standards.

Reynolds technicians worked closely with the rocket scientists and engineers in Huntsville and incorporated changes in the shell while they were being fabricated. The aluminum, produced at Listerhill, had to be perfect with no scratches, blemishes, or weak spots. The width and thickness of each plate and sheet, rolled at Listerhill, was measured to precise tolerances. The Reynolds plant in Phoenix, Arizona, provided the extrusions and tubing and more missile tubing came from the Grand Rapids, Michigan, plant. From Sheffield, the ballistic shells went to Detroit where prime contractor Chrysler Corporation installed the engines and completed the Jupiter-C for the Army.

The Jupiter was 69 feet long and 9 feet in diameter. It was capable of striking targets at ranges up to 1500 nautical miles and successfully tested a re-entry nose cone on Aug. 8, 1957. A few months later, President Eisenhower displayed the nose cone at a news conference. That test solved the difficult problem of preventing the cone from burning up when it re-entered Earth's atmosphere.

During the late 1950s, the Navy was trying unsuccessfully to blast a satellite into orbit with its Vanguard missile. The technicians at Reynolds Missile Plant in Sheffield contributed greatly to the success of the Jupiter-C, which gave the Army the honor of putting America's first satellite into an orbit around the

Earth. This provided a vital key to America's future success in rocket development and space travel.

The author is indebted to James E. Bowling, of Florence, who worked on the missile project and contributed reference material for this column.

From Northern Lithuania To Northern Alambama

By Sam J. Israel

At the request of my daughter, I shall attempt to write my autobiography, including the family history of my parents. I cannot be sure of exact dates, but they are fairly accurate or as well as my memory permits.

We lived in a rural area of Lithuania. I was born on a plantation about eight miles from the small town of Ponadel. Lithuania was one of the Baltic States. It was an independent kingdom until the nineteenth century, when it was absorbed by Russia. After absorption, each of the Baltic States retained their own language and culture.

My father served five years in the Russian Army as a petty officer. The regiment he was assigned to was composed of men from surrounding states and this gave him an opportunity to learn from them, their customs and language.

His father, my grandfather, was in the wholesale flour business and my father joined him in business on his release from the army. One of his customers was in the bakery business. It was there that my father met the baker's daughter and they married shortly thereafter.

Not long after their marriage, Father heard of an opening on a plantation owned by a Polish baron. The baron was looking for a qualified man - preferably a bi-linguist to take over the production of his cattle herd and to handle sales of the crops. My father traveled forty miles to apply for the job. The baron was favorably impressed that my father could speak Polish, as well as several other languages of nearby states -an important asset in this business.

The contract included a comfortable home, land for a garden and two cows and two horses. Our home was next to an orchard, and we were privileged to take fruits and berries for our family. The baron set the price my parents were to pay him for the milk for his entire herd of approximately two hundred cattle, and they converted it to butter. My parents worked very hard, especially in the summer, during the heavy production.

The principal market for butter was the city of Riga, in Estonia, which was about 100 miles from our home…a long way by horse and wagon. It took four days to make the round trip. During the summer heat he would drive all night to prevent the butter from melting and during the day he would drive into barns until night fell. The mid-day heat would have melted the butter.

They had a unique way to chill the freshly churned butter. It was placed in 30 pound tubs and stored in the ice house for several days. The ice house was built on a hillside. During the winter months, they would have men saw big ice blocks from the frozen river. They threw the huge ice blocks through a trap door on the high side of the hill. When the ice house was completely filled they would pour all the water it would hold into it. With the below zero weather, it soon became a solid block of ice.

On the summer days when my father was going to Riga with his load of butter, the wagon was loaded for the trip after sunset, well covered with ice and tarpaulin. When the butter market was good, he came home happy.

The milk production fell off during the autumn. At that time the harvest season began, and our whole family worked in the field gathering potatoes, cabbage and other vegetables.

Father devoted part of his time to going on trips selling the crops that were produced by the estate of the baron. That was part of the agreement. The baron considered himself too dignified to stoop to dealing with potential buyers – and father was his business agent.

There were eight children in our family (four boys and four girls). I was the fifth child, born in December, 1891. There was one brother older than me - then the three girls about two years apart, then myself - two brothers younger than me and the youngest girl, Ida, who was the pet of the family.

When we were small, we were not allowed to get too far away from our home, or play too closely in the area of the baron's mansion. My father was a good disciplinarian and stern on occasion. He was tall and generally well-dressed. My parents were frequent visitors at the mansion on business. The baron would speak often with my parents and the several foremen who were in charge of the various departments.

Although life was not easy, my parents had a great deal of pride and we were considered among the privileged people, compared to the unskilled workers and mostly illiterate peasants who did the menial work. The houses they lived in were not much more than shacks and crowded together much farther away from the mansion than where we lived. The mansion itself was very pretentious on top of a hill, and the grounds were beautifully landscaped. There must have been several thousand acres.

When father had to go on a business trip for the baron, he was allowed to use a special vehicle and a fine horse, thus giving him a rather prestigious position.

As I said before, my parents had a great deal of pride, and saw to it that we were always well-dressed, and they were eager for us to have a good education. As our family grew, we would have our clothes and shoes made at home, our parents arranging for a tailor and shoe cobbler to come to our house for a week or so.

My mother was very thoughtful and generous. She would constantly make up little bundles for the poor in Ponadel. When we would go into town on market day, our arrival was greeted with love and tears by the poor families as mother would have packages for them of bread, cheese and vegetables.

There was no such thing as public school for the peasants who worked for the baron. Even in the small town of Ponadel, there were only a few small private schools for those who were able and willing to pay. When we reached the age of seven we were taken to Ponadel, where we would stay in the teacher's home for about two years, seeing our parents perhaps once a week. When we reached the age of nine, we were taken to a larger town where there were better facilities and where our grandparents lived, the town of Kupisac. It was several hours ride in a horse and wagon.

I remained with my grandparents about three years and at the age of twelve my parents wanted me and my brother, Manuel, to go to a religious school of higher type, about 500 miles away.

The climate there was colder. I remained in that school two and one half years. However, I was not a good student, mainly because I had in the back of my mind hopes of going to the United States. My brother and my sister were already there and my brother, Max, had written me, calling America "the land of the free."

When I caught a cold at school, I wrote my parents. They responded that I should come home immediately for a rest. I enjoyed the few months at home, and my parents were somewhat disappointed that I did not seem to want to go back to school. They seemed to realize it would be a waste of time for me to go back to school, and they also realized that I would be subject to draft into the Russian

Army in less than two years. Because of that they reluctantly gave their consent for me to go to America.

A period of sadness ensued. My brother, Max, sent me a ticket and knowing that my mother already had two sisters and a brother who had previously emigrated to the U.S., made our hour of separation a little easier. In due time my parents took me to the port of Estonia. At the embarkation center, my father met some people he knew who were also on their way to America, and they offered to look after me. That helped to lighten the emotion of departure. We sailed August 1, and landed in Boston the last of August.

When I landed in Boston my sister, Rose, came from Worcester to meet me, and took me immediately to my Aunt's home in Worcester--my Aunt Grace. There I spent the new year's holidays, and my brother, Max, from Henniker, N.H., was there also for holiday. As they were discussing my future, my uncle had an idea that I remain in Worcester with them for the time being. The Grace family were exceedingly gracious and hospitable-their home open to relatives and friends always.

But my brother, Max, thought that the best way for me to become adapted to American life, and to learn the English language was to join him in the small town of Henniker, N.H. So after a couple of weeks in Worcester visiting with my sister and other relatives there, I joined Max in Henniker. He was already established there in business and had many friends.

I worked with him for six months, meanwhile learning the English language and adjusting to American life. After about six months, the 1908 depression came along and cleaned Max out of his entire small capital. So we decided to return to Worcester, hoping to find jobs.

Soon afterwards, friends of Max, my brother, came upon a small grocery store for sale, and they offered to loan him the money to buy it. I acquired it finally, knowing that the business was limited and would bring in only enough for one person to live on. Meanwhile I went to Boston job hunting, but due to my youth and inexperience and language barrier, and the short time I had been in the U.S., job finding was very difficult.

In Boston, I was living with a cousin of my father's and they were most kind and hospitable. One day shortly after my arrival, we noticed an ad in the local newspaper that because news boys were out on a strike, the newspaper was offering a dollar a day for news boys, regardless of age or experience. I took that job, which lasted about two weeks--after which I tried selling song books on the streets of Boston, but knowing it was only temporary. My next venture was peddling knickknacks such as pins and needles from door to door. My relatives financed the project, totaling about $15.00. I worked hard at this job until the Chelsea fire in 1908. The house I was staying in temporarily was wiped out in the fire, so that was the end of that business venture, which I disliked anyway.

In the meantime, I was offered a job in a grocery store and I told my relatives about it, as I wanted to take it and hopefully in time be able to repay them the money they had so kindly lent me. But much to my surprise they advised me not to take the job. They knew the owner and knew that he had never been able to keep a boy any length of time due to the extremely long hours, and the unreasonably hard work. They reiterated that I was most welcome to continue to stay with them, until something better came along and they were anxious for me to continue going to high school which was free. As it happened they were among the fortunate ones whose home was some distance from the Chelsea area which had been wiped out by the fire.

But I was determined to be self-supporting and took the grocery job anyway, knowing it would be backbreaking. The store was filthy, the hours long- from 5 AM to 10 PM daily and on Saturday from 5 AM to 12 PM. The salary was huge, $2.00 a week with room and board. The room was a narrow cot in a corridor, which led to the owners' living quarters in the rear of the store. The meals consisted of the owners' leftovers after they had finished eating and seldom was really enough.

My first job there was to clean up the basement which normally would have taken two boys a great length of time to clean up. But I was determined to do the best I could, sometimes working up to 16 hours a day, and then cleaning and trying to improve the main part of the store. When old customers walked into the store and complimented the owner on the improvement in the looks of the store, he freely admitted--"that boy did it," which naturally pleased me, and made me feel it might be time to remind him I deserved the raise which he had promised when he hired me. He readily agreed to raise me a dollar a week. That did not entirely satisfy me, as besides the heavy work in the store, my job also included delivering groceries--heavy packages which I had to carry on my shoulders to customers living on 3rd and 4th floors. I also resented having to work every night, as I wished to attend night school in the fall. I suggested to him that I would work three nights a week in the summer, but when I started night school, I could work every other Saturday night. His answer was "you are telling me what you will do." At that he called in his wife, who was twice as mean and greedy as he. Telling her of my conditions, she said "Kick him out." I said "you don't have to"--and took off my work apron. At this his mood changed, and telling his wife to leave the room, he said to me, "You and I can get along, you should have enough time off to attend night school." After that, I worked for him about a year, and when I left my wages were $7.00 a week.

I then joined my brother Max in a new venture of his – half interest in a wholesale cracker business appeared to be fairly attractive. The partners of the company, by name, The Star Biscuit Company, misrepresented the facts to Max, telling him there was no debt against the company, but after a month or so, creditors sued the company. Thus, Max again lost his entire capital.

We both left Boston going to Worcester, practically penniless. After awhile Max found a new connection and I went to live with the Grace Family. My uncle Grace succeeded in finding a job for me which did not pay much, but gave me free time to attend night school. The job was to work in a hot basement unpacking winter blankets, sweaters, etc. That was in August, 1909, and though the upstairs was hot, the basement was unbearable.

Shortly afterwards, a friend of Uncle Grace's told him he knew of an opening for a young boy in Alabama, preferably a boy who had some grocery experience. The store was owned by a relative. I recall asking my Aunt and Uncle's advice, as they were like parents to me and I had misgivings about going so far way, as did they. My Aunt Rachael finally said, "Go, but only for a few years, and remember, don't get married there." I was then nearly 18 years old.

The company in Alabama advanced me travel expenses which was less than $30. As I began to think of it seriously, I naturally felt a little blue, leaving my Aunt and Uncle Grace, their family and leaving my sister Rose and brother Max to travel such a long way 1200 miles approximately and where I knew no one.

I nervously boarded the train in August, 1909, with $10.00, that I had borrowed, in my pocket and tears in my eyes. I went to New York and changed there to go to Washington. Changed again in North Carolina, arriving in Spencer, N.C. about midnight. The agent told me there was a hotel close by, called to get a room for me, but when he told me it was a dollar, I decided to save the money and instead sat in the depot all night.

I left for Atlanta the next morning and had to stay over night there. On arriving in Atlanta, I became extravagant, bought a new shirt for a dollar, registered in a hotel for another dollar, and splurged by having a good supper in the coffee shop. Next morning about 7 o'clock, I boarded a train for Chattanooga, having to change trains again there, arriving in Sheffield that afternoon. I remember it was Sunday.

That night I was to go to the Philip Olims' for supper--my new boss. Both Isaac and Adolf Kreismans' family were there that night also and all appeared to be very friendly. Naturally I was wondering what they thought about the newcomer. They told me I was to stay in their home, and that the store would open at seven o'clock the next morning.

The next morning, on going to the store, I recall being favorably impressed. The store was clean. They had two drivers who delivered the orders as they came in by phone. When they finished deliveries they would clean up the store, wash windows, etc. What a contrast that was with my previous backbreaking job in E. Boston. It did not take me long to familiarize myself with the stock, and where each item belonged, and soon I began waiting on customers.

Mrs. Olim was very kind to me, and I was comfortably settled with adequate food or more than adequate. But on inquiring of her about a night school, she told me there was none. This bothered me as I was eager to learn and improve my vocabulary. She promised to talk to some of the teachers she knew, and tried to arrange some private tutoring for me. When those she spoke with were not interested, she mentioned that her sister, who had graduated from State Teachers College might be willing to tutor me. She, the sister, was then away on a buying trip.

On her return, Mrs. Olim talked with her, telling her I would pay for her time. She readily agreed saying she would give me two lessons each week. She lived in Florence and transportation was available as street cars operated on a regular schedule. Miss Bessie Kreisman proved to be a good teacher. She was very helpful, patient, and gave me homework between lessons. We started in September, 1909. I had ample spare time to study and between lessons to read the outside books she suggested.

It was in January, 1910, the boss, Mr. Olim, decided to sell the retail grocery store, and start a wholesale grocery store. This suited me, especially as the change included a raise for me, and I had a hunch it might give me an opportunity to show what I could do. He put me in charge of the warehouse, receiving and shipping, filling orders and taking care of the stock. Mr. Olim devoted most of his time to calling on customers.

Another phase of the change pleased me. The Kreisman family closed the Florence store and moved to Sheffield, where Miss Bessie worked in the wholesale business as bookkeeper, billing, etc. Working with her during the day as I did, and twice weekly for lessons at night, drew me closer to her. She helped me learn some bookkeeping methods, making deposits, etc.

Soon the business began to show growth, enough for them to hire an experienced accountant, or so they thought. This job included selling on the road, three days a week, and spending the other three days in the office. Bessie respected his ability, but became a little suspicious after awhile. She told the boss of her suspicions. In September the combination salesman and accountant became ill. We sent out statements to the customers who had fallen behind paying their bills--they were offended, replying they had already paid said bills. To adjust this discrepancy, Mr. Olim decided to send me out to find out the true story, not to collect, but mainly to get the facts. I was a little reluctant to undertake this, due to having been in the United States only three years and having a limited vocabulary. But the boss and Miss Bessie gave me confidence, saying I could do it.

Early the next morning, I was on the train with a list of all the customers. Some resented me at first as they liked the former salesman, not knowing he had pocketed their money instead of turning it in to the company. Other customers who had paid by check, were mostly friendly to me. It took three days of hard, strenuous work for me to finally adjust the accounts.

The Boss then told me I would be the new salesman and when I left the following Monday to pursue my new job, I had a price book and samples with me. I also had a feeling of confidence. The accounts came in a little slow at first but in about three months my sales exceeded my predecessor. I began to make friends on the road, more and more, and enjoyed the new job. I also opened up new territory, thus keeping me away from the office all week. I began to realize I missed seeing Bessie, except on weekends. Then as my sales grew my salary grew likewise.

Bessie and I married in January, 1912. We bought a small house on Atlanta Avenue, in Sheffield. It was anything but luxurious, costing us all of

$2,000. It had a living-dining room with a coal stove, a fireplace in the bedroom and a small kitchen. The electric lights were only on strings, no fixtures, but we were satisfied with it, and did not wish to go in debt.

I continued on the road another year. And the business showed growth. Then it was decided that I was needed inside and another salesman was employed for the road. The government started construction of Nitrate Plant No. 1 at that time and it resulted in bringing in many new people, thus resulting in increased business volume

In 1914 Bessie's father who was up in years and who owned 50% of the company, decided to retire; he sold his interest in the business to his son, Philip Kreisman, and to me. Philip Olim owned the other 50%. Soon afterwards the government started construction of Nitrate Plant No. 2, which was larger than the initial plant, bringing more people into the area. We had more business than we could handle comfortably, and as our company was the largest wholesale grocer in the Tri-Cities, the government contractors largely depended on us to supply them with food.

War in Europe threatened and there was talk that the U. S. could become involved. As the draft came along, we had difficulty hiring enough men to unload cars and to load trucks each day. We all worked long hours. Philip Kreisman was drafted, but being married, I was exempted. This heavy rush continued until 1918 when the armistice was signed.

From that date, business began falling off, but we were glad to return to near normal hours. That was also the year of the dreadful flu epidemic that touched countless families. My sister Rose in Worcester, Mass., was struck down after a couple of weeks illness. She left three children, one less than three years old. Bessie and I traveled to Worcester to see what we could do to help the situation. We decided to adopt Beatrice, the youngest. The older sister, Lillian was taken in by the Grace family. The father said he could take care of the oldest, a boy. Bea has been a joy to Bessie and me. At the time we really wanted to take both Bea and Lillian, but Bessie was not too strong and was, therefore, reluctant to take care of two small children.

In 1919, I contracted a severe case of malaria, which failed to respond to normal treatment. My doctor advised me to leave Sheffield. There was no such thing as mosquito control in those days.

My brother-in-law, Philip, who had been released from the army wanted to go east. After deliberating, we decided to sell our half interest in the business to the senior partner, Philip Olim. In discussing the terms and conditions of the sale, he insisted that if we sold out, we must agree not to return to the wholesale grocery business within 200 miles of Sheffield for five years. Although we had no plans to do so, we both felt the requirement was unfair but he was persistent, and we finally yielded to his demands.

Philip Kreisman left for New York. But I decided to take a leisurely vacation. Bessie and I sold our modest home, purchased a new car, and started out with our little daughter to Waukesha, Wisconsin, which had been recommended as a good health resort. We traveled leisurely in the east for about three months, and by the time we reached Boston, I felt good. We rented an apartment there.

By that time, I was getting anxious to return to work. It seems that Philip Kreisman, who was in New York had the same feeling. He phoned me one day saying he thought he had found something in which we both would be interested.

So I went to New York to look into it. It was apparent there was a short supply of manufacturers in men's underwear line, due to a break in the cotton market, causing many manufacturers to go out of business. Consequently, the two of us decided to open a plant in Patterson, N. J., where there were experienced operators and supervisors.

We stayed in business in Patterson about three years, and in that time did fairly well. But in 1923, another large manufacturer contracted with two southern penitentiaries to use their labor to make underwear at much lower prices than we could afford to sell ours.

Meanwhile, my younger brother, Milton, who was in Sheffield working for our former company, as a salesman, along with another young man decided they wanted to go into the wholesale grocery business. They started in late 1919, and operated as a partnership about 2 1/2 years. At that time his partner withdrew and Milton continued on alone, working very hard, naturally. In 1924, Milton wrote me, explaining that the business was holding up satisfactorily, but the business was undercapitalized. As I indicated before the underwear business was not as good as formerly, especially the popular price line. Also, I was beginning to look forward to the time when I could return to Sheffield, pending the expiration of the five year restrictive period.

I made the trip to Sheffield to tell Milton that there was a six month interval before I could return to Sheffield and enter the grocery business. My partner in the underwear business, Philip Kreisman, and I were convinced after checking our figures that it would be wise to liquidate the business. It was not easy, as we had to dispose of equipment, etc. The liquidation was slow and resulted in a considerable loss. When I finally returned to Sheffield by the end of September, 1924, my capital was much smaller than when I had left five years earlier. Nevertheless, the capital was big enough to match Milton's. Our partnership business was sound enough to enjoy good credit. Business began to pick up and for several years we did well.

Also, about 1928, Milton's health began to deteriorate. Soon it became necessary for him to go into a sanatorium in Asheville, N.C. His family remained at home, as his family and mine had built a new duplex apartment in 1925 on Montgomery Avenue in Sheffield. Business continued to hold up well and I had no trouble at the time making payments on the mortgage. We had merged our business with two other firms in 1927, which necessitated borrowing $10,000.00 from one of the large corporations with whom we did business. But the economy as a whole was good and we drew adequate salaries. There was no reason at that time to feel cramped in meeting obligations.

By 1930 conditions changed, generally, and began growing worse. In 1931, we began to reduce expenses, but not enough to prevent a loss. Milton's salary could not be reduced because of his sanatorium expenses in Asheville. Also, by that time his family had moved to Asheville to be near him.

The depression became nationwide. Some of our merchandise had to be sold at a loss. Banks were closing in many cities, including one in Sheffield. As it happened, Milton and I had our personal accounts there, which included money we had put aside for the semi-annual mortgage payment on our home. When the date for payment arrived, I wrote the Birmingham agent for an extension, giving them the reason for our inability to meet the payment. They replied, giving us a thirty day extension, saying a failure to meet payment in thirty days would be subject to foreclosure. Many homes in Sheffield had already been foreclosed. My best efforts to meet the payment of $688.00 in thirty days failed. I could only raise $588.00 short $100.00. I made a trip to Birmingham hoping they would accept the $588.00. Their reply was that instructions from headquarters were for full payment or foreclosure. By the hardest pleading, telling them we were still operating a wholesale grocery business and my brother's ill health, etc., they accepted the $588.00, provided the balance of $100.00 was paid within one week. This was just a sample of the countless problems I had to overcome in 1932. It was a daily occurrence, trying to hold things together. Fortunately, within a week, I was able to send them $100.

Our inventory had run down pretty low and some of our sources would ship us only a limited amount. The year 1932 was the depth of the depression. No one knew from day to day how long our business could survive. The experience with the mortgage on our home was a semi-annual payment and another payment would be due in six months.

Another crucial situation was with the New York corporation who had loaned us $10,000.00 in 1927. The interest was delinquent for a year. I wrote to them we would pay for each shipment as we received it, but regretted that we were unable to pay the interest. They responded that would have to resort to legal methods to collect the interest. I wrote them again reminding them that we had been good customers for many years and wished to continue our pleasant business relationship. About a month later the company sent the division manager to see me. I had known him (Ben Redmond) for many years. He had with him the stock certificates which we had formerly given them for collateral. His firm had instructed him to try to sell the stock certificates by advertising in our local paper.

I took him through the warehouse to let him see for himself how low our inventory was. Then I let our bookkeeper show him our bank account, convincing him we had very little, and that the figures of our total indebtedness proved we were almost broke. I reminded him that all he could accomplish by advertising our stock for sale would mean to close us up completely. Also, I reminded him that if we were given more time, and hopefully the economy would improve, we would work out of the situation together. He agreed to try to convince his firm that the collateral was worthless and to give us a chance, which they did.

My daughter, Bea, graduated high school in 1932. We had hoped to send her to the University of Alabama, but because of business conditions, we decided to enroll her in our local college, Florence State, for her first year. She was most understanding and agreeable. By 1933, as the economy improved, she did enroll at the University of Alabama. It was necessary even then that we hold down expenses for clothes and spending money, but she never complained. Even though some of the girls in her sorority had fine clothes and more allowance for spending, she was happy there and made good friends. In fact her Junior year, she was elected Sorority President. She graduated 1936.

Early in 1932, the news media began writing about the coming Presidential election. It seemed that Franklin Roosevelt had an excellent chance to defeat Hoover. Perhaps the economy would materially improve. That brought us some hope. After Roosevelt was elected he made statements about plans to create employment. What was more significant, he said he would make a trip to Muscle Shoals very shortly. At that, business became more active, and there was encouragement in the air. When he did come to this area, and looked over the possibilities of development in this area on the Tennessee River, he said as he was boarding his train on departure "I will put Muscle Shoals on the map." From that day our area took on new life.

Soon after Roosevelt took office, Congress enacted legislation to organize the Civilian Conservation Corps (CCC) to give work to countless unemployed people who had been walking the streets. Wide publicity informed the country that people joining the CCC would receive a moderate salary. It would be similar to a military organization as they would also receive housing and food. As jobs were available later they could resign. There were four companies of 200 men each sent to this area. Each company was commanded by military officers.

The Chamber of Commerce was given advance notice of the train arrival of the CCC companies and I was on the welcoming committee. We went to the train at six o'clock one morning and I was introduced to the officers as the wholesale grocer. The senior Captain told me they had sufficient supplies for only a couple of days. I assured him that we were in a position to serve them. We had about a week's advance notice so I phoned brokers in several cities for rush shipments of any staple food.

That fact only greatly encouraged our whole area. People who had money began to spend it as business improved generally. The President's proposal to Congress to enact legislation to organize a program to develop the Tennessee River, which had been our hope for many years, took a few months more. Then the Tennessee Valley Authority was organized and adequate funds appropriated.

As soon as the TVA Board was set up, they proceeded to buy land adjacent to the river, then to build dams which in a few months started to generate power. All of this brought in thousands of new people to the entire valley for construction and housing. This demand for food and all sorts of supplies reversed our economy from a depression to a boom.

When I returned to Sheffield in 1924, I joined the Kiwanis Club. I was put on the committee for underprivileged children. Consequently, I came in contact with children of the very poor. Some were physically handicapped, some could not walk to school, and others underfed and inadequately clothed. We did what we could to help. The first object of Kiwanis is "To give primacy to Human and Spiritual values rather than material values of life." That had an impact on me. In 1929 I was elected President of the Sheffield Club and the following year, Lt. Governor of the North Alabama district, which included all Kiwanis Clubs north of Birmingham.

During the depression years we learned from the schools that many children came to school without food. There were no school lunches provided at that time. Our Kiwanis Club organized a campaign to appeal to the public by radio or otherwise for help to buy food for hungry children. WLAY radio station gave us free time each evening. The appeal was successful and in helping the needy, we found many physically handicapped children. We were informed by the teachers of many children who needed eye glasses. Dr. McGrath examined the children free and the local optometrist supplied the glasses to the Kiwanis Club at his actual cost.

There were no facilities for helping the other handicapped children until the mid-thirties. Mr. W. T. Archer became involved in organizing the Alabama Society for Crippled Children (1926). He called a meeting to organize county chapters in 1935 which I attended. That was the beginning of this program on the local level. The Society arranged clinics for the handicapped in each county in church basements. An orthopedic doctor accompanied by trained personnel came from Birmingham semi-annually to examine and prescribe treatment for the handicapped. It was necessary to send the children to Birmingham for treatment.

About the same time, a group of young women organized the Muscle Shoals District Service League. This group cooperated with the clinical progress doing the clerical work and providing lunches for the children. The results were impressive as we saw many children improve. As for myself, I was deeply interested and attended the clinics. I also attended the annual conventions of the Society where they demonstrated what was being accomplished for the needy patients, and pointed out that because of limited facilities and shortage of trained therapists as well as orthopedic doctors that only a small percentage of the overall handicapped were being reached and treated. In our own area, it was found that 3% of the school children had speech defects. That was surprising to everyone. We started to work on it.

It took several years to obtain the funds to establish a speech clinic at the Florence State College. As chairman of the Colbert County Chapter, I received considerable material on the subject.

Meanwhile, the economy of our district continued on the uptrend. The TVA brought in many new people, both skilled and unskilled. Our business was good and we were able to pay off our debts. Although our staff had been increased, I still had to work long hours. Milton's condition was not good. He had now gone to Arizona for his health and could only come home once a year for two or three weeks. The long hours, overwork, and strain and worry during the depression years caught up with my own health. I was unable to get away for vacations or to reduce my work hours. Therefore, I felt bad most of the time. Dr. Littlepage kept warning me that medications were not a "cure all" and told me I needed rest. When I told him I could not get away for a vacation he suggested I at least stay home in bed for about ten days. Two days later he saw me calling on customers. He called me to his office saying he wanted to inquire how Milton was doing, but mainly to advise me and said, "If that is the route you want, you are on the way." I answered that I realized it and was ready to do anything he suggested. He suggested I go to a diagnostic physician in Memphis for a complete checkup immediately. He made the appointment for me and when I finally got into the office of Dr. Alperin in Memphis, he told me that he did not have time to waste on patients who did not cooperate. Knowing I needed his help, I promised to do everything he instructed.

After a complete examination he dictated a list of "dos & don'ts". He also prescribed a month vacation, no cigarettes, no alcohol, etc. Also, he limited my normal work hours, and a rest of an hour midday. On leaving he said if I followed his instructions to see him again in six months, otherwise, not to return.

That was in 1936. Fortunately for me I did precisely everything he directed. at the end of six months, when I returned to his office, he was highly pleased. I continued seeing him twice a year. I have enjoyed good health throughout the years, much of which I attribute to Dr. Jacob Alperin.

After Beatrice graduated from the University of Alabama, she and two of her sorority sisters decided to go to New York. She worked for the Navy and while there she met Jack Muhlendorf. It developed into a romance which she revealed to us on her return home. After she invited him to our home for a visit, we approved and they married in 1942. He was stationed in Texas at the time and the wedding was there. After about a year, he was sent to Europe, and she returned home with their first born child, a son, Alan. Jack was overseas approximately 2 ½ years. They now have three fine sons.

Alan is Executive Vice-President of our family company. Kenny, the second son, is a medical doctor and presently practicing in Norfolk, Va. and doing extremely well. David, the third son, is a Certified Public Accountant, associated with a national organization and also doing well. All three are married to fine girls.

When Jack was released from service and shortly after returning home, they built a home on River Bluff Drive in Sheffield. Our house on Montgomery Avenue was on a high lot--there were too many steps for Bessie, therefore, we found a house a block from the children that suited our purpose. We enjoyed the beautiful neighborhood.

Prior to the war, I had been involved in several civic projects. Boy Scouts, Salvation Army, United Fund, Chamber of Commerce, Jewish Federated Charities, and County Chapter of Crippled Children. By that time I had a good staff in our business, having procured an experienced man in the wholesale grocery business as assistant manager and buyer.

Milton's health was getting worse. He came home for a couple of weeks in December, 1941, returning to Arizona in January. He passed away ten days later. His wife was in poor health also. In line with the provisions of his will, I bought his interest in our partnership business.

When the United States became involved in World War II, it became necessary to ration many food items. Ration boards were organized in every county. I was asked to serve as Chairman of the food section of the local ration board. Ration stamps were allotted to each family according to the size of the family. We received direction from the authorities on how to handle special cases. Because of illness, some people were entitled to extra stamps. Doctors would give their patients prescriptions or vouch that the patient needed extra butter or meats for example. Naturally, some families took advantage of this situation, and some people were unreasonable. We handled the situation as best we could, but often opened up more trouble for me.

A few months before the U. S. became involved in the war, the government sent a Coast Guard unit to our area to guard the power house and Wilson Dam. But after Pearl Harbor, the Coast Guard left immediately for sea duty. The captain of the port called a meeting to organize about 150 men to be temporary coast guards to patrol above and below Wilson Dam. I was among the group.

We were given brief indoctrination because of the urgency of the situation. My hours were to be 12 hours each week on a schedule of noon to midnight. Most of my time was on Saturday. Our duty was to check every barge that came thru and check their identification card. When I had an important business trip to make, I had to get permission from the Captain of the Port.

I also served on the United Service Organization (U. S. O.) Board for military personnel, as I found it hard to refuse at that time.

At long last, the European war came to an end in the Spring of 1945. What a relief. The Japanese were still fighting, until Hiroshima. Japan paid for her victory in Pearl Harbor. Most of the men from the European war were released and returned home. Some were sent to the Pacific area. The country was gradually returning to normal and restrictions on securing merchandise, food and otherwise slowly lifted.

At that time the food business was largely handled through small stores, including some small chain stores averaging three to five thousand square feet. The independently owned groceries sold most of the food. A major canning corporation employed the Neilson survey to make a study of what the retail food business would probably be after the war. The result of this report was given in 1945 at the annual convention which I attended. We were convinced that after three or four years hence, the corporate chains would have super markets in the area of thirty to forty thousand square feet. That would gradually eliminate most independent grocers, as well as wholesalers. Naturally, I began to think about the necessity for change of business.

We had been handling paper bags and wrapping paper in our grocery company. So it occurred to me that perhaps this area is becoming large enough for a paper wholesaler. When Jack returned home in 1946, he worked in our grocery company a couple of years pending a final decision of his future plans.

Thus in 1948, we started the Paper & Chemical Supply Company on a small scale. This was a new experience. We started with one salesman and limited inventory. Jack, meanwhile, spent a couple of weeks in Tuscaloosa with a friendly experienced paper merchant to get some pointers which were helpful.

The out of town paper suppliers continued soliciting business here, so we expected very little growth the first few years. The grocery business continued to do well through 1952-53; but was easing off gradually. In 1954 we decided it was time to liquidate the grocery business. Two of our best grocery salesmen were brought in and more capital and space enlarged our paper company. I began devoting full time to the paper company with Jack in charge. The territory was increased. I worked full time for ten or eleven years.

We operated on a partnership basis. Bessie and Beatrice had an interest in the grocery company and it was transferred to the Paper Company. When we decided to incorporate, Jack's three sons were given stock. I chose to retain a small interest in the company and work about half time. The Paper Company has made good progress--Jack is President; Alan, Executive Vice-President. I have no desire at present to retire completely and still have a deep interest in the business.

Getting back to my civic duties…After the war, I was elected to serve a three-year term on the State Society Board for Crippled Children. I was delighted. Board members cannot succeed themselves but after a years's absence from the board, one is eligible. I was elected again in 1953. In the third year of my second term on the Board, I was elected Vice-President of the State Society. The friends I had made serving as a Board Member had been a great experience for me.

Mr. Frank Spain, a distinguished lawyer from Birmingham, was on the Board the same time I was, and his friendship had a great impact on me. We had met before when he was State Chairman on rationing during the war years. Being county chairmen gave us the opportunity to meet several times.

When I was elected to the Board, Mr. Spain mentioned to me that we had mutual interests and often when we both had to go to Montgomery for meetings, he suggested that I come to Birmingham, meet him there, and ride on to Montgomery with him. He had a chauffeur to drive us and these drives together gave us an opportunity to become even more friendly. His law firm carried on while he devoted most of his time to his civic interests during the war years. To me, he was and is a great philanthropist, as he indicated to me he was critical of people who devote all their time to themselves, ignoring the less fortunate. We discussed our interest in the Society which had formerly gone under the name of

Sam Israel, president of the Muscle Shoals Hotel Corporation, presided at the opening of new hotel (now Park Place), March 30, 1950. Standing behind Mr. Sam are his grandson Alan Muhlendorf, Officer Howard Kelly, Mrs. Howard Griffith and her daughters Carolyn and Christine. Courtesy of Sheffield Public Library

Society for Crippled Children. At this point it was changed to Society for Crippled Children and Adults, thus enlarging their program. The Board had to devote much time to enlarging the entire plan, to construct Rehabilitation Centers throughout the State, training therapists, and trying to promote the interest of the medical profession in Rehabilitation.

Prior to the Second World War there were very few orthopedic doctors in the nation. Dr. Howard Rusk of Missouri is due the credit for bringing attention to this fact. Dr. Rusk, a surgeon, was unhappy with the treatment that seriously injured war veterans were given. He told the commanding general of the Air Force that the seriously injured were getting only a "patch up job" and sent home to die. He also noted that the hospitals were poorly equipped and often the doctors poorly trained. Statistics of World War I showed that about 80% of the seriously injured died in a relatively short time. His idea was to reverse this situation.

He finally convinced the general of the Air Force and after that Dr. Rusk was determined to get his message over to the President. He had hopes of convincing other military departments to improve their hospital facilities. After a while he succeeded. Mobile, Alabama, built the first Rehabilitation Center; Birmingham followed with a relatively small center called 365 Club. The Society built a comprehensive center in Montgomery which opened in 1960. Huntsville followed shortly thereafter.

Frank Spain became deeply impressed. He acquired land in Birmingham in the medical center area and employed an engineer and architect. The three of them went to New York to consult with Dr. Rusk and observe the center there. Federal matching funds became available through the work of Senator Lister Hill for Rehabilitation Centers and Hospitals. The Spain Center was opened about 1962. Spain himself gave $667,000 for the center. Dr. Howard Rusk came to Birmingham for the dedication. I attended and it was a great privilege to meet and hear Dr. Rusk. He said that the $2,000,000 structure was the most complete Rehabilitation Center in existence. It is a fitting tribute to Frank Spain.

In the early fifties, when we were having our one-day clinics semi-annually in church basements and having to send our patients to Birmingham for treatment, we realized and spoke of our need for a Rehabilitation Center in this area. Dr. E. B. Norton, president of the Florence State College, had been active in the Alabama Society and was very helpful in the planning and execution of our Center.

My wife's health began deteriorating and she was hospitalized for several weeks. When she returned home, she required nursing care. She never complained when I had to go out of town, whether on business or board meetings and always encouraged me to continue my various interests--especially my civic interests.

After the war, the area began talking with TVA about developing an airport here. They had a small landing field. The TVA advised a board be appointed to take over the existing limited field and develop an airport. Each town and county could appoint one man on the board. Sheffield appointed me. I served seven years as Vice-Chairman and continued to serve fifteen years as Chairman. We had to acquire several hundred acres of land and build a terminal with mostly federal and state funds.

In 1959, I was elected President of the Alabama Society for Crippled Children and Adults. It was the culmination of my deep interest in the program. Personally, at first I was reluctant to accept it, considering my limited education and thinking of the stature of the men who had previously filled that position. When the nominating committee called me, I told them I questioned my qualifications. They persisted, citing my strong interest in the Society and my experience having served on the Board. Officers serve a year and I was elected for a second term. My good friend Frank Spain consented to become Vice-President of the Society.

I had been heading up and working very hard on a literacy program. About 1957 Miss Nell Peerson of Florence came home from Baltimore where she had been working with Dr. Frank Laubach, who developed a new method to teach illiterate adults to read and write in a short time. Mrs. James Massey, Sr., a friend of Miss Peerson, heard about it. She also went to Baltimore, learned the method and when they came home they were determined to organize a group of volunteers to learn the method to be able to teach others. It was all new to me when I was approached to head up the organization. I was involved in the airport program, the Society, (so many things), etc. They reminded me that I was illiterate when I came to the U. S.--I could not say no. I agreed and we organized many school teachers and others. We raised a little money. The hardest part was to get the illiterates to come. They were ashamed to admit it. After a few weeks it was proven. It was very rewarding work, but when I was elected president of the State Society, I had to resign.

The new center at Montgomery was dedicated during my first year in office. Sen. Lister Hill delivered an appropriate speech, stressing the possibilities of benefiting the handicapped. I made brief remarks saying that there would eventually be centers in various parts of the State, and that Sen. Hill was due the major credit. He had made it possible through the Hill-Burton Act to construct these facilities. Privately, I told him that we would build a center in Muscle Shoals soon; that the land had been acquired and plans were underway locally to raise funds. At that time I felt it advisable not to divulge that I had purchased the land myself. Our executive secretary who knew it, urged me to let it be known, thinking it would help in raising the $150,000.00 in our relatively small community. On returning home, I began inquiring about a capable person to run our publicity campaign for the drive. The Service League suggested one of their members, Betty Schuessler, a most charming and capable lady. But Betty thought I should let it be publicly known that I had purchased the land and it was a gift, thus making it easier to raise money. I had no choice but to consent. Betty's articles were excellent and the Service League members helped in soliciting potential donors. I contacted a select list of people whom I felt could give $1,000.00 or more in memory of a deceased loved one.

Dr. E. B. Norton assisted and the campaign was successful. In three months approximately 75% of the money had been raised from the $1,000.00 donations. Several persons gave voluntarily, including blacks; the black community also had a committee to solicit funds. We reached our goal of $150,000.00, which enabled us to secure $300,000.00 from the Hill-Burton program.

Meanwhile, I had been talking with a friend of mine who had had considerable experience in construction. Mr. Donald Dugger was properties manager of TVA for many years. He had reached retirement age and became interested in our project. He readily agreed to serve on our local board and assume responsibility of Chairman of the Building Committee. He did an excellent job of overseeing the building.

I was becoming concerned about my wife's health. The person we had looking after her was more interested in the salary than in the patient. After many inquiries we found a lady who was kind and thoughtful. Mrs. Carter exemplified "tender loving care." In November, 1963, Bessie felt better. The National Convention of the Society was to meet in Miami. I thought I should skip it, but Bessie insisted that I go. Knowing Mrs. Carter and Bea were nearby, I left home Sunday morning. Monday about noon, Bea phoned that her mother had to be taken to the hospital. Within an hour I was on a flight home. The doctor assured us the patient was now out of danger, but should remain at the hospital for a couple of weeks. She did improve.

When Bessie felt good enough, she inquired when we would start construction on the center. We were then in the preliminary stage. In 1964 she felt well enough to be taken out for short rides and was able to enjoy TV, etc.

In November, 1964, the National Society Convention was scheduled to be held in Pittsburg. Mrs. Deal, my secretary, asked me whether I planned on going and if so would I be home the following weekend. I would like to add here as I look back over the years, it was always Mrs. Deal, my valued friend and secretary, who aided me in all civic projects, and in all difficulties in which I became involved. She was not only capable, but her sense of loyalty and concern made my accomplishments possible. She was our valued employee for 30 years.

When Mrs. Deal hinted that I should be home that coming weekend, I was unaware of why. But on Saturday, she told me I should attend the D.A.R. meeting on Sunday. So on Sunday afternoon we went to the High School Auditorium, with Bessie in a wheelchair. Surprisingly, we found a sizable audience already assembled, and many of my old friends with whom I had worked. It was a program similar to "This is your Life", with me as the subject. Seven or eight people told what I had done heretofore--Crippled Children, United Fund, Boy Scouts, Literacy Movement, etc. At that time I received the D.A.R. Award for naturalized citizens.

Bessie was so proud. I was expected to make some brief remarks. It gave me the opportunity to say that when I came to Sheffield I was "fundless and friendless. Bessie Kreisman was my tutor, friend and advisor." A reception followed the program. That occasion meant more to her than to me. It was a great day for both of us.

Bessie's health seemed to be improving in early 1965; she kept asking when we expected completing and dedicating the Center; she said on one occasion "don't put it off too long." June 15, 1965, was the date set. The Alabama Society Board Meeting was the day before; the Board met that Sunday morning and the dedication was scheduled at 2 PM. By 1:30 every chair was occupied. Bessie in her wheelchair appeared happy. So many friends spoke to her.

When the original building was completed we thought we had adequate space for many years. About 4 years later the professional counselors told us we needed additional space. We proceeded to raise more money. The second time it was not so easy. Then, too, the government funds, especially, during the Viet Nam War were hard to secure. By 1971 we let the contract for the addition; which is almost as large as the first. Now some of the departments are too small, a second addition is in the planning state. Fortunately, we have ample land. Activities of daily living and occupational therapy needs to be enlarged.

The executive director of the National Society delivered the dedication address, followed by Dr. Woodrow Elliot. He was a past president of the Society and made many complimentary remarks in presenting me the highest award (The Bronze). Bessie was overwhelmed to hear so many flattering things about her husband. About two weeks later she was able to attend another function which gave her much pleasure--the wedding of Alan and Sally Mullendorf, which took place at the Tuscumbia Country Club. That was the last time she was able to go out. She was in bed until early in August, when her health took a sudden turn. On the morning of August 15, 1965, the end came.

SAM J. ISRAEL---
"Citizen Of The Year" At Muscle Shoals

Now came a period of sadness and I seemed to be living an empty life. Bea suggested that I move in with them. But I did not think that was practical. Bea had always been a devoted and loving daughter. I saw her and Jack daily and often had meals with them.

For years I had wanted to go to South America where we had relatives, but could not leave Bessie. So in March, 1966, I took a 34-day cruise. I enjoyed the trip and meeting my niece and her family in Brazil--also her brother and family in Argentina. Coming home to an empty house was not pleasant.

After that, I began to see an old family friend, Hilda Shipper. She had been widowed several years. She was very nice and had formerly been thoughtful to Bessie. When I told Bea that Hilda and I were considering marriage; her answer was "wonderful." By the same token Hilda's two sons approved warmly.

We were married December 16, 1966. I sold my house in Sheffield and we now live on Shoals Creek. We both enjoy being near the water and close to the Country Club (Turtle Point). Hilda became a golf tutor and we play often. We have also taken many cruises and trips. I am still keeping in close touch with the business, having cut my hours recently to half a day.

I have been honored with many awards--including "Citizen of the Year," D.A.R. Award, "Silver Beaver" by Boy Scouts of American, National Rehabilitation Association Distinguished Service Award, United Fund and the Bronze Award given by the Alabama Society of Crippled Children & Adults.

Recently I received "The Book of Golden Deeds Award" from the Florence Exchange Club, which was a complete surprise.[1]

When I came to the United States my goal was to be a good American. I have experienced good times and bad. I have a great deal to be grateful for as I have been given a generous share of blessings. I am proud of my family, including my niece Lillian, who is almost like a daughter, and proud of the reputation I have acquired in business. Fortunately, I enjoy good health, considering my age, Hilda and I are congenial and we are hoping for many more years together in good health.[2]

---

[1] For more information on Sam Israel, see Chris A. Eckl, "Mr. 'President' – that's Sam Israel of Sheffield," Tri-Cities Daily, Dec. 8, 1963; Louis A. Eckl, 'All American off the field – that's Mr. Sam!" Times Daily Apr , 1965.

[2] Sam J. Israel completed and signed his autobiography, June 5, 1978. He died in Florence, AL, Nov. 21, 1990 at age 99 years and was buried in Sheffield's Oakwood cemetery. His obituary in the Times Daily, Nov. 24, 1990, recalled many of his humanitarian deeds.

Index

Adams, Harvey, 57
Adams, Raymond, 119
Agee, Capt., 33
Airdome Theater, 20
Alabama Avenue Grammar School, 153
Alabama Avenue School, 9, 158
Aldred, Bill, 118, 127, 128
Aldred, Johnny, 127
Allen, Annie Louise, 43
Allen, Harriet Elanore, 43
Allen, Joseph V., 32, 33, 43, 44
Allen, Joseph, Jr., 43
Allen, Mel, 46
Allen, Porter Weakly, 43
Allen, Susan Pendleton Ball, 43
Allen, William W., 43
Alleyn, C. J., 59
Annie, Cynthia, 139
Archer, W. T., 213
Ashcraft, C. W., 62
Azbell, Peggy, 184
Azbell, Raymond, 43
B'Nai Israel Temple, 14
Banister, Bill, 191
Baptist Church, 21
Barber, Ethylene, 173, 176, 184
Barksdale, Ethel, 115
Barksdale, Ruth, 116
Barnes, Crawford, 139, 140
Barron, Mary Joyce, 115
Bartee, W. Glenn, 57
Bassaham, Oscar, 153
Beard, Charles L. "Chuck", 1, 55, 73
Beard, Leonard, 77, 78

Belle, Zora, 139
Berheiser, H. W., 12
Bethel M.E. Church, 21
Birmingham, Sheffield & Tennessee River Railroad, 45
Black, Ray, 93
Blackburn, Al, 140
Blair, Bettie, 52
Blair, Hugh A., 48
Blair, Hugh W., 7, 48
Blake, Wyatt, 57
Blake, Wyatt H., 49
Blankenship, Lloyd, 139
Blanton, Alice O., 149
Blanton, Joyce, 149
Blanton, Lawson Haynes, Sr., 148
Blanton, Lawson, Jr, 149
Block, Max R., 14
Boeckh, Charles, 4, 5
Bond, Max, 185
Bowling, James E., 199
Braun, Wernher von, 198
Brooks, Bazzle, 139
Brown Temple C.M.E. Church, 21
Brown, Alberta, 116
Brown, Alice, 116
Brown, Janet, 116
Buchanan, C. H., 5, 10
Buford, Julia, 152
Buford, Rosalie (Betty), 152
Burt, Reynold B., 1, 32, 61, 68
C. M. Brewster School, 98, 99
Calvary Baptist Church, 21
Campbell, Phil, 39, 45, 46
Caparn, Harold A., 84

Carmichael, Judge, 24, 31
Carter, E. C., 17
Carter, Mary Jo McWilliams, 137
Carton, John, 140
Carton, Myles, 140
Carver, George Washington, 185, 186, 187
Castle Heights School, 65
Chamberlain, Oliver, Jr., 84
Chambers, W. L., 7
Chambliss, R. B., 85
Chase, W. B., 66
Christian Church, 52
City and County Hospital, 55
Civilian Conservation Corps (CCC), 22, 23, 28, 90, 212
Clark, Capt., 33
Clemens, Samuel, 75
Clement, John W., 88
Cleveland Hotel, 8, 9, 11, 33
Clifford, E. H., 81
Clingan, Bob, 140
Cloud, Capt., 33
Coast Guard, 92, 119, 120, 122, 154, 164, 165, 216
Coffee, John, 3
Colbert County Hospital, 56, 57, 58, 77, 79
Colbert Theater, 166
Cooke, Samuel Claiborne, 54, 56
Copson, Leslie, 116, 118
Cornelius, A. D., 139
Corner, B.L., 34
Cottrell, Kathrine, 46
Craft, W. L., 151
Crosby, Don, 116
Crosby, Oscar, 118

Crowe, Isabella, 65
Crowe, James R., Sr., 65, 66
Crowe, James Richard, Jr., 65, 66, 67
Cumberland Presbyterian Church, 7
Curtis, A. W., Jr., 186
Damsgard, Harold, 45
Darby, Charles, 139
Davis, Ethel, 78
Davis, Lt., 33
Davis, Ruby, 139
Dean, Capt., 33
Debardeleben, Henry, 61
Deshler High School, 2
Dexter, Ralph, 191
Dimic, L.W., 32
Doud, C.C., 34
Driskell, Carole Edwards, 1, 38
Dugger, D. O., 95, 97, 100
Dugger, Donald, 221
Dugger, Donna Ann, 115
Dugger, Mary Sue, 115
Dyar, Betty, 44, 48, 52, 54, 58, 59, 60
Edison, Thomas, 63, 76, 141
Eisenhower, Dwight, 130
Elliot, Woodrow, 222
Elmore, Isabel, 131
Elmore, Kelly, Jr., 124, 125, 128, 131
Elmore, Stanley M., 1, 103
Episcopal Church, 51
Farneman, James, 132
Fell, Richard, 57
First Baptist Church, 18, 21
First Methodist Church, 45, 51, 57
First Presbyterian Church, 14
First United Methodist Church, 14

Flynn, Catherine, 46
Foot, Aubrey, 180
Foote, Edith, 180
Ford, Gene A., 1, 3
Ford, Henry, 18, 63, 76
Foster, Capt., 33
Foster, Ellen, 136
Foster, George W., 136
Foster, Ida, 136
Foster, Joe, 137
Foster, Martha Ellen, 137
Foster, Owen, 137
Fould, A. J., 5
Frear, Evelyn, 116, 118
Frear, George L., 185
Funke, John F., 16
Furnace Hill, 8, 70, 91, 141, 155, 178
Furnace Hill Kindergarten School, 54
Galloway, W. J., 21
Gamard, Walter T., 46
Garner, Bryce, 152
Garner, Buford, 152
Garner, Buford, Jr., 152, 155, 157, 159
Garner, Roy, 139
Garner, Ruby, 139
Garrett, Reba, 60
Gibb, V., 12
Goodloe, Buster, 139
Goodloe, Forrest, 139
Goodloe, James (Doodley), 139
Gordon, Walter S., 3, 40
Grace Episcopal Church, 14, 33, 57, 59
Grace, Rachael, 203

Graham, Mike, 34
Gray, Fred, 134
Green, Milborne, 163
Green, Ray, 163
Green, Roy, 163
Green, Ruth, 163
Green, Zelma, 163, 175, 179
Greer, Hoyt, 59, 60, 78
Greer, James Julian, 60
Greer, Jordan, Reba, 78
Greer, W. H., 55
Griffith, Howard A., 20, 28
Grimes, Mary, 98
Grizzard, W.W., 142
Habbeler, Henry, 17, 54
Habbeler, Julia, 54
Habbeler, William (Will) H., 54
Hall, Mary Jane, 115
Harbin, Rozanne, 179
Hardy, Joseph, 51
Harris, Dora, 48
Harris, James Craig, 43, 44
Harvey, Ann, 115
Hatch, W. S., 14
Haynie, Martha, 115, 117, 118
Heaton, Donald, 115
Heaton, Gordon, 118
Heaton, Roy, 129
Heffernan, Barney, 119
Heffernan, Dorothy, 115
Heffernan, John, 119
Helen Keller Hospital, 56, 58
Helgoth, Richard, 192
Henderson Hotel, 17
Henderson, George, 14
Heron, W.W., 34
Higdon, Junior, 175, 179

Hill, H. G., 168
Hill, L.L., 34
Hill, Lister, 166, 219, 220
Hill, Richard Randolph, 59
Holt, B., 34
Holtzclaw, Jim, 34
Hopeman, Edgar, 12
Hotel Astor, 76
Howell, A. L., 20
Huff, N. D., 100
Humphreys, G. P., 7
Huston, Robert, 140
Israel, Max, 202, 203, 205
Israel, Milton, 209, 210, 214, 215
Israel, Sam J., 1, 200, 224
Jacks, Joe, 89
Jackson, Andrew, 3
James, Virginia W., 93, 98, 99
Johnson, John W., 16
Johnson, Kenneth R., 5, 94
Johnson, Rollen, 192
Johnson, W. A., 51
Jones, E. M., 100
Jones, H.J., 32
Jones, J.A., 26
Jones, R. M., 100
Jones, T., 34
Jones, Thomas D., 34
Keller, Sam, 5
Kelly, Paula Jean, 115
Keyes, George, 7
Kienker, J. J., 16
Kimbrough, J.C., 139
Kimbrough, Williams Harold, 139
King, Joe, 140
Kinnard, Herbert Marshall, 57
Kirkby, Arthur, 85

Koonch, Goober, 158
Kreisman, Adolf, 206
Kreisman, Bessie, 206, 222
Kreisman, Isaac, 206
Kreisman, Philip, 208, 209, 210
L & N Railroad, 36, 81
Ladd, Martha McWilliams, 137
Lagomarsino, John B., 7, 52, 141
Landers, Obbie, 139
Lata, Sam, 33
Laubach, Frank, 220
Lee, James, 73
Lee, James Earl, 139
Lee, Jim, 139
Lee, Lillian Margaret, 73, 74
Lee, Rossie, 139
Lee, Sarah Miller, 73
LeMay, Bruce, 91
LeMay, Ralph, 91
Lewey, Jim, 139
Lindsay, Maud, 1, 66, 67, 98
Lindsey, Bill, 114, 115, 117, 118, 119, 120, 129, 131, 133
Long, Joe, 95
Louisville and Nashville Railroad., 43
M.E. Church, 14, 18, 19
Mae, Connie, 139
Marks, H., 13
Martin, E. J., 83
Martin, W. H., 141
Mason, W. F., 162, 168
Massey, James, Sr., 220
McCluskey, Agnes, 166
McCollum, Tom, 139
McCroskey, Alfred, 95
McCullum, Lois, 179

McGregor, George T., 42
McGuire, Dall, 140
McWilliams, Alma, 139
McWilliams, Andy L., 135
McWilliams, Charles, 137
McWilliams, Floyd, 139, 140
McWilliams, George, 137, 140
McWilliams, Jack, 140
McWilliams, James, 135, 140
McWilliams, John Alexander, 135
McWilliams, John Hubert, 137
McWilliams, Lillian Taylor, 137
McWilliams, Mary Lou Willingham, 135
McWilliams, Robert Lee, 1, 135, 137
McWilliams, Walter, 137, 140
McWilliams, William, 137
McWilliams, William C., 135
Mead, Bill, 92
Mead, Charles Morris, 42
Mead, Mary Elizabeth Morris, 41
Mead, Mrs. W. J., 41
Meadows, Robert H., 1, 151, 184
Mefford, Betty Jean Greer, 60
Methodist Church, 7
Miller, A. M., 100
Mills, A.C., 188
Mills, Laverne, 2, 188
Mize, Garnie, 139
Mize, Leroy, 139
Mize, Orbert, 139
Mobile and Montgomery Railroad, 43
Moore, Harry, 191
Moore, Jimmy, 158
Morris, Alma Bertrand, 41
Morris, Caroline, 56
Morris, Charles Thomas, 41
Morris, Charlotte Naomi, 41
Morris, Cornelius VanCleef, 41
Morris, Ida Caroline, 41
Morris, Jane Warren, 41
Morris, Mary, 158
Morris, Mary Elizabeth, 41
Morris, Myrtle, 158
Moses, Adaline L., 39
Moses, Alfred H., 3, 7, 34, 39, 40, 41, 43, 54
Moses, Alfred, II, 39
Moses, Henry, 39
Moses, Joseph W., 39
Moses, Lee J., 39
Moses, Levy, 39
Moses, Mordecai, 39
Moses, Sarah A., 39
Mothershed, John C., 2, 94
Muhlendorf, Alan, 215
Muhlendorf, David, 215
Muhlendorf, Jack, 215
Muhlendorf, Kenny, 215
Muhlendorf, Sally, 54
Mullendorf, Sally, 222
Munsom, J. G., 84
Muscle Shoals Hotel, 28
Nathan, Janett, 39
Nathan, Joseph H., 16, 34, 39, 62, 66
Neff, John, 12
Newsome, Gabe, 139
Newsome, Ozzie, 139
Nitrate Plant, 8, 15, 16, 17, 18, 19, 21, 22, 24, 25, 72, 75, 76, 77, 78, 83, 94, 95, 97, 98, 102, 103, 105, 107, 135, 140, 155, 197, 208
Norris, George, 21, 63, 99, 104

Norton, E. B., 79, 219, 221
Nyhoff, John J., 19, 76, 82
O'Neal, Edward A., 39
Olim, Philip, 18, 148, 206, 208, 209
Olive, Willie, 140
Opera House Hotel, 33
Owen, Catherine Maddox, 78
Owen, Ralph, 139
Page, Amos, 139
Page, Neal, 139
Page, Tracy, 139
Page, Wilson, 139
Page, Winnie, 139
Page, Wyomia, Raze, 139
Painter, Charles, 100, 101, 126, 132
Painter, Charlie, 100
Painter, Donald, 132
Parsons, Charles, 62
Parsons, George, 62
Parsons, Henry, 62
Patten, John H., 62
Pauls, Roger, 193
Payne, Mary Ida, 41
Peerson, Nell, 220
Perkins, Ace, 139
Perkins, F.W., Sr,, 139
Pershing, John J., 89
Polk, Mrs. Charles, 137
Ponders, Odes, 140
Posey, Carl, 139
Poyet, Anthony, 88
Poyet, Evangeline, 92
Poyet, Garnette, 92
Poyet, Isabell, 92
Presbyterian Church, 21, 50
Proctor, W. E., 33
Rather, John D., 62

Redmond, Ben, 211
Reeves, Betty, 116
Reeves, Bobby, 120
Reeves, Wesley, 122
Rhodes, Della Gwynn, 129
Rice, Katherine Boyd, 78
Richardson, W. G., 13
Richeson, William Hal, 58
Ritz Theater, 20, 156, 157
Roberts, Ray C., 98
Roberts, Tillman, 178
Robertson, Fred W., 88, 90
Robinson, Caroline R., 54
Rodell, W. H., 12
Rogers, Wayne, 134
Rolls, W. A., 7
Roosevelt, Franklin, 64, 77, 99, 104, 212
Rose, Jake, 191
Roulhac, Allen Jones, 56, 57
Roulhac, Annie Bee Cohen, 57
Roulhac, Julia Erwin Jones, 56
Roulhac, Thomas Ruffin, 56
Roulhac, Thos. R., 7
Rusk, Howard, 218, 219
Russell, James, 130
Russell, Roy, 130
Rutland, Bridge, 140
Rutland, Fred, 140
Rutland, James, 139
Rutland, Wallace, 139
Saffold, J. R., 34
Saffold, J.O., 34
Sanders, Vernon (Buck), 168
Scates, Gloria Dawn, 115
Schall, Charles, 12
Schmidt, Curt, 74, 75, 79

Schmidt, Lillian Margaret Lee, 75, 76, 77, 78, 79
Schmidt, Therese Augusta, 74, 77
Schuessler, Betty, 220
Scott, Betty Lou, 115
Sellers, Samuel, 193
Shackford, Capt., 33
Sheffield and Birmingham Railroad, 6
Sheffield High School, 25, 28, 70, 93, 98, 124, 131, 137, 185
Sheffield Hotel, 9, 11, 16, 17, 20, 27, 33, 43, 61, 85, 140
Sheridan, Richard C., 5, 2, 35, 46, 65, 80, 83, 148, 185, 197
Shipper, Hilda, 223
Sibley, R. Y., 42
Smith, Elbert, 140
Smith, Jim, 139
Southern Railroad, 14, 121
Spain, Frank, 217, 219, 220
Stanfield, Corelia, 177
Stanford, George, 129
Stansell, L. F., 51
Stansell, S. L., 12
Steamboat, 35, 36
Steele, John A., 39
Sterling, R. L., 149
Stewart, John Righty, 88
Stewart, Mose, 88
Stewart, Ocie, 88
Stewart, Sarah, 88
Stout, Patty Lee, 115
Streit, Charlie, 143
Streit, Charlie "Bud", 2, 143
Streit, Christian, 143
Streit, David, 140
Summers, G. O., 85
Swoopes, P.B., 24
Tennessee Valley Authority, 1, 2, 22, 23, 24, 25, 26, 28, 30, 31, 60, 64, 77, 78, 83, 86, 90, 92, 94, 95, 98, 99, 100, 101, 102, 104, 105, 107, 110, 114, 115, 119, 121, 122, 124, 125, 126, 128, 129, 144, 185, 186, 212, 214, 219, 221
Thompson, Ambus, 139
Thompson, Freddie, 139
Thompson, Humphrey, 139
Thompson, Nora, 78
Thomson, A. D., 13, 52, 54
Thomson, Elizabeth (Beth), 53
Thomson, Hugh Blair, 53
Thomson, Louise, 53
Thomson, Margaret, 53
Thurmond, Richard J., Jr., 47
Tidwell, Jim, 158
Tidwell, Mary, 158
Timberlake, Lewis, 38
Tschantre, Susan, 116
TVA Elementary School, 107
TVA School, 107, 119
Union Railroad, 13
Village One, 8, 2, 27, 83, 84, 91, 92, 94, 95, 96, 97, 98, 100, 101, 102, 103, 105, 107, 110, 126, 128, 129, 130, 131, 133, 134, 165, 179
Village School, 98
Virtue, D. Roy, 100
Virtue, Susanna, 116
Waddell, Lena, 33
Wade, Peggy, 116
Walthall, Patsy, 116, 118
Wann, Horace C. "Chick", 2, 83

Watkins, R.L., 34
Watson, Lt., 33
Weakly, Annie Lou, 43
Weakly, Capt., 33
Weddell, B., 33
Wedemeyer, Fred, Jr., 118
Weston, W. R., 50, 51
White, Evelyn, 184
White, J. G., 84
Whitfield, C.D., 21
Whitlock, Owen, 140
Wilhoyte, Benjamin Allen, 52
Wilhoyte, Nancy Snyder, 52
Wilhoyte, Robert H., 51, 52
Williams, Dennis, 91
Williams, Febby Ann, 115
Williams, Johnny, 89, 90
Williams, Warren, 91
Willis, Nila James, 139
Willow, R.D., 34
Wilson, Bobby, 179, 182
Wilson, Woodrow, 94, 135
Woodard, Thomas B., 47
Woolrych, Ed, 128
Worthington, Billy, 120
Worthington, Jimmy, 120
Worthington, John Warren, 61, 62, 63, 64
Wright, Walton, 176
York Terrace, 26, 27, 60
Young, Audrey, 115
Young, Bill, 118
Young, Charles, 100, 118
Young, Nancy, 115

Bluewater Publications is a multi-faceted publishing company capable of meeting all of your reading and publishing needs. Our two-fold aim is to:

1) Provide the market with educationally enlightening and inspiring research and reading materials.

2) Make the opportunity of being published available to any author and or researcher who desires to be published.

We are passionate about preserving history; whether through the re-publishing of an out-of-print classic, or by publishing the research of historians and genealogists. Bluewater Publications is the Peoples' Choice Publisher.

For company information or information about how you can be published through Bluewater Publications, please visit:

www.BluewaterPublications.com

Also check Amazon.com to purchase any of the books that we publish.

Confidently Preserving Our Past,

Bluewater Publications.com

www.ingramcontent.com/pod-product-compliance
Lightning Source LLC
Chambersburg PA
CBHW050458110426
42742CB00018B/3303